WORLD CRUISING
ESSENTIALS

A Note from the North American Publisher

World Cruising Essentials was published in the United Kingdom in 2002 as *World Cruising Survey*, second edition, and is a much revised and expanded sequel to Jimmy Cornell's *World Cruising Survey*, which was published in 1989 and has been out of print for several years.

Other titles by Jimmy Cornell

World Cruising Handbook
3rd edition
ISBN: 0-07-137610-0

This unique bestselling book contains invaluable practical information on all aspects of cruising worldwide. The third edition has been thoroughly revised to bring it in line with the enormous changes brought about by the Internet revolution. Now covering 187 maritime nations of the world, this book brings together in one single volume all the practical information anyone would need when planning to sail to any country in the world.

World Cruising Routes
5th edition
ISBN: 0-07-1408690-X

World Cruising Routes is a comprehensive guide to nearly 1000 sailing routes covering all the oceans of the world. This book is geared specifically to the needs of cruising sailors and contains essential information on winds, currents, regional and seasonal weather as well as valuable suggestions concerning optimum times for individual routes. This thoroughly revised fifth edition features new data collected by the author on his recent voyage from Antarctica to Alaska via Tahiti and Hawaii.

WORLD CRUISING
ESSENTIALS

The Boats, Gear, and Practices that Work Best at Sea

Jimmy Cornell

International Marine / McGraw-Hill
Camden, Maine • New York • Chicago • San Francisco
Lisbon • London • Madrid • Mexico City • Milan • New Delhi
San Juan • Seoul • Singapore • Sydney • Toronto

To Barry Esrig

For never losing his sense of humour

The McGraw·Hill Companies

Visit us at: www.internationalmarine.com

1 2 3 4 5 6 7 8 9 0 DOC DOC 9 8 7 6 5 4 3

Library of Congress Cataloging-in-Publication Data

Cornell, Jimmy.
   World cruising essentials : the boats, gear, and practices that work best at sea / Jimmy Cornell.
       p.   cm.
   Rev. ed. of: World cruising survey / Jimmy Cornell. c1989.
   Includes index.
     ISBN 0-07-141425-8 (hardcover : alk. paper)
     1. Yachting. 2. Yachting—Equipment and supplies—Evaluation.
   3. Recreational surveys. 4. Seamanship. 5. Seafaring life. I. Cornell, Jimmy. World cruising survey. II. Title.
     GV813 .C753 2002
     797.1´246—dc21   2002152867

First edition published 1989 by Adlard Coles. Second edition published 2002 as *World Cruising Survey* in Great Britain by Adlard Coles Nautical, an imprint of A & C Black Publishers Ltd., London.

Contents

Acknowledgments

Several thousand sailors were involved in the many surveys that form the basis of this book and listing them all would take up far too much space, so in the Introduction I have mentioned by name only those who had taken part in the most recent surveys: the Global Cruising Survey and the Sailing Women Survey.

This book also contains the results of a recent survey on the worldwide movement of cruising boats, and I am particularly indebted to the following officials for providing me with statistical data pertaining to their port, region or country: Juan Francisco Martin of Las Palmas Port Authority, Canary Islands; Richard Garcia of the Ministry for Tourism and Transport, Gibraltar; Joao Carlos Fraga of the Azores Tourism Office; Mick Floyd of the Falkland Islands Customs; Susan Kloulechad of the Palau Tourism Office; Scott Bretherton of the Australian Quarantine Service; Allen Jones of the New Zealand Customs Service; James Findlay and Joe Pagnam of the Radio Control Centre, Bermuda; Galo Ortiz of the Puerto Lucia Yacht Club in Salinas, Ecuador; Cuthbert Didier of Rodney Bay Marina, St Lucia; Dee Siebert of the Royal Cape Yacht Club, South Africa; Donald Stollmeyer and Angeli Elliot of YSTT, Trinidad; Nick and Carolyn Wardle of the Bahamas Search and Rescue Association; Y P Loke of Raffles Marina in Singapore; Mark Ray of the Republic of Singapore Yacht Club; Jason Lim of the Changi Sailing Club, Singapore; Yongli Ong of the Royal Selangor Yacht Club, Port Klang, Malaysia; Dick McClune of Bali International Marina, Indonesia; Sam Mann, Director of Maritime Traffic, and Teresa Arosemena, of the Panama Canal Authority; Francois Le Brun of Port Moselle, Nouméa, New Caledonia; Alex Wopper of Alwoplast in Valdivia, Chile; Judy Nip of the Royal Hong Kong Yacht Club; Frigg Jørgensen of the Governor's Office, Svalbard, Norway; Lieutenant Héctor Aravena Salazar, Port Captain of Hanga Roa, Easter Island; Andy Stephens of Yacht Haven Marina in Phuket, Thailand; Pamela Young, of the St Helena Tourism Office and Barry Williams, harbourmaster, St Helena; Roban Clarke of the Cocos (Keeling) Islands Administration; Ann Lee, US Customs Marine Section, Honolulu, Hawaii; José Zacarias of Centro Nautico da Bahia, Salvador, Brazil; Phil Watt of the Northern Territory Immigration Office, Darwin, Australia; Lavinia of the Royal Suva Yacht Club, Fiji; Ashraf Soukar of the Prince of the Red Sea yacht agency, Suez, Egypt.

I am also grateful to my various personal contacts for their help with the survey on the global yacht movement, who put me in touch with local officials, or who supplied relevant data when my efforts fell on deaf ears: Daniel Kuntschik and Skip Novak on Patagonia and Antarctica; Ricardo Arenas and Roslyn Cameron on the Galapagos Islands; Gill Outerbridge on Bermuda; Luc Callebaut on French Polynesia; Bill Stocks on Japan; Penny LaSette on Darwin; Tom Williams on

Jamaica; Bill Tschan on the Cook Islands; Gonzalo Yanzi on Ushuaia, Argentina; Salah Medani on Port Sudan; Mike Grubb, formerly of the Falmouth Coastguard, on the United Kingdom; Jan and Nick Wooller on Chagos, Seychelles and Madagascar; Brian Hull on Papua New Guinea; Tom Muller on Chagos and Madagascar.

Likewise, I am extremely grateful to the following participants in the Millennium Odyssey for providing detailed figures for my survey on the costs of cruising: Ann Harsh and Ralph Nehrig, Stu and Julie Conway, Matt Rollberg and Margaret Reichenbach, Klaus Girzig, Hannes Pfeiffer and Lou Morgan Jr.

One participant in the Millennium Odyssey who has made a substantial contribution to this book is Michael Frankel. During the round the world rally he conducted his own surveys on a wide range of subjects and these he generously put at my disposal.

Grateful thanks are due to my old friend Peter Noble, who, assisted by Louise Abrams, prepared the list of medical supplies, which is given in Appendix 3. I am also grateful to Barry Esrig for checking that all medical terms are understood on both sides of the Atlantic.

The World Cruising Club, as organizer of the ARC, has provided me with valuable data on its current events and I am particularly grateful to Tony Mark, Jeremy Wyatt and Louise Griffin.

Special thanks are due to *Yachting World* magazine, and its editor Andrew Bray, for allowing me to use the results of the various equipment surveys conducted among participants in the ARC. These surveys are regularly updated on www.yachting-world.com.

Similarly, I am indebted to the Seven Seas Cruising Association for permission to use the results of the wide-ranging equipment survey conducted among its members in 2000. Having been a member of the Association for the last quarter of a century I want to use this opportunity to urge anyone interested in cruising to join this worthwhile organization, which is open to any sailor: SSCA, 1525 South Andrews Avenue, Suite 217, Port Lauderdale, FL 33316, USA (www.ssca.org; e-mail: office@ssca.org).

As always, grateful thanks are due to my publisher, Adlard Coles Nautical, and its helpful staff: Carole Edwards, Linda Carroll and Carrie Goldsworthy, and in particular to my editor Janet Murphy, who suggested that I wrote this book, and subsequently gave it her wholehearted support. Across the Atlantic I have enjoyed similar support from my US editor, Jonathan Eaton, at International Marine.

Introduction

"Cruising around the world is not as difficult as it sounds. More people should spend less time worrying about it and just do it."

MICHAEL FRANKEL

A lot has happened both in my professional and private life since the first edition of *World Cruising Essentials* was published in 1989. Then, the memories of my six-year voyage with Gwenda and our two young children, which had concluded in 1981, were still fresh in my memory, but I was already involved in a very different activity professionally. Starting with the first ARC (Atlantic Rally for Cruisers) in 1986, the organizing of transoceanic rallies had pushed my journalistic career to one side and led me in a totally new direction. The year 1989 was also the one when my second *Aventura* was launched, and the new boat was the embodiment of the findings of the various cruising surveys that had resulted in the first edition of this book. While the findings of those early surveys had greatly influenced the choice of my second yacht, the lessons learned during the six years that I owned her have led to the current *Aventura III*.

The rallies

The various surveys, which I have conducted over the years (see complete list in Appendix 1), allowed me to probe deep into the experience of hundreds of sailors. An important source of data on all aspects of cruising were my contacts with the estimated 15,000 sailors and 3,000 yachts that had sailed in the various rallies I was involved with over a period of 15 years starting with the first ARC in 1986. Those rallies included 13 ARCs, many other transatlantic rallies, as well as five round the world rallies. The boats that sailed in those rallies totalled some 18 million miles of ocean sailing. During that same period, first on *La Aventura*, and then on *Aventura III*, I covered some 75,000 miles myself. This included a second circumnavigation, two trips to Antarctica, and as I am writing these lines I have already embarked on a new voyage that may take me around the world once more.

Having decided in the year 2000 to leave the organizing of rallies to others and do more cruising myself, I consider myself to be extremely fortunate to have been the recipient of the vast pool of knowledge that so many sailors have shared with me over the years. Therefore this new and fully revised edition is an excellent opportunity not only to share that knowledge with anyone interested in offshore cruising, but also to step back and take a detached look at what has happened on the world cruising scene during the last decade of the twentieth century. I hope that these findings will be of real value to any sailor preparing to set off on a world voyage in this new millennium.

The surveys

My first survey was born almost by chance. The year was 1978 and we had been cruising for nearly two years in the South Pacific. As we sailed from one island group to another and shared anchorages with other cruisers like ourselves, I was increasingly puzzled by the variety of cruising boats that we came across during our peregrinations. Although almost every one of those boats had some feature that made it stand out, there was not a single one among them that came anywhere near to what I believed in those days to be a feasible goal: the ideal cruising yacht. That first survey attempted to find out the kind of boats that sailed the oceans, how they were equipped, and how they lived up to their owners' expectations. The success of my first survey led to a more ambitious survey the following year that concentrated on the human factor and attempted to present a comprehensive picture of life afloat. More surveys followed and dealt with a host of subjects, from the role and attitude of sailing women, to the lessons learned from their circumnavigation by the crews of a dozen yachts that had just completed a voyage around the world. The unexpected outcome of a survey conducted early in 1986 on both sides of the Atlantic was the birth of the cruising rally concept and the first ARC. In the following years the ARC provided a fertile ground for several surveys on a variety of subjects: the quality and performance of yachting equipment, advances in cruising boat design, marine communications, practical aspects of life at sea, and many others. The findings of all those surveys were distilled in the first edition of this book, which since its publication has helped countless sailors in their choice of boat and equipment, as well as in their preparations for the voyage of their dreams.

I have been influenced by the findings of those surveys just as much as many of my readers, and my present yacht incorporates many of the lessons learned from those surveys. As I wrote recently to a couple seeking my advice and who were planning to set off on a world voyage, and were obviously very concerned about their lack of offshore experience, 'cruising is only 25 per cent based on experience, the rest is commonsense'. Indeed, so many of the comments made by the sailors who took part in my various surveys were based on sheer commonsense. What struck me most when I re-read the previous edition of *World Cruising Essentials* was just how little some aspects of cruising had actually changed.

In the years since the first edition of this book was published, more valuable data was provided by participants in the various round the world rallies, the first of which took place in 1991–2. Nearly 200 yachts have sailed in these rallies, and the resulting surveys concentrated on the practical aspects of life on a cruising yacht: maintenance, repairs and breakages, financial considerations and the cost of cruising, the problems of crew, or the pressures on family life afloat. Many of the findings of these surveys have not been published before. The cost of cruising was investigated among participants in both the Expo'98 round the world rally and the Millennium Odyssey. These two rallies also provided the material for a survey of breakages and equipment failure during a round the world voyage. The performance and reliability of marine equipment was also examined in the light of the comprehensive survey conducted by the Seven Seas Cruising Association (SSCA) among its members in 2000, and the wide-ranging surveys undertaken by *Yachting World* magazine among participants in ARC 1999 and ARC 2000.

Therefore the main aim of this edition is to bring together the largely unused data of my later surveys and project it onto the findings of my earlier surveys. This is why, whenever relevant, reference is made to the results of earlier surveys as I consider them to be a valuable term of comparison against which to assess the changes that have occurred in the intervening years. Many of the suggestions made by skippers interviewed five, ten or even twenty years ago are often just as valid now as they were then. To bring those earlier findings up to date, and to find out how much the cruising scene has changed in recent years, in the winter of 2001–2 I conducted a wide-ranging Global Cruising Survey that confirms, reinforces and occasionally contradicts those earlier findings. Rather than conduct the survey with a sample that was chosen randomly, as I used to do in the past when I usually interviewed all skippers that I met in a port or anchorage, this time I felt that a more selective sample might yield better results. Therefore my latest survey includes several highly experienced sailors of various nationalities, several circum-navigators, well-known naval architects, enthusiastic offshore sailors, as well as many former participants in the various rallies. It is, I feel, a good cross-section of the current offshore sailing scene, and the valuable suggestions and comments made by these outstanding sailors have greatly enhanced the findings of my previous surveys. Their comments and suggestions have also made a unique contribution to the search for that hypothetical perfect cruising yacht.

Women have played a major part on the cruising scene and the success of many outstanding voyages is often due to them, yet the role of women on cruising boats is rarely discussed and their contribution is simply taken for granted. In order to bring up to date the findings of a previous survey on this subject, in the winter of 2001 a wide-ranging survey was conducted among 20 women in which their participation in the successful running of a cruising boat, their concerns and expectations, were examined in great detail. In most instances the women inter-viewed in the Sailing Women Survey were the companions of sailors participating in the Global Cruising Survey.

The sailors

The various rallies that I have been involved with in the last 15 years, whether transatlantic or around the world, have brought me into contact with many sailors, some of whom have since become personal friends. They were, naturally, my first choice when I started working on the Global Cruising Survey and I am very grateful both to them, and to all others who agreed to collaborate in this ambitious project, for their valuable and selfless contribution. Their names will crop up again

The latest
Aventura *has*
taken the author
to many corners
of the globe, often
accompanied by
Gwenda, Ivan or
Doina Cornell.

and again in the following chapters as I decided to quote many of their comments in their own words, rather than distil them into arid statistical data.

The Millennium Odyssey round the world rally brought together several sailors who had sailed in previous rallies. It was indeed a very special event as the 40 yachts that sailed in it carried around the world a symbolic flame of peace for the new millennium. Don and Lois Babson on *Que Sera Sera*, Charles and Saundra Grey on *Sea Gem*, and Bob and Judy Hall on *Hornblower* are all veterans of America 500, another symbolic event that in 1992 had crossed the Atlantic along the historic route of Christopher Columbus to commemorate the quincentenary of that momentous voyage. One remarkable sailor who stands out all on his own is Michael Frankel. On his small *Sabra* he accomplished several singlehanded voyages, including America 500. He joined the Millennium Odyssey as crew on *Hornblower* and used the opportunity to conduct a wide-ranging survey among the participants in that round the world rally. Michael generously allowed me to use extracts from his valuable survey, as well as some of its results, in this book.

The Global Cruising Survey brought together other Millennium Odyssey participants, such as David Hersey and Steve Spink of *Company*, Javier Visiers of *Antaviana*, Ann Harsh and Ralph Nehrig of *Harmonie*, Klaus Girzig of *Alparena*, Chris Harding of *Futuro*, Volker Reinke of *Vegewind*, Matt Rollberg and Margaret Reichenbach of *Santana*, and John and Alison Wicks of *Dreamtime*.

Other circumnavigators who contributed to the Global Cruising Survey were Carlton and Jody DeHart, who had sailed on *Miss Muffet* in a previous round the world rally, as had Astrid and Wilhelm Greiff on *Octopus*, and Terence Brownrigg on *Fiskery*.

Another participant in America 500, who left an indelible mark on that rally, and who made an invaluable contribution to the Global Cruising Survey, was Bill Butler. In 1989, with his wife Simonne, he left Florida on the 38-foot *Siboney* to sail the long way around the world to join America 500 in Spain. En route to the Philippines, the wooden yacht was sunk by pilot whales. Bill and Simonne spent 66 days in their liferaft before being rescued. Undeterred, Bill bought the 40-foot *New Chance*, sailed across the Atlantic, and was there for the start of America 500. Several years later, after successfully completing a circumnavigation of South America and crossing Europe via the Rhine and Danube, *New Chance* was lost off Newfoundland.

Antti and Nina Louhija's 33-foot *Pegasos* also sailed in America 500 and later set off on a round the world voyage. While sailing in the Red Sea, only a few hundred miles short of completing her circumnavigation, she was lost on a reef off the Sudanese coast. Also from the class of America 500 is Eduardo Gallardo of *Argo*, whose boat is currently based in Croatia.

Several of the contributors to the Global Cruising Survey had sailed in one of the ARCs such as Mirek and Lucy Misayat of *Kaprys*, Barry Esrig of *Annie B*, Tom Muller and Lilly Vedana of *Miz Mae*, and Klaus Bartels of *Cythera*.

Well known to participants in these various rallies was John Ellis, an accomplished New Zealand sailor who took part in the first round the world rally, and afterwards managed several rallies as my trusted and hard-working deputy. A similar role was played in the Millennium Odyssey by Jamaican Tom Williams.

Two major contributors to the survey need no introduction as they are well-known writers in their own right: Arthur Beiser and Steve Dashew. Arthur and Germaine Beiser are now cruising in the Mediterranean on their *Ardent Spirit*, while Steve and Linda Dashew criss-cross the oceans on their state-of-the-art *Beowulf*.

Skip Novak is a well-known racing skipper and participant in several Whitbread round the world races. His *Pelagic* has sailed on numerous expeditions to Antarctica, South Georgia and Patagonia, and is now permanently based in the Southern Ocean.

Other sailors who have contributed to the Global Cruising Survey are Silvana and Giuseppe Italo Masotti, whose *Freedom* is based in the Mediterranean, John and Marilyn Morgan on *Sheerwater II*, and David and Glynn Beauchamp on

Milady Candida, both currently cruising in the South Indian Ocean. Temporarily land-based sailors are circumnavigators Marc Labaume and Paulette Vannier, Peter Förthmann, the well-known manufacturer of the Windpilot self-steering gear, Helmut van Straelen, who lives in Kalkar, Germany, and Dr Thomas Wilm from Port Elizabeth in South Africa.

Our website www.noonsite.com has put me in touch with several cruising sailors who have made valuable contributions to this survey, such as Dorothy and Richard Walker, whose *Mariposa* is currently cruising in South-East Asia, Luc Callebaut and Jackie Lee, based in the South Pacific on their trimaran *Sloepmouche*, and Ann and Clyff Huggett, currently in the eastern Caribbean on *Koncerto*.

Two singlehanders who have shared their experience with me are Zoltan Gyurko of *The Way* and Michelle LaMontagne of *Wooden Shoe*. Michelle is one of three female skippers who contributed to the Global Cruising Survey. The others are Ann Harsh of *Harmonie* and Annelie Rollfing, whose *Maresa II* is engaged in charter work in the Caribbean.

In the following chapters these remarkable sailors will help me answer some of the questions that I am frequently asked at lectures and cruising seminars: what kind of boats sail the oceans? How are they equipped? What equipment works, and what doesn't? Who are the people who cruise today? What is the best age to go cruising? How feasible is cruising with children and is it recommended? Can women share equally in the handling of a cruising boat? How dangerous is cruising today? How much does it cost to cruise full time? What are the essential features of the ideal cruising yacht? Which are the most popular cruising grounds? How overcrowded are those popular areas? What is the future of cruising?

1

From Dream to Reality
OFFSHORE CRUISING YACHTS TODAY

"I will never have a boat so large and complicated that I cannot with my own eyes and hands check everything regularly and be able to fix almost any defect that may arise."   ARTHUR BEISER

"I don't believe there are good or bad construction materials, only good or bad builders."   JAVIER VISIERS

"As my wife puts it, the design of a boat starts with an icemaker and works outward."   CARLTON DeHART

Everyone who has been cruising, and even those who just dream about it, has in their mind a picture of the perfect cruising yacht. That this picture is not the same for everyone is clear from the enormous variety of yachts one sees in marinas and anchorages all over the world. While some people have very clear ideas about the essential features of a cruising boat and how it should be equipped, many others, particularly the less experienced, find the choice bewildering.

The basic parameters of size, construction material, displacement, rig and keel configuration have to be decided before one comes to the equally difficult decisions over equipment. This is not helped by the fact that even designers are rarely agreed on the optimum characteristics of an offshore cruising yacht. It was to try and find some consensus on this subject, or the reasons for a lack of consensus, that I first started questioning experienced cruising skippers in my surveys. While some of them had bought or built their boats specifically with an offshore cruise in mind, others had just set off in the boat they happened to own at the time, which may have been purchased originally for a very different kind of sailing. To try to assess the essential features of a cruising boat qualitatively, in my earlier surveys the skippers were asked to give a rating to the various features of the boat they were sailing on at the time, while in the latest cruising survey skippers were questioned on both what they considered to be the essential features of an ideal cruising yacht, and also to comment on how close their present boat comes to that elusive ideal. In a few cases the two views coincided, as the skippers were already sailing on what they considered to be their ideal boat but, as will become clear from the findings of the Global Cruising Survey, these were obviously the exception.

The search for the ideal cruising yacht can be a complex and difficult task, fraught with doubts, mainly because the choice confronting a buyer is so enormous. Several of the surveys I conducted during the last quarter of a century tried to answer this complex question and, although cruising yacht design has evolved greatly since my earlier surveys, the requirements of those sailing have remained largely the same. Therefore the main aim of this chapter is to present first an overview of the kind of cruising boats that are sailing the oceans at this moment, and compare the current situation with what some experienced and well-travelled sailors think should be the best choice of boat or equipment for an extended cruise. It will soon become apparent that there is a great difference between what one sees in marinas or popular anchorages now and what those questioned regard as the 'ideal' cruising boat. As Arthur Beiser, whose very successful book (*The Perfect Yacht*) deals with this subject in great detail, points out, 'There are four essentials for a proper yacht. These are, not in order because all four are needed, that the boat be (1) beautiful; (2) fast under sail and under power; (3) able (well designed and engineered, strongly built and well equipped); and (4) comfortable at sea and in port, on deck and below.'

Although everyone will probably agree with that description, there may be situations when a different set of priorities may apply, as explained by Skip Novak: 'A pragmatic approach is needed when considering the design of a boat built for expeditions in difficult areas. Style counts for little. With this philosophy four considerations come to mind: hull material, lifting appendages, simple sailing and mechanical systems, and good cockpit protection.'

Whether one approaches this subject by applying Arthur Beiser's basic parameters or takes Skip Novak's pragmatic stance, the choice of the ideal cruising boat is a complex undertaking, with many details that make up the whole, so in this chapter only the essential features of such a boat will be discussed: length, displacement, draft and construction material.

On many occasions in the past, my own interest in the ideal cruising boat made me look more critically at the vast range of cruising boats that I saw every year in the rallies I organized. Thousands of participants have taken part in successive ARCs, providing a constant source of data on various aspects of offshore cruising. From standard production boats to luxurious custom-built yachts, from light displacement cruiser-racers to heavy classics of yesteryear, the variation in the ARC boats is only matched by that of the skippers: from those on a tight budget to millionaires, from those making their first ocean passage to veterans of many transatlantic voyages. Nevertheless, compared to the boats surveyed in other parts of the world, the majority of the yachts taking part in the ARC are standard production boats. Walking down the dock in Las Palmas one can see among them some of the latest offshore cruising yachts from the drawing boards of the best naval architects in the world today. There is no doubt that great strides have been made in offshore yacht design since my first survey, and that both designers and builders have learned a lot from earlier mistakes.

Size

Undoubtedly the first decision to be made by anyone contemplating acquiring a boat is its size. The length itself depends on many factors, such as the number of crew, the length of time intended to spend afloat, the cruising area envisaged and,

All kinds of boats take part in round the world rallies, but is the ideal cruising boat among them?

of course, the size of one's wallet. For most people the latter reason is the determining factor, and I know of many cases where a larger boat would have been acquired if the funds available had allowed it. Nevertheless, financial considerations should not be permitted to override all other criteria in the choice of boat for an extended cruise. As Ian Allmark, who had cruised for many years on his 35-foot *Telemark*, advised, 'Don't go for a bigger boat than you need, and most certainly do not buy a large boat just because you can afford it.' I remember these words of wisdom every time I see a shorthanded crew arrive in a port on board a large yacht, which they obviously cannot handle comfortably on their own. As Bill Butler points out, 'Too many of my friends follow the erroneous belief that a yacht should be as long in feet as the years of your age.'

Unfortunately that useful yardstick – one's own age – may not necessarily coincide with what is best. The findings of my various surveys may provide a more objective approach to this subject, and in fact all earlier surveys show a remarkable consensus between what was regarded as the optimum length and the actual size of the cruising boats of the day. The one notable exception is the latest Global Cruising Survey, which is remarkable for the absence of a consensus among those interviewed on the optimum size of the ideal yacht. There was, however, a much closer relationship between the size of the yacht owned by most of those sailors and what each regarded as an ideal length.

The optimum size of a cruising boat was investigated on several occasions and it is very interesting that after all these years most of those interviewed point to virtually the same 'ideal' size. Let us first consider the size of boats that people are actually cruising in at the moment. In ARC 2001, the average length of the 219 boats was 48 feet, an average that was obviously affected by the higher than usual number of very large boats that sailed in the ARC in 2001. In fact, nearly half the yachts in the fleet (44 per cent) were between 40 and 50 feet, showing that this continues to be the most popular size among owners joining the ARC.

The trend towards larger boats was confirmed by Tony Mark, who is in a better position than anyone else to assess the changes that have occurred in the ARC over the years, having been chief safety inspector ever since this popular event started in 1986: 'The boats are getting bigger every year, also smarter and better equipped. Their age is also getting lower. Ten years ago there were a lot of older boats, whereas now the average age is between one and three years. There is also a much higher proportion of proprietary brands from large-capacity builders such as Hallberg Rassy, Swan, Oyster, Beneteau, Bavaria, etc. Many of the small builders are now gone, as are home-built boats.'

I can well remember the very different boats that sailed in the early ARCs when often we were concerned about the seaworthiness of some boats, and every year rejected one or two that were considered to be unsafe for an Atlantic crossing. I realized just how things had changed when I saw, among the 2001 entries, a smart brand-new Swan 48 flying the Russian flag and remembered the last time we had a Russian entry in the ARC. It had been a crudely home-built boat, equipped with a huge radio and radar more suited for a Soviet Navy destroyer, from which they had probably been liberated. The boat lacked many essential items, but other ARC participants stepped in and donated spare sails, provisions, an EPIRB, even money. Ten years later, one of the best-equipped yachts in the ARC hailed from Russia. The world has certainly moved on!

The average size has been steadily increasing, not just in the ARC but also among the boats sailing in round the world rallies. In the Millennium Odyssey the median boat size was 52 feet in a fleet that ranged from 37 feet to 73 feet. Fabio Colapinto, who had participated in a similar round the world rally on his 62-foot *Taratoo* five years earlier, remarked that boat lengths are increasing everywhere. According to Michael Frankel, 'This may be due to power winches and power furling gear that make large boat handling easier. It may also reflect an inflation in people's wealth and an ability to afford larger boats.'

Although the ARC provides a valuable cross-section of current cruising boat design, only a small proportion of their owners plan to embark on a world voyage. Therefore, the average size of boats taking part in the ARC, or in a round the world rally for that matter, may not be the best indication of the actual size of cruising boats on the global scene. A more significant sample was therefore needed, so I decided to analyse the size of the boats that stopped at the Royal Cape Yacht Club during 2000 (Table 1). There is little doubt that most of the 78 cruising boats that were hosted by that welcoming club were true world girdlers, and indeed several of them were on their way to completing a circumnavigation.

LOA (ft)		Monohulls	Catamarans
30–35	17	17	–
35–40	18	16	2
40–45	26	21	5
45–50	12	9	3
50–60	3	2	1
Over 60	2	2	–
Total	**78**	**67**	**11**

Table 1: The length of cruising boats that called at Cape Town in 2000

The average length of the 78 boats, which included 11 catamarans, was 42.6 feet. Although the sample in Table 1 includes a surprisingly large proportion of boats under 35 feet, the average is none the less close to the ideal length indicated by the majority of skippers interviewed in previous surveys, and also by many of those who took part in the Global Cruising Survey.

In the summer of 2001, while sailing from the south of France to the Canaries, we stopped for a couple of days in Gibraltar. By an incredible coincidence our first *Aventura* was also there, being sailed by her new owners to the Mediterranean. I had last seen *Aventura* in Greece in the summer of 1982 when I had handed her over to her new English owner. Her latest owner had bought her in a sorry state a few years previously but had done an excellent job in turning the 27-year-old hull into a beautiful yacht again. While both Gwenda and I were quite moved to be on board our beloved ship again, what struck us most was how small she appeared to be. The main cabin, especially, looked so small that Gwenda could not refrain from exclaiming, 'Did we really spend six years on this boat?' We were indeed amazed that not only had she been a comfortable home for us and our two children, but occasionally had hosted as many as four guests, including both our mothers. But we were young, and that was all we could afford then. Nor were we in any way exceptional as very few of the cruising boats in the 1970s were larger than our own modest 36 footer.

In this respect, too, expectations have changed radically in recent years, as soon became apparent from the ideal length indicated by many of the skippers interviewed in the Global Cruising Survey (Table 2). The first part of that survey dealt with the characteristics of their ideal cruising yacht, and one thing that soon became evident was the lack of consensus among those experienced 40 skippers as to what they considered to be an ideal length. This was in marked contrast to the results of the Ideal Boat Survey conducted in the early 1990s, when both the ideal size and the actual length of the boats that were sailing the oceans were more modest. The Global Cruising Survey confirmed this trend towards larger yachts, and although well over half of those interviewed would prefer their ideal yacht to be between 40 and 50 feet, several skippers would only consider a substantially larger yacht to meet their requirements.

LOA (ft)	Number of skippers
35–40	4
40–45	11
45–50	13
50–55	4
55–60	3
Over 60	5
Total	40

Table 2: The ideal length of yachts indicated by skippers in the Global Cruising Survey

Not all the skippers in this latest survey would prefer much larger yachts than their current ones. Bill Butler, whose latest boat is a 40-feet steel sloop built in Germany in the late 1940s from material destined for wartime submarines,

A sturdy steel boat like Pelagic *is well suited for high latitude sailing.*

considers the ideal length to be: '38 to 43 feet overall. Under 38 feet, in heavy weather conditions, you will soon find out that your boat is too small to handle overwhelming waves safely, and too small to stow provisions and safety equipment for long ocean passages. Over 43 feet, again, in heavy weather, you will need to have adequate crew to handle the boat safely in difficult conditions.' Antti Louhija fully agrees: '40 foot is perfect as it is big enough for comfort and small enough to be handled by my ideal crew of two.' Zoltan Gyurko, as a singlehander, would prefer something smaller, 'around 35 feet, so it can still fit in the trough of a hurricane swell'.

Marc Labaume feels that a larger boat has certain advantages: 'It should be between 40 and 46 feet. Under 40 feet, seaworthiness could be a problem, over 46 feet, maintenance costs and the ability to sail the boat alone or with a small crew (such as a couple) would become negative factors.' David Beauchamp shares those views: 'Our current boat is 42 feet LOA, but she was based on a 36-foot one-ton design and is basically just that as far as accommodation is concerned. This is too small for a live-aboard couple so we are currently looking at bigger boats, something about 40–45-feet deck length. This would seem about right for two fit and able people – providing she is rigged right. Still small enough to be handled by two people but large enough to carry and be sailed by a crew of six or even eight if required. A 36 footer can perform the same service (almost), but there is just not enough space for the necessities of life that make the difference between cruising and racing.'

Tom Muller would prefer a smaller boat than the 60 footer he is currently cruising on: 'For a couple I consider 40 feet to be adequate as it is spacious enough, can be a safe sea boat, with enough load capacity and enough freeboard to stay dry. Anything larger quickly increases costs dramatically, and requires much more maintenance, which is the time one could spend playing.'

Terence Brownrigg reached a similar conclusion, albeit for various reasons: 'It really depends on the number of people you wish to have on board regularly and, of course, what you can afford. When I bought *Fiskery* I was able to lift the genoa on my own without too much struggle, but having had a heavier cloth genoa made in South Africa, and being that much older now, it is a real struggle. I suspect that dyed-in-the-wool blue water cruisers are usually a couple, and I think that the sail lifting point is very important, so I would probably opt for a 42- to 43-foot boat with conventional rig.'

Matt Rollberg subscribes to that view: 'Our *Santana* is a Beneteau First 405. When we bought her in 1992 we knew we could sail her without any electric winches and with just the arm power of two of us aboard. We started our ocean adventures in 1994 by crossing the Atlantic and then cruising in the Med. We liked it so much we sailed back to the USA in 1995 and joined the Expo'98 round the world rally one year later. There was too little time to get a bigger boat, so we upgraded and went with what we had. We are still out here and she's working beautifully with just the two of us. However, if we had to do it all over again, based on our experiences since 1994, we'd get a bigger boat – say 44-foot – mainly to have extra storage space and more room for guests. We would particularly like to have two aft cabins so that the guests don't have to sleep in the saloon if we do an overnight sail.'

Luc Callebaut put the question of ideal length into perspective: 'The length depends on everything you plan on carrying on your voyage, and at the same time to be manageable by the crew. The waterline has to be long enough to still be able to go at an acceptable speed despite the weight carried. In our case, our first boat was a 28-foot catamaran, which we quickly overloaded, making it slow, so our present boat is a 46-foot trimaran that just makes it! 45 to 50 feet should be about right.'

Arthur Beiser, who sails mostly in the Mediterranean, prefers something larger: 'Depending on details of design, 55 to 60 feet would be closer to my ideal length. We have owned seven boats from 21 to 70 feet, two of them 58-foot LOA – the ketch *Minots Light* for 17 years and the cutter *Ardent Spirit* for 14 years thus far. The latter two were the most satisfactory of our boats, taking everything into account. Other people with different tastes and circumstances may well be happier with smaller or even larger boats, but this size has worked for us.'

Charles Gray, who recently completed a circumnavigation on the 54-foot *Sea Gem*, almost agrees: '54 feet is as large as two people (at least Saundra and I) can comfortably handle. I think for blue water sailing a larger boat is safer, as well as more comfortable in port.'

Skip Novak's 55-foot *Pelagic* is about that size, although he is planning to have a larger boat built that is better suited to his high latitude expeditions: 'The length depends entirely on the purpose of the boat and how many people will sail on her. If we are speaking about a couple or maybe four people, and your goals are to explore remote areas rather than make long fast ocean passages, then not more than about 50 or 55 feet. If you are interested in making fast passages, I would say a slightly bigger boat, which can sail easily at 10 knots, would be preferable. But at 55 feet a boat is big enough for comfort and yet small enough to handle. Electric winches and other needless complications are not necessary. Also, if your priority is to get close into shore and really get protection (rather than anchoring in big open spaces), then 55 feet or smaller is preferable.'

Chris Harding fully agrees: 'For myself I would consider the perfect length to be between 48 and 55 feet depending on what kind of cruising was planned. For longer cruising plans, I would prefer 55 feet.' John Ellis has something slightly larger in mind as his ideal cruising boat: 'Sixty feet as a maximum length would feel comfortable and could be handled by two people. This is assuming cost is no problem.'

Volker Reinke feels that for sailing in high latitudes, 60 to 70 feet would be more suitable, bearing in mind that he is used to sailing with large crews as part of his school of seamanship and navigation based in the north of Germany. Carlton DeHart is more concerned about waterline length than overall length: 'There is nothing more frustrating than having a slow boat that is heavily laden with all the cruising toys necessary to have a good time and all the cruising comforts to keep the crew happy. I feel that a waterline around 60 feet is the best length that will carry all the weight, yet is still manageable by two people. A yacht with a 60-foot waterline and 60-foot deck length would be ideal. It can carry all the weight and still clock 300-mile days. This is also a safety issue in that you can leave in good weather, stay with that weather pattern, and arrive in good weather. A smaller boat, doing 200-mile days at best, will catch all the weather patterns, use more provisions en route, and be at sea much longer. After all, fast is fun!'

Javier Visiers, whose maxi yacht *Fortuna* once held the world record for the fastest 24 hours in the Whitbread round the world race, entirely agrees that speed can be fun: 'The question of ideal size is very difficult to deal with and, in my own case, I must admit that over the years I have changed my mind several times depending on many factors such as age, financial possibilities, cruising plans, etc. Just now my ideal length is a 80-foot monohull with a displacement of 40 tons.' In other words, quite close to Steve Dashew's current 78-foot *Beowulf* which, not surprisingly, Steve considers to be the ideal size.

As several skippers pointed out, the size of crew also has a bearing on the size of boat, but a change of attitude has occurred in this respect too and many people are now prepared to handle boats that until not so long ago were considered to be fit only for a crew of Tarzans. This was particularly obvious in some of the round the world rallies in which boats well over 40-foot LOA were sailed only by a couple, many of them not even that young. Indeed, if one looks at existing boats rather than an ideal model, it was interesting to find that most of the boats in the various surveys did suit their owners' requirements, whether large or small, yet in every survey there were some disgruntled skippers. A few complained that their boats were too large to handle, but the majority of dissatisfied owners complained about their boat being too small. The feeling of being overcrowded or the lack of space can have a negative effect on morale and lead to friction among the members of the crew. Another cause of complaint was not having enough space to store all the gear necessary for a longer voyage. Often this meant that surplus gear was stowed on deck, which can lead to a potentially hazardous or unseaworthy situation. Having been on the dockside in St Lucia watching the ARC boats coming in to dock after their Atlantic crossing, I have been amazed at the clutter on the stern of some boats, as the person throwing the lines struggled to clear a forest of obstructions, from wind generator pole to danbuoy, radar mast, fishing rods, flagpole, spare anchor, whip aerial, outboard engine, barbecue and even a bicycle! In an emergency, one might need to throw a line to a man overboard or launch the liferaft past all such obstructions. Undoubtedly there is a great safety factor in having clear uncluttered decks. However, it does not follow that larger boats necessarily have tidier decks, but that the amount of cruising gear to be carried and how it will be stowed should be given serious consideration when acquiring a boat for extended cruising.

Larger boats also mean more living space and many of the owners of smaller boats stressed the importance of privacy, particularly on long passages. A separate cabin for each crew member is the ideal solution, or at least a provision to shield a bunk from the rest of the boat. Having a separate cabin for the children was stressed as extremely important by several parents. Another interesting suggestion concerned those who may be planning to set off on a joint adventure with another couple, in which case the boat should be designed in such a way as to give privacy to both couples.

Draft

Keel configuration and draft were examined in earlier surveys, whereas only the ideal draft was discussed in the Global Cruising Survey. Different concerns came to light in the latter compared to the Ideal Yacht Survey, in which skippers were asked to indicate their preferred keel and the maximum draft they would consider acceptable. Being concerned by the vulnerability of a fin keel on a cruising boat, several skippers stressed that fin keels should be matched with well-supported rudders protected by strong skegs. Two of them went even further and also specified a watertight bulkhead forward of the rudderstock. Several skippers qualified both their choice of keel and maximum draft by pointing out that a final decision would depend on the particular cruising area the boat was being built for. Just over one decade later, it was remarkable how much more importance most of the skippers interviewed in the Global Cruising Survey attached to shallow draft compared to those questioned on the same subject in the previous survey.

Skip Novak spoke for many when he explained: 'If your priority is to explore, rather than see from a distance, then some lifting appendage is necessary. My preference is for a lifting ballasted keel and lifting rudder so that drying out can be achieved. A centreboard allows you to get into shallower places. However, if you are cruising in deeper, well-charted waters, and staying in marinas, not getting too close to tricky situations, then a fixed keel would be better, as the lifting appendages need some care and judgement in their operation.'

Arthur Beiser prefers a less radical solution: 'The keel-centreboard on our former Swan 47 *Quicksilver* (6 feet board up, 10 feet board down) provided excellent performance and was trouble-free for the ten years we owned the boat.

A centreboard can be an advantage when cruising in shallow waters. While cruising the Chilean canals, Aventura III dries out between tides for a coat of antifouling paint.

Not all other boats with centreboards have given us such service, however. I would say it depends on the experience of the builder: if a builder has not had sufficient satisfactory experience with centreboards, I would probably prefer a moderately shallow fixed keel.'

Terence Brownrigg had a similar experience: 'My previous boat had a lifting keel which I much appreciated. The trouble was awful windward performance, but I believe this has now improved. If starting from scratch I would have either a lifting keel or a centreboard. Ideal draft would be as shallow as possible and the maximum would not matter – presumably the deeper the better for windward performance.' It is something that Marc Labaume fully agrees with: 'Less is best. With four feet or less, you can go almost anywhere. Centreboard could be the solution for a monohull, skegs for a multihull.' This was a view shared by Clyff Huggett, who sails a catamaran: 'Beaching keels with a draft of around 3 feet would be best, and also for better control when manoeuvring at slow speeds with the two engines. Drop keels or daggerboards to increase draft to six feet for windward work.'

For Bill Butler, the 'ideal draft is between 6 and 7 feet. Much less than 6 feet means that performance is handicapped, particularly in heavy weather, and there is no real need to go over 7 feet. A fixed keel is the way to go. It eliminates the maintenance hassle of a centreboard. Fin keels help you go a bit faster with their reduced wetted area but by necessity are not attached to the hull anywhere like a full keel. I like a semi-full keel design, with the leading edge of the keel being led up towards the waterline.'

Chris Harding, who has cruised extensively in a deep-drafted Swan 65, is fully aware of the disadvantages: 'The ideal draft would be 1 metre; unfortunately, this is not very practical for my ideal 55-foot boat. A compromise on this would be a draft of about 7 feet, depending on how performance-oriented you wish the boat to be. There are several options for lifting keels and daggerboards available, but most daggerboards tend to be quite noisy if at all loose and the risk of getting blocked either up or down from barnacles or mud seems to be quite high. As for lifting keels, because of the need for complicated hydraulic systems to deal with all the weight involved, I would not consider one of these systems.' Javier Visiers agrees: 'The least draft is always best, but only if this is possible by avoiding any kind of lifting arrangement or moving parts.'

Volker Reinke, who sails mostly in high latitudes, takes a similar view: 'I prefer a fixed keel on an ocean-going vessel as I was once caught by a storm in the north Atlantic and found that the light displacement aluminium centreboard yacht was not easy on my crew (all of whom were sick) and I would have wished to be able to set more sail, but considered this to be too risky.'

Klaus Bartels, who also sails in the North Sea, would prefer 'a fixed keel, as it needs no maintenance and there is not much that can go wrong'. Michael Frankel shares that view and is supported by Luc Callebaut who 'would prefer a fixed keel around 5 feet. A centreboard is one more source of trouble and annoyance with rattling noise.' Steve Dashew is also in favour of a fixed keel: 'The draft would depend on the size of the boat – on our present *Beowulf* it is just under 8 feet.'

John Ellis, who has raced and cruised on a variety of yachts, comments: 'I swing back and forth on this one, but if I had to make a choice I would go for a fixed keel with a torpedo bulb. Draft would be about 8 feet, certainly no more than 9 feet. This would be the ideal compromise between performance and draft restrictions in certain anchorages and marinas.' Steve Spink also prefers 'a traditional fin keel, which does restrict the draft but a fin/bulb combination could bring the draft to under 5 feet'. David Hersey, who Steve sails with, disagrees: '*Company*'s draft is 8 feet which I regard as an absolute maximum. If I ever change yachts I will want some sort of lifting keel arrangement so as to be able to reduce draft.'

Carlton DeHart, who sailed around the world on just such a boat, now seems to have certain doubts: 'I think that you greatly limit the places you can go in the world by having a deep draft. Our last boat had a draft of 6 feet with the centreboard up and 11 feet with the board down. This worked really well and allowed us to get into places most other boats could not reach. The only downside was that the board was noisy when sailing off the wind. Also, when running with the board up, the boat would roll from side to side more than a boat with a deep draft. Next time I'd probably go for a shallow 6-foot draft version of a fixed keel and keep it simple.'

Matt Rollberg arrived at the same conclusion: '*Santana* has a shallow draft keel and draws 6 feet. If we had a fin keel, we'd point 5 degrees higher, which would be nice, but since we're not racing, it's OK. I'd be wary of a centreboard because of the extra maintenance. *Santana* has explored the Bahamas three times, admittedly plowing from time to time, and a centreboard wasn't really necessary.'

David Beauchamp agrees: 'My experience has been with a draft of around 6 feet. This is great for passage making, but I must admit having on many occasions wished for less draft when close inshore or passing through reef areas. A centre-board in a big boat seems to me to be just one more item that could go radically wrong at a dangerous time – so I wouldn't have one. Maybe a catamaran could be the answer.'

For Don Babson the ideal solution would be 'fixed keel for mid-ocean, unless sailing downwind in the trade winds, centreboard for shallow waters. We have owned two 38-foot centreboard yachts previously, and would do so again, but our fixed keel of 6½ feet served us well in the many conditions and mostly deep water found on our recent circumnavigation.'

Tom Muller is pleased with his present system: 'We have a centreboard and I feel it is a great bonus for many anchorages, also when sailing downwind, even if upwind performance is affected. However, it is a problem if you have to maintain it in Third World countries.'

Michelle LaMontagne would choose her draft depending on 'my cruising destination. For coastal cruising (Bahamas, Mexico, Med, etc.) I would prefer maximum 5 feet or a centreboard.' Wilhelm Greiff stressed the advantage of 'being able to dry out upright so I'd be prepared to let the shape of the keel of my ideal yacht to be dictated by this requirement'. Such a boat should therefore have a fairly flat bottom and be provided with either a centreboard or swing keel. The rudder itself would have to be either retractable or a twin rudder configuration. My own *Aventura III* comes close to Wilhelm's specifications as she has a flat bottom and a draft of 8 feet with the board down, and 3 feet with the board and rudder up.

One skipper who went the opposite way is Alastair Duncan, who switched from a centreboard aluminium boat to a deep-drafted fibreglass yacht: 'There are times when I regret not having the ability to slip into those shallow sheltered anchorages, but all this is blown away as soon as you realize that going to wind-ward is no longer the trial it used to be and indeed is something to be enjoyed.'

Among those for whom a catamaran was the ideal cruising boat, low draft appeared to be one of the main attractions. Another attraction of catamarans outlined by their supporters was the possibility of providing them with sufficient positive buoyancy to render them unsinkable. Three catamaran owners mentioned that they would make sure that their ideal cats incorporated extra buoyancy chambers, which could keep them afloat even if the boat was partially flooded.

Multihulls

It is interesting that in spite of the undeniable advantages of multihulls for cruising, their popularity is still limited. There are several reasons for this, mainly the reservations many people seem to have about the safety of multihulls in offshore sailing. The well-publicized disasters involving racing multihulls have certainly not helped the cause of cruising multihulls, in spite of the fact that several outstanding voyages have been accomplished in cruising catamarans. Indeed, among the skippers interviewed for the Global Cruising Survey there were at least two who had sailed around the world in a catamaran, and a few more are cruising at this very moment in a multihull.

I cannot think of any other subject that can cause so much controversy among sailors as the debate of monohulls versus multihulls. Most monohull sailors regard multihull sailors with suspicion, while many multihull sailors regard the others with derision. I will never forget the furore created by an advertisement placed by *Multihulls* magazine in various other US sailing publications showing side by side the photograph of an upright catamaran and a monohull being raced so hard that it was showing most of its underwater body as well as much of its keel. The photo was accompanied by the caption 'Do you really want to cruise on your ear?', or words to that effect.

The Global Cruising Survey was a perfect opportunity to ask all those experienced sailors whether they would consider a multihull as their ideal cruising boat. Not surprisingly, there were no doubts about their choice among the multi-hull owners, such as Clyff Huggett: 'I have been sailing since I was 16 years old and that's over 45 years of experience. I have sailed boats from Optimists to big square-riggers, and boats with one, two and three hulls. We now sail a catamaran that has space and grace and does not require you to live at 45 degrees for days on end when on an ocean crossing. It is therefore a lot less fatiguing. We can sit at the table and have our meal on a plate without it or the coffee spilling on the floor. We do not need hand holds and straps in the galley to prepare a meal. If we hit something hard at speed and hole the boat, it will not sink under our feet. Yes, we do have to be careful not to fill up all the space with gear and overload the boat because she will then become too stable and unyielding, thus putting too much pressure on the rig. Nor would she be able to accelerate in strong gusts of wind. The only reservation I have for sailing any boat is: wherever it is, it must be warm!'

Luc Callebaut agrees: 'I would *only* consider a multihull for cruising! Stability (so nice not to live at an angle!), space (a big cockpit and a huge deck to relax and entertain) and safety (unsinkable and rarely tipped over, never rolled over!), all show the advantages of multihulls. Supposedly speed is also an advantage, but as you tend to overload a cruising multihull, there goes the speed edge! We prefer a trimaran to a catamaran because you have more feeling about the sailing and you slam less. If I have reservations about going some places on a multihull, then I think perhaps I should not go there at all! As far as we are concerned, difficult cruising areas are better read about or seen on TV. We are happy to stay between the tropics, where the weather is generally nice and warm.'

Marc Labaume is another convinced multihull sailor: 'Definitely our choice, even for some areas prone to heavy weather (high latitudes either in the south or the north). My only reservation is the safety factor in very heavy seas, also if you have to find your way through brash ice or are confronted with many growlers. In those situations, a multihull is obviously not the best answer. While in the far north of Alaska we decided to sail on a monohull.'

Javier Visiers, probably the best-known Spanish naval architect, who designed the highly popular Fortuna range (monohulls), proved his pragmatism when for the Millennium Odyssey round the world rally he chose a catamaran, which he sailed with his wife Barbara and friends. As he pointed out: 'I was very happy with the performance of our Lagoon 47 during our recent circumnavigation. I believe that it was the ideal boat for that voyage, for that route, and also for our budget.

In spite of which, I feel that if you want to sail in the Southern Ocean, a monohull would be better, but not just any monohull.'

John Ellis agrees: 'A cat is a perfect boat for destination cruising, such as for a group of friends to charter a yacht in the Caribbean for a couple of weeks. Long ocean crossings on a multihull are probably OK in some areas, although I still prefer a monohull for this, but I would stay away from the Capes and any high latitude sailing.'

Arthur Beiser is among those who have certain doubts about multihulls: 'It depends on how and where you cruise. For us a monohull is the right boat. I would not like to have a boat that limits how much I can carry, is not awfully strong, and can turn over and stay over – plus is not convenient in many harbours. For certain of our friends, catamarans seem to have worked out well, but we have never been tempted except for exciting daysails.'

This is a view shared by Carlton DeHart: 'I am very uncomfortable with the idea of any boat being more stable upside down than right side up. I think that multihulls have their place such as cruising the Bahamas, where they present a comfortable platform with lots of room for four couples to explore the islands. However, with a short crew and lots of weight, I think their advantages start to disappear. Multihulls are fast when kept very light, but start loading all the gear and they become as slow as a monohull. There is something very comforting about a monohull that is self-righting. I have been in situations where I was very happy not to have a multihull. I'm sure that we could have done it, but we would have been very close to our Creator. I had a long talk with the owner of a catamaran from New Zealand, after the Queen's Birthday Storm. They were experienced boatbuilders and sailors and made it through that storm dragging warps and drogues to slow their progress. They sustained structural damage where the cross-beams attach to the hulls and broke their rudders. They were no longer happy with a catamaran and were quite shaken by the experience. That was good enough for me. It will always be a monohull, just a fast one.'

Some of the skippers interviewed in the Global Cruising Survey who own monohulls are planning to switch to a multihull for their new boat, such as David Beauchamp: 'I am, indeed, considering a catamaran for cruising, but not a trimaran. A big catamaran over 12 metres that can be handled by a couple with, on most occasions, more ease than a monohull. I have spoken to owners of large cats. They are best kept between 30 degrees north and 30 degrees south for safety's sake.' Tom Muller shares that view: 'We are planning to go for a multihull ourselves. We have no reservations unless you want to go to the Arctic or Antarctic.'

The fear of being caught out in heavy weather was mentioned by several skippers, such as Bob Hall, who: 'would consider a multihull, but not in the Roaring Forties'. This is also how Bill Butler feels about them: 'I am not sold on the ability of a multihull to maintain its stability during severe oceanic conditions. If I did sail a multihull I would do so only when and where weather conditions would assure me of no severe weather.' Volker Reinke has had just that kind of experience: 'I consider multihulls, especially heavily built or overladen cruising catamarans, as too risky in heavy weather. Maybe I am being biased as I was once caught out by bad weather in the North Sea in a 55-foot blue water catamaran. The crossbeams and daggerboard casings were badly damaged, as were the supports of

the rudders. This particular catamaran had a weight of 12 tons, which proved to be too much to keep it going fast enough to avoid some of the worst seas.'

Antti Louhija and Chris Harding expressed similar doubts, as did Steve Dashew: 'Would I consider a multihull? Never! They are too slow and unsafe in extreme weather.' Don Babson is equally adamant: 'No! I can't forget what happened to the guy who invented them . . . Arthur Piver, who was lost at sea on one of his own trimarans.'

John Wicks is not so concerned: 'A multihull would seem an ideal craft if making sure it had an escape hatch and twin engines.' This is exactly what Michelle LaMontagne seems to dislike: 'I would have a problem buying a boat that has a built-in escape hatch on the bottom! However, for coastal cruising it is probably fine and easier for the guys to get a woman on board when the galley does not tip over.'

Skip Novak is also of the opinion that multihulls are a good choice for certain areas: 'If I was concentrating my cruising in the tropics and doing mainly trade wind sailing, and was heavily involved in diving or other activities, then a multihull makes a lot of sense. Plus the passage times will be halved. The only reservation is being caught out in a tropical storm, so you would have to really be aware of the seasons and the weather in the short term – especially in areas like the North Pacific where you can have a typhoon in any month. They are certainly not suitable for high latitudes, and arguably so for mid-latitudes where it is more likely you will be going to marinas where it is always difficult to find a place.' Klaus Bartels agrees: 'Having a multihull in the Baltic is completely impractical because of the beam that would not fit into most of the small ports and narrow pontoon spaces.'

My personal views reflect those of Skip Novak. We very nearly sailed around the world in a catamaran in the early 1970s, but none of the builders would sell me a bare hull, which was all that we could afford, so we ended up with a monohull instead. My decision was justified during the following summer in Greece where we sailed in company with a 37-foot catamaran, identical to the one I had planned to buy. One day we had to sail to windward against a not very strong meltemi, and our friends on their heavily laden cat simply could not make it. It was a scene I saw repeated in Las Palmas every time we had a windward start for the ARC, when some catamarans, fully laden with provisions for the Atlantic crossing, had great trouble clearing the start line.

Several skippers stressed how important it was not to overload a catamaran, however tempting it may be to fill up all those empty spaces. This is why some of the skippers quoted earlier suggest that larger catamarans are better suited for cruising as they are able to carry sufficient weight. Indeed, for a crew of two, provisions for an ocean passage weigh the same whether loaded onto a small or a larger boat. But whereas on a small boat one ton of provisions, fuel and water can be as much as 25 per cent of its total displacement, the same ton only amounts to 10 per cent on a considerably larger cat.

Displacement

The variety in boat design that I came across in the various rallies prompted me to examine more systematically the factors that can influence the choice of a cruising boat. One conclusion that I drew was that a surprisingly large number of people do not consider displacement to be of sufficient importance to influence greatly the choice of their future boat. It seems that many people are quite happy to leave this decision to the designer, particularly such niceties as the displacement to sail area or displacement to ballast ratio. In an earlier survey, when asked if they were satisfied with their present ratio, a considerable number of skippers did not even know what their displacement to ballast ratio was, let alone comment on it.

The fact that displacement is something that many cruising skippers treat with indifference was shown every year by the number of blank spaces or obviously incorrect figures given for displacement on the ARC entry forms. I was always puzzled by this, and I am convinced that the performance of many cruising boats would be significantly better if their owners had given displacement the consideration it deserves when they were in the process of choosing a suitable boat for their cruising plans. Often it is only when they start cruising and meeting other boats that this important element of yacht design attracts their attention, invariably much too late to do anything about it. This attitude was summed up by Erick Bouteleux, who never failed to show his disdain for some of his fellow Frenchmen, who had slavishly copied Moitessier's ultra-heavy *Joshua*, 'What fun can anyone get from sailing in a floating safe?'

Displacement was examined in various surveys and the majority of those questioned favoured a medium displacement boat, able to carry sufficient stores and provisions, but without being sluggish. One valuable suggestion concerning displacement underlined the importance of the designer taking into account the additional weight of water, fuel, stores and gear that are carried by every cruising boat, when calculating the displacement of the fully laden boat. This should then determine the amount of ballast to be added. Obviously with production or secondhand boats, the prospective owner can do little about this, but otherwise it is in the owner's best interest to inform both designer and builder of his weight requirements and how it will be distributed, especially heavy items such as batteries, extra anchors or the amount of chain.

Construction material

Most people have a fairly precise idea about the kind of construction material they prefer long before they choose the actual design of their boat. As far as standard production boats are concerned, in most cases the choice boils down to any kind of material as long as it is fibreglass. A wider choice is available to those who can afford a one-off, who plan to build the boat themselves, or who decide to circumvent all these problems and buy a used boat.

Although fibreglass continues to be the dominant construction material for the large-scale production of cruising boats, other materials still have an assured slice of the market. A tendency highlighted by my earlier surveys was the increasing popularity of metal hulls. Many sailors who cruise among the reefs and coral atolls of the South Pacific feel safer in a metal boat. The preference for strong hulls is not such a priority in the Atlantic, where the proportion of metal boats is generally lower. Although the proportion of metal boats is much lower in the Atlantic than among those cruising in the Pacific, the concern for strength was still manifested by many of the skippers participating in the Ideal Yacht Survey, several of whom indicated a metal hull as their ideal choice. Ten years later in the Global Cruising Survey an equal proportion of skippers showed a preference for a metal hull in their choice of ideal boat. However, there were fewer who showed a preference for steel instead of aluminium, the latter usually being the choice of those who wanted to combine strength with a lighter displacement. Indeed, as mentioned in the section on displacement, the latest surveys reveal a shift towards lighter displacement boats. However, from talking to many of the skippers, it was clear that they were not prepared to sacrifice strength for the sake of speed, but rather it was the other way around: they expected designers to produce cruising boats that were strong as well as fast.

Although the majority still consider a GRP hull to be the ideal construction material, there is now a higher proportion of metal boats among those undertaking world voyages. This is not the situation in the ARC fleet, in which the proportion of metal hulls continues to be quite low. Among the 219 boats that sailed in ARC 2001, the majority were fibreglass (202), with only 8 aluminium, 7 steel, and 2 yachts made of wood. It is quite interesting that if given the choice to name their ideal material, the results are very different from the actual state of affairs. Indeed, when it comes to actually buying a boat for an intended voyage, whether new or used, many other elements come into play, with availability and price often proving to be the determining factors.

In the Global Cruising Survey several skippers declared in favour of fibreglass – even, surprisingly, some who had good reasons to prefer something more resistant to impact, such as Bill Butler: 'Any heavy-duty hull material such as epoxy resin impregnated fibreglass below the waterline. The hull must be safely able to resist collision, grounding, or impact as may be expected during a severe hurricane.' Or, maybe I should add, a collision with a whale, or grounding on a rock – as this is how Bill lost his last two boats. Antti Louhija, who, like Bill Butler, also had the traumatic experience of losing his boat, also considers GRP 'almost ideal. Steel would of course be stronger, but needs much more maintenance.' Marc Labaume agrees: 'When well constructed, GRP/sandwich is OK, perhaps reinforced with Kevlar in some critical stress points, such as chain plates, etc. Alternatively, aluminium also looks interesting, but as far as any material is concerned, I am mostly concerned by the maintenance-free aspect. The idea of a steel boat strong enough to endure grounding on a reef is for me like the idea of driving on a road in an armoured tank.'

Carlton DeHart, who circumnavigated the world in his fibreglass Bowman 57 *Miss Muffet*, tends to agree: 'An alloy boat would be much stronger and take hitting a container better than most materials. The downside would be trying to keep paint on it and being ever mindful of electrolysis. For longevity, I would go with a single lay-up of non-cored fibreglass with a Kevlar outer skin around the bow for impact resistance, and use a non-blistering resin. I don't really think that there is an ideal material. It is a compromise at best. Either material has good points and bad.' Javier Visiers underscored that point: 'There is no good or bad construction material, but unfortunately there are good and bad boatbuilders! For any kind of boat, and depending on budget and availability, one can choose one or the other. In my own case the next boat will be made of aluminium.'

Peter Förthmann was very scathing about the poor standard of some fibreglass boats: 'When installing my self-steering gear on some fibreglass boats I am amazed at the thinness of the hull in the stern area. I really wonder if they use only 3 mm for the transom, how much stronger the hull itself could be?' For this reason, Terence Brownrigg felt that older fibreglass boats were so much stronger, and buying an older well-built boat was probably a better idea: 'They didn't know how to build *thin* hulls in those days.'

Luc Callebaut was unequivocal: 'The ideal material is one that doesn't exist! Everything is a compromise. Our first boat was fibreglass and, except for some minor blistering problem, was fine. Our present boat is made of double diagonal plywood, covered with Unitex [a little-known British product designated to protect underground piping for 30 years] that we covered with a few coats of epoxy when the boat was already 14 years old, and we are very satisfied as the boat is now 22 years old. When I see new steel or aluminium boats, they look fine, but after a few years they start losing the battle against corrosion. Electrolysis is also difficult to fight. I once maintained an old aluminium boat whose metal was showing signs of age fatigue. Finally, ferro-cement is heavy and has its own problems with age. The ideal material would be light, resilient to stress and impact, resistant to corrosion and electrolysis, easy to glue things on, and affordable! Is this a dream? Until then, wood/fibreglass/epoxy or fibreglass hulls are my favourite.'

Tom Muller agrees and prefers fibreglass: 'A 40-foot boat in steel would be too heavy for my taste, while alloy would be expensive and I'd worry about electrolysis. Wood is simply not practical.' For Clyff Huggett the answer is simple: 'Fibreglass over foam. Easy to repair with modern materials, especially in a multihull which will still float after being holed.' David Hersey agrees: 'Modern reinforced composites seem pretty strong, are long-lasting with excellent thermal and sound properties.' For Don Babson, who circumnavigated in his fibreglass 43-foot *Que Sera Sera*: 'My choice hull material would be cored glassfibre. You certainly would not want to go to Antarctica with a cold aluminium hull, would you?' A barbed question pointed at myself, as we sailed together to Patagonia and beyond and Don knew too well that, if anything, my well-insulated *Aventura* was never cold. Chris Harding, who sailed the same route on the Swan 65 *Futuro*, also considers a fibreglass hull as coming closest to being the ideal material: 'Steel is not an option because of the amount of maintenance involved and aluminium, while if unpainted requires little work, still has the corrosion problems when connected to stainless steel.'

Arthur Beiser, who has owned several fibreglass boats, would be ready to change: 'Probably aluminium, although cold-moulded laminated wood sheathed in fibreglass is also attractive. The final choice would probably depend on the builder's skills and experience.' Charles Gray is attracted to the idea of an alloy hull, 'but only if all proper measures are taken to eliminate dissimilar metal as well as condensation problems. Otherwise fibreglass.' John Ellis has no doubts about aluminium: 'It is light, strong and requires low maintenance. Light – so the boat is fast, strong – so you can bounce off rocks and icebergs. Low maintenance is a high priority, as you want to spend your time enjoying your cruise and not polishing and varnishing.' Steve Dashew is also keen on aluminium, which he suggests should be left unpainted. An aluminium hull would also be the choice of Matt Rollberg: 'Our Beneteau is relatively thick plastic and because of that we don't push *Santana* into tight situations. We think it would be nice to have aluminium, especially if we go through the Straits of Magellan. Even then we would probably continue to sail cautiously.'

For David Beauchamp the choice is clear: 'My individual preference is for steel. I am aware of all the arguments for and against it and the same applies to all the other materials. Properly and consistently maintained, a 50-year-old steel boat can be in as perfect condition as one just launched. Alternatively, a steel boat that has been badly neglected can be cut and patched, welded and sandblasted, re-coated, and still come up as good as new. I know this can and has been said for most of the other materials currently used in yacht construction. It's all a matter of what can be proven and what can't. I just know that when I'm out there with a couple of miles of salt water under the keel and container ships shedding their cargo like a winter coat, I'm glad I'm cosseted in steel!' Clyff Huggett could not agree more: 'Maybe steel is the ideal material, so you can hit logs or be run down by freighters and survive.' Michael Frankel shares the same opinion regarding steel: 'Strong, easy to repair worldwide.' Steve Spink *almost* agrees: 'Steel would be safer, but on a practical side GRP is cheaper and easier to maintain.' For Michelle LaMontagne: 'Fibreglass is probably preferable . . . or steel if you sail by Braille' (a singlehander's sarcastic comment directed at those who sail without a proper lookout).

I leave the final word to Skip Novak: 'For rugged world cruising I'd choose aluminium – and then not paint it. Steel is, of course, stronger and can be repaired more easily, but the downside of constant cosmetic maintenance to control corrosion in and out is, on balance, not worth the effort. Also you get a light boat in alloy, you save on fuel, and it is actually cheaper to maintain as long as you don't fill, fair and paint the alloy hull. In any case, metal is better than plastic, unless you are a very careful sailor and treat your boat as a precious object. Wood is a waste of time unless you enjoy the work on board rather than the actual sailing. You can extol the virtues of carbonfibre, Kevlar and composite materials, but the first time you run aground in uncharted waters or have to careen on a rocky bottom you will regret the choice of any hull material except alloy or steel. Even if you give up some sailing performance, this will be more than compensated by integrity and peace of wind.'

The main reason for the current concern with the strength of the hull among world voyagers is the fear of collision with an unidentified object, of which there seem to be rather too many lurking on or just under the surface of the oceans. Several collisions have been reported by participants in the various rallies and, more recently, two of the boats taking part in the Millennium Odyssey collided with whales – fortunately with little damage to themselves. These examples show that such fears are not exaggerated. Not surprisingly, every one of the skippers who had experienced such a collision indicated either steel or aluminium as the preferred construction material of his ideal boat. The one notable exception was Bill Butler, who indicated fibreglass as his ideal material, but whose latest boat is about the most solid boat one can build . . . in steel!

The fact that more metal hulls were specified as the ideal material than are found in reality, where fibreglass continues to be the most common construction material, reminds me of the conclusion of a marketing survey among new US car buyers. Apparently the majority of men enter a car showroom determined to buy a sports car . . . and walk out having settled for a staid family sedan. In the case of boat buyers, the reason so many end up with a fibreglass hull is probably because for most buyers a production boat is the only feasible option and metal hulls are not so easy or economic to produce on a mass scale, although some French boatbuilders are producing competitively priced aluminium boats. As to the comments concerning the longevity of alloy hulls, Luc Callebaut may have been unlucky with his aluminium boat when I think of all those wrecked planes from the Second World War littered on land or in the sea on countless Pacific islands, without showing any ill-effects after six decades of exposure to the elements.

Safety

An overall concern for safety was apparent from the large number of suggestions made by skippers on this subject. The provision of collision bulkheads and watertight compartments was a common suggestion as it was felt that more should be done to reduce the risk of losing the boat as a result of collision. Also with this consideration in mind, it was suggested that water or fuel tanks should be built into the sides of the hull to reach above water level so as to act as a second skin in case of collision. Another improvement in safety was the suggestion that ideally there should be only one seawater intake through the hull, and that generally the number of through-hull openings should be kept to an absolute minimum. Criticism was levelled at boat designs with a bottom so flat that there is no bilge, and it was suggested that even on flat-bottomed boats provision should be made for a well. The ideal boat should therefore have a deep bilge and be provided with good bilge pumps, ideally one of which should be engine driven. Giuseppe Italo described one obvious advantage of a generous bilge: 'The old-style bilge on my boat can keep 100 bottles of wine cool, which makes it a real cruiser.'

The fact that the engine should be easily accessible in an emergency was a requirement mentioned by many skippers. Another interesting suggestion was to make the engine compartment watertight so that the engine could continue to operate even if the rest of the boat was partly flooded. An engine-driven large-capacity bilge pump could possibly save the boat in such an eventuality. Many other interesting features were suggested – some adding to safety, while others made life more comfortable for the crew. Non-slip floors, especially in the galley area, were recommended as contributing to safety, as was the absence of sharp edges anywhere below decks. Permanent boarding steps on the transom were suggested by many as a safety feature, as was the provision of a transom platform or skirt, both of which would make it much easier to retrieve a man overboard. The stern scoop also serves as a bathing platform and can be designed in such a way as to protect the self-steering gear. Steve Spink went further than that: 'As fishing is such a big part of cruising I would customize the stern of my ideal boat to be perfect for fishing.'

Several skippers stressed the importance of good preparation, which is just as crucial whether you plan to leave on a new or used boat. As Peter Förthmann put it: 'Too many people decide to buy a new boat in the hope that everything will be all right. Wrong! Even if buying an expensive boat, this will not avoid the teething problems. Every year there are very expensive brand-new yachts in the ARC that have major problems. Any boat, new or used, will need between six and twelve months to get it right.' It is a point that was reiterated by Erick Bouteleux, who has fitted out many cruising boats for long voyages, including my own: 'All essential jobs should be done before you go as everything will take a lot more time and cost twice as much in some foreign location.'

Interior

Many additional suggestions made by skippers for their ideal yacht concerned comfort. Good ventilation was considered essential throughout the boat, which should have several opening portholes and reversible hatches. Some skippers went as far as providing their ideal boat with air conditioning, whereas others praised the advantages of good hull insulation, which many boats lack, and which can make life on board more comfortable both in hot weather, and particularly in cold climates. *Aventura III* had been heavily insulated down to the water line in preparation for her cold water sailing, but we discovered that the boat is also cool and comfortable when sailing in hot climates. Adequate sound insulation for the engine room was also recommended, as was the provision of good ventilation for the engine itself. On the subject of ventilation, it was also suggested that the stowage area should be adequately ventilated as fresh stores kept much better if air circulation was not restricted. Particularly in the galley area, it might be better to fit wire baskets instead of shelves. It was also suggested that provision should be

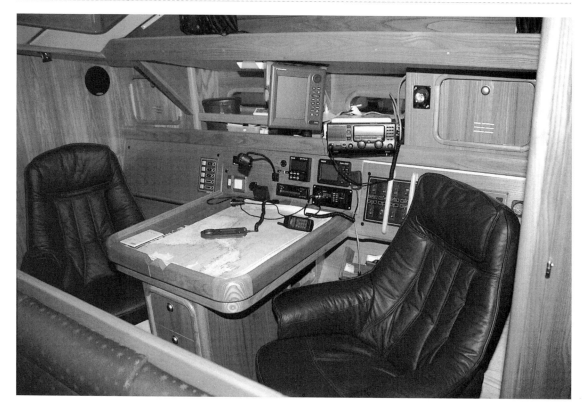

Comfort is high on everyone's list of priorities. On Aventura III leather armchairs provide comfortable seating in port and at sea.

made for more gimbaled facilities apart from the cooker. A good suggestion was a gimbaled shelf for serving and stowing prepared food in plates, cups or mugs. On *Aventura III* a stainless plate with cutouts for four mugs and one bowl in the centre can be placed on the gimbaled cooker, and provides a safe stowage for the full mugs while at sea.

The importance of good comfortable sea berths, at any angle of heel, was stressed by many and it was also suggested by one skipper that if the saloon bunks were not used for sitting at sea, they should be easily convertible to coffin-shaped berths on passage. John Wicks and Richard Walker listed a comfortable double bed as one of the six essential features on their ideal yacht. The attraction of a double berth in port was also underlined by many – and rather more graphically by one singlehander!

The heads attracted a whole range of comments, several skippers saying they would be prepared to pay anything for a good-quality toilet that did not break down at the most inconvenient moment. According to Erick Bouteleux: 'Ideally one should have two toilet compartments, so if space is limited the second one can be used for storage on long passages.' One interesting suggestion was to provide the shower tray with a high sill so that it could be used as a tub for bathing children or for soaking laundry. One of the conclusions I drew early on was that many boatowners appear to be obsessed with everything on board having a double function. For instance, among some rather unusual comforts listed was a sauna, which could double up for stowage when not in use.

The need for ample storage space was often repeated, as was the suggestion to use the forward cabin for storage – but to provide it with collapsible berths that could be used for extra crew if necessary. The forward cabin was also suggested as a possible workshop, with several skippers stressing the importance of having a workbench on a cruising boat. David Hersey was among them: 'A workshop area not in the middle of the saloon would be a great improvement.' Concerning the navigation table it was stressed that ideally the navigator should always face forward and have a properly shaped seat that provides firm support even when the boat is heeled.

Essential features

Having processed all the data and worked my way through the results of the various surveys dealing with the essential features of the ideal cruising boat, I had no doubt that if most suggestions were put into practice, the result would be a very attractive yacht. The skippers in the Global Cruising Survey were asked to list the six most desirable features on their ideal yacht. The most quoted items were a powerful electric anchor winch, watermaker, a dependable refrigeration system, autopilot, powered furling gear and electric winches. The complete wish list is included as Appendix 2. However, to narrow down their main priorities, the skippers were also asked to indicate the first three essential features they would like to have on an ideal boat. Several stressed the overall importance of a strong seaworthy hull – among them, not surprisingly, were two of those who had recently lost their boats. The priorities for Bill Butler were quite clear: 'a strong seaworthy 40-foot hull with semi-full keel, rigged as a cutter with all lines coming to the cockpit'. Antti Louhija also would like: 'a solid, sturdy and comfortable boat even if it means sacrificing some speed. If you are comfortable you gladly spend more time on passage. Finally, large enough fuel tanks to be able to run the engine for about ten days.'

Dave Beauchamp has a similar order of priorities: 'A sound, well-found hull and well-conceived deck. A well-designed and easy-to-use rig and rigging. Enough storage space to stow all those items that make life comfortable, not just bearable.' Steve Dashew considered the following features to be essential: 'watertight bulk-heads, the ability to hit the ground at slow speed without having to go into a boatyard, and a good turn of speed when one needs it'. Charles Gray would like to have 'a watertight bow locker which would protect against collisions and could be used to store sails, anchor handling gear and fenders'.

John Morgan's ideal boat would have to be 'seakindly, go reasonably well to windward, and be very strong'. It was also what Marc Labaume expected: 'good seaworthiness, shallow draft and generally speaking easy maintenance', whereas for Bob Hall the three most important features were 'seaworthiness, comfort and easy sail handling'. Carlton DeHart considered shallow draft as a desirable feature and for the boat to have an efficient underbody, a sugar scoop transom and large capacity tanks.

Several skippers stressed the importance of good sailing capabilities. Both Terence Brownrigg and Klaus Bartels wanted a boat that could point high under most conditions. Besides their natural concern with safety and performance, several skippers stressed the importance of comfort. Carlton DeHart said: 'Because I wish to go to high latitudes, I would like to have a pilot house with inside steering capabilities.' Antti Louhija also wanted 'total shelter over the cockpit and still to be able to navigate and manoeuvre as much as possible from inside, with good visibility'. Having good protection, ideally a pilot house or hard dodger, was mentioned by both Charles Gray and Skip Novak, whereas Giuseppe Italo Masotti wanted to have 'cockpit protection from waves and bad weather in general, and also the possibility of reducing sail area quickly from the cockpit and without excessive effort'. Finally, John Ellis praised 'the ability to sail the yacht singlehanded and preferably without leaving the cockpit'.

In an earlier survey, skippers were asked to indicate their preferred position of the cockpit, but without going into detailed design considerations. Aft cockpits had more adherents than centre cockpits, but as some sort of cockpit protection is high on most cruisers' list of priorities, the skippers were also asked if they would choose a canvas dodger or a more permanent arrangement. With the majority preferring an aft cockpit, permanent protection for the steering position was not so practical, and therefore most skippers opted in favour of a canvas dodger. However, over one-third of the skippers specified a permanent structure providing shelter to a centrally placed cockpit, which is one of the main attractions of a cruising catamaran. Designers have obviously recognized this trend as several production yachts now have this feature. Among the Millennium Odyssey boats, two had a raised cabin – *Company*, a Wauquiez 54, and *Risque*, a Swan 57 – and both owners were delighted with this arrangement. What was once described as a desirable feature on the ideal cruising yacht has now become reality by being incorporated into the design of several production boats.

2

The Driving Force
RIG, RIGGING AND SAILS

"We love our cutter rig, for when the going gets rough our little staysail gets tough."
DON BABSON

"To choose a standard mainsail is to deny any progress in the 80 years since the Marconi rig appeared."
GIUSEPPE ITALO MASOTTI

A tendency that has manifested itself in recent years among cruising boats is the switch to a one-masted configuration on even the largest yachts. The reasons are many, although the single most important contributing factor has been the improvement in furling gear, both for headsails and mainsails.

Rig

The rig of the boats taking part in ARC 2001 reinforced the findings of previous surveys, with 92 per cent of the boats having one mast. The proportion is quite different to the findings of the Bahamas Survey, in which of the 115 boats, 19 had two masts (17 ketches and 2 schooners). In the ARC, even the largest yachts were rigged as either sloops or cutters. This confirms the trend towards single masts on all but the largest cruising boats and spells the end to the old theory that a two-mast configuration is to be preferred because smaller sails make handling easier. Smaller sails are indeed easier to handle, particularly in strong winds, but furling gears, which are now used on most cruising boats, have taken care of that aspect. For long distance cruising it is just as important to have a rig that is efficient to windward, and this is where a sloop or cutter wins hands down. Several skippers pointed out that whichever rig is chosen, it should be of ample proportions, as there is nothing more frustrating than an under-canvased boat. The same view was expressed in an earlier survey by Peter Ibsen, an experienced Danish sailor, whose Sigma 41 *Baldur* won many races, both in strong and light winds. He stressed the advantages of a generous sail plan: 'In light airs one can set a good spread of sail, while in a blow one can always reef down to manageable proportions.'

This ability to perform satisfactorily in light winds is obviously not a matter that many people consider seriously when choosing the rig of their boat. Usually heavy weather preoccupies them more, and in fact many skippers admitted that initially they had thought a ketch rig would make life easier in heavy weather, only to find later that they did not meet much heavy weather along the trade wind routes and that their boats were slow and under-canvased most of the time. This was the painful observation that I made myself on my first circumnavigation on the ketch-rigged *Aventura*. With a split rig, as well as a trysail and storm jib in her sail wardrobe, she was prepared for the worst. What happened instead was that during a six-year circumnavigation of 72,000 miles we only twice encountered sustained winds of over 40 knots, and it was in the frequent light winds that our shortcomings were so apparent. It still pains me to see well-designed cruising boats that simply cannot move at any speed once the wind drops below 10 knots. This was quite apparent during the Millennium Odyssey, which attracted a variety of very different boats. In strong winds their performances were fairly evenly matched, but when the wind was light, which was often the case, some of the heavier cruising boats were left wallowing far behind the lighter cruiser-racers, which continued sailing at a fair pace. Gauging the right amount of sail area for a particular boat is something that some designers are obviously far better at than others. One Millennium skipper vented his frustration when he said, 'For comfortable cruising there is little to fault our boat, but why hasn't the designer added another 5 feet to the mast to make her into a perfect all-rounder?' It was a question that probably went through the minds of several sailors taking part in the rally as they watched other participants pull ahead in the light breeze and show a clean pair of heels.

The comments made earlier about the ideal material are just as valid when one considers the perfect rig, as in the ARC the vast majority of boats were sloops with very few cutters among them. Indeed, most production boats are rigged nowadays as sloops as this is, for the builders, the cheaper solution. Modifying a sloop to cutter rig is usually a complicated and costly affair. It is therefore telling that a majority of the skippers interviewed in the Global Cruising Survey indicated a cutter rig as the ideal arrangement for a long distance cruising boat.

While in the Bahamas early in 2002, I conducted an ad hoc survey in two popular anchorages at Great Exuma where I counted a total of 115 boats, almost all of which could be described as typical cruising boats (Table 3).

Sloops	68
Cutters	28
Ketches	17
Junk schooners	2
Total	**115**

Table 3: The rig of cruising boats anchored at Stocking Island

What was interesting to note was the much higher proportion of both cutter-rigged boats and ketches than in the ARC. Among the 28 cutters, 11 had their forestay mounted on a bowsprit. Even among the 68 sloops, 5 had made arrangements for a temporary staysail, so could be converted into a cutter if needed. Finally, 4 of the 17 ketches were rigged as cutters with permanently installed inner forestays. Another interesting observation was that cutters were much more common among the Canadian boats, making me wonder if this was maybe just a matter of fashion?

My present *Aventura III* is cutter-rigged with both yankee and staysail on furlers. The arrangement has worked perfectly throughout well over 35,000 miles of sailing under all kinds of conditions, from Antarctica to Alaska and the Mediterranean to the South Pacific. The yankee is a high-cut sail that has the advantage over the standard genoa, which I hardly ever use, in that it keeps a much better shape when furled and also does not obstruct the view forward when full.

Among the skippers interviewed for the Global Cruising Survey, Arthur Beiser has no doubts that a cutter rig is the most suited for long distance cruising: 'No other rig makes sense these days except in very small boats when a simple sloop might be OK.' Clyff Huggett agrees wholeheartedly: 'This rig can give the best sail combination when the wind strengthens as one can furl the genoa and use the staysail.' Bill Butler stressed the same advantages: 'Masthead cutter rig provides the ultimate versatility. It would be ideal if all three sails could be reefed from the cockpit.'

Antti Louhija would prefer 'a ketch with cutter foresails to keep every single sail small enough'. This was the system used by Carlton DeHart: 'We sailed around the world on a ketch, which had many sail possibilities. Sailing across the Pacific, we had the mizzen staysail up most of the time and found the boat loved all the sail power. Sailing up the Red Sea with 35-knot headwinds, a storm staysail and reefed mizzen, along with the engine at slow revs, gave us a fast comfortable ride. We had manual slab reefing, which worked well, but was not fun to deal with when conditions were really bad. We also had a Reckmann roller furling headsail and staysail, which I would want again. They worked like magic, always. My next boat will probably be a sloop, with a fully battened main that reefs into the boom only because of convenience. My last choice would be an in-mast furling main. They are noisy and will not sail to weather. The best advice is to never buy a yacht that will not sail to weather.'

Many skippers consider a cutter rig to be an optimum solution. On Aventura III the yankee and staysail are provided with identical furling gears.

A ketch rig was considered more suitable for shorthanded crews before furling gears became common on cruising boats. Aventura *under full sail off Papua New Guinea.*

David Beauchamp also praised the simplicity of a cutter rig: 'A cutter rig with furling on both jib and staysail gives as much sail as is possible to handle shorthanded, but is still possible to put on and take off sail reasonably easily.' Don Babson agrees: 'We love our cutter rig, for when the going gets rough our little staysail gets tough. We nearly wore it out on the Red Sea bash.' Javier Visiers believes that 'it is essential to have a sail arrangement that can be easily handled by a small crew in both light and strong winds. The ideal rig for my next boat will be a sloop, with a self-tacking jib, and a removable forestay where a staysail can be set when needed. The mast will have swept back spreaders to do away with the need for running backstays.' Matt Rollberg has a similar arrangement, with a removable inner forestay: 'We have the ideal rig – a sloop which goes to weather efficiently and a cutter set up for heavy air.' This is also the system preferred by Tom Muller: 'A cutter will ensure best speed even upwind. Both foresails should be on roller furling, with masthead rig and swept spreaders, so as to avoid having running backstays, and a deck-stepped mast to keep the boat dry.'

Skip Novak is convinced that 'for small boats of less than 60 feet a cutter rig with two headsails on roller furling gear is the way to go. On these boats, a mizzen is arguably a waste of time, and just gets in the way of the cockpit area. A well-balanced cutter rig can be tuned to sail in a variety of conditions. A small staysail doubles as a storm sail and can be used to heave-to.' Chris Harding fully agrees: 'For ease and the possibilities of sail combinations, a cutter makes a perfect rig as long as the proportions are kept realistic. A high aspect rig would cause too much work, constantly reefing for small changes in wind speed. If more sail area is required, it would be preferable to have a standard height mast with a longer boom.'

Not all skippers were sold on the idea of a cutter, such as Zoltan Gyurko, who would rather have 'just a simple sloop, less headache'. Steve Spink agrees: 'I'd go for sloop rig with two furling headsails side by side, which is a good combination. The downside is having to move the genoa by hand when tacking. Also, I would choose wire rigging, which is not as strong as rod but is easier to spot arising problems and also easier to repair or jury rig.'

In the case of Steve Dashew, 'the ideal rig depends on size, but over 65 feet it should be ketch, with a good separation between main and mizzen'. Terence Brownrigg feels that 'on a smaller boat of 40 to 45 feet a mizzen is a bit of a clutter, so I'd rather go for masthead cutter rig'.

Michael Frankel, who has sailed extensively in the North Atlantic on his junk-rigged *Sabra*, has no doubts that this rig suits him best: 'A junk rig is my preferred choice for low maintenance and easy handling by one or two persons.'

Sails

Tremendous strides have been made in recent years in the design and making of sails, an area where the cruising market has benefited enormously from the advances made in racing. Although some of the newest materials may not be found on cruising boats, designing and even cutting sails by computer is now common-place. These developments have resulted in much better-quality sails, particularly in the case of furling sails, both headsails and mainsails. Light weather sails are also much better designed and cut, while the provision of dousers on spinnakers have made these exciting sails manageable even by shorthanded crews.

In spite of the general improvement in the quality of sails, both in design and manufacture, I still find that many cruising skippers do not pay this subject the attention it deserves. This is particularly obvious on the starting line of the ARC, where there is a grandstand view of some 200 boats. The contrast is enormous, and while some sails seem to have been cut and put together by a trainee tent-maker, others are perfect examples of the present state of the art.

Standard sails have been examined in several surveys and it was interesting to compare the sail wardrobe of various boats. Thus it was pointed out in an early survey that some boats carried a complete second suit of sails, while almost half the boats also had a trysail as well as storm jib to be used in strong winds. Better sails, stronger material, and sturdier furling gears mean that nowadays very few skippers deem it necessary to carry such extra sails on board. However, the importance of carrying storm sails, which can actually drive the boat to windward in a blow, was mentioned by some of the more traditionally minded skippers. Bill

Butler is one of those who feels that furling gear and better sail material may have made storm sails obsolete: 'In heavy going, a deeply reefed main and reefed staysail can drive the boat to windward in over 50 knots. A high-cut number one genoa and a full main, both reefed, should easily handle any conditions up to 30 knots.'

DOWNWIND SAILS

Being aware of most cruising sailors' dislike of going to windward, I concentrated on finding out what kind of preparation skippers had made for downwind sailing. Several people told me that they had made special provision for extended downwind runs, some having twin jibs or genoas to be set on poles of equal length. On some boats the twin jibs could be used with existing furling gear. One highly praised system consisted of twin furling genoas set in separate grooves on the same extrusion and poled out on booms of equal length so that they could be reefed simultaneously with the help of the furling gear. As Terence Brownrigg explained: 'On my circum-navigation I was very happy with my twin headsails with twin poles, both on the same headfoil so they could be rolled up together. We had twin grooves on the forward headfoil and also a furling staysail. The trouble was that you had to be sure that you could keep them up for a reasonable time as it took a lot of trouble to drop and fold the genoa, and then hoist the twins. The solution might be to keep the twins furled on a forward headstay and to have as big a sail as practical on a furling inner forestay, but having this as near as possible to the bow, perhaps as a seven-eighth rig.'

Over half the boats in an earlier ARC survey had spinnakers on board, most of them fitted with a douser, as were the cruising chutes. Not all the owners of the chutes were totally satisfied with their performance, some stressing that these sails were not as good as expected when reaching and that it was a mistake to regard them as an all-round light weather sail. Another criticism levelled at cruising chutes was that often these were advertised as a hybrid spinnaker, but with the great advantage of being set without a pole. However, several skippers mentioned that if there was any swell combined with a light wind, the sail tended to collapse and the only way to overcome this was to pole it out, in which case one might as well have a proper spinnaker. This has not been my own experience, perhaps because the new asymmetric spinnaker I use on *Aventura III* is so well cut that it rarely collapses, compared to my previous one, which was so badly made that it was useless in most situations.

Downwind sailing techniques were examined closely in an earlier ARC survey when the skippers were asked to comment on the sails they used, their setting arrangements, and the effect on automatic pilots or self-steering gears. Although just over half the boats in the survey had spinnakers, these had been used very little during the transatlantic crossing. Cruising chutes were set just as infrequently and the main reason given for the limited use of spinnakers and cruising chutes was the need to steer by hand, or at least keep a watchful eye on self-steering gears, when these sails were in use in boisterous trade wind conditions. The fact that most boats had small crews was another reason why spinnakers were used so little. One shorthanded skipper who tried to fly his spinnaker pointed out that he only managed to get it wrapped around his furling gear. He was forced to climb the mast to untangle it, and protected himself from the constant banging against the mast by wearing a lifejacket. I should add that during this particular ARC crossing, the winds were quite strong so there was little need for spinnakers.

Even a large spinnaker can be easily handled with a good douser.

On most boats the preferred running technique was to use the mainsail, often reefed, in conjunction with a poled-out foresail. This arrangement worked reasonably well on most boats, although in some instances the mainsail had to be well reefed to balance the jib, either to minimize weather helm or to reduce the risk of broaching. On some cutters the staysail was also set, but sheeted in hard so as to stop some of the rolling. The constant rolling was in fact the main drawback of the traditional trade wind technique of running with poled-out twin jibs. In most cases, the twin jibs had to be dropped when the wind exceeded 20 knots, and a smaller sail set, either with or without a reefed mainsail.

Skippers were also asked to comment on the effect their particular downwind sailing arrangement had on the behaviour of self-steering gears or automatic pilots. Windvanes appeared to function best in conjunction with twin jibs, although the rhythmic rolling induced by this particular set of sails was not appreciated by some crews. Mostly because of the rolling, but also due to stronger than expected winds, even on boats fitted with twin jibs, a reefed mainsail and poled-out jib were often substituted for running. Self-steering gears did not always cope well on extended downwind runs, and were occasionally thrown off balance not because of the wind or sails, but by the swell. On some boats that were less well balanced, the danger of gybing the mainsail while running on self-steering meant that the watchkeeper had to be close at hand all the time. This was not such a hazard when the boat was on automatic pilot, so several skippers reverted to this option when the going got too rough. Matt Rollberg of *Santana* commented: 'We used the spinnaker on the crossing from the Canaries to St Lucia and it was too hairy. We sold it and bought a second pole to use two headsails going downwind in the Pacific.'

LONGEVITY

The wear and tear of cruising sails had been examined in an earlier survey in which the average mileage per sail worked out at almost 30,000 miles, although this does not mean that every single sail was actually used for all those miles. Some of the circumnavigators taking part in that survey completed their voyage on one suit of sails, which shows the kind of care they gave to their sails. As Carlton DeHart pointed out: 'My best advice is to stay away from exotic fabrics for sailcloth and go for longevity. We used Dacron sails with great results.'

The longevity of sails depends on two main factors, both of them equally important: first, the quality of the material and workmanship, and second, the care taken in looking after those sails. Continuous exposure to the sun, particularly in the tropics, exerts a heavy toll on any sail, although some materials appear to be more resistant to ultraviolet rays than others. Usually it is the stitching that disintegrates long before the material itself, and one way to overcome this is to have cruising sails provided with triple stitching, ideally by using one of the ultraviolet resistant threads. Furling jibs need to be protected by sacrificial anti-ultraviolet strips, which may have to be replaced after the sail has been in use for a few years.

Taking good care of sails can undoubtedly prolong their life considerably, but still you see boats left in marinas for long periods with their mainsails left unprotected by a sail cover. It is an operation that rarely takes more than a few minutes, but one that pays dividends in the long run. The most meticulous people I came across in this respect were Herbert and Ilse Gieseking of *Lou IV*, who always put on the sail covers immediately after dropping anchor, folding away carefully the sails that had been used, and giving all the sails a rinse ashore with fresh water whenever this was possible. After four and a half years, they completed their circumnavigation of 46,000 miles with all their original sails intact. It is a valuable lesson that I have learnt myself, and I now look after my sails much more carefully than in the past. On *Aventura III* the fully battened mainsail drops into a so-called lazy-bag, which can be quickly zipped close to protect the sail from the sun, while both staysail and yankee are shielded by a protective strip when furled. All original sails are still in good condition after more than 35,000 miles and four years of use.

Furling gear

The preference for single masts discussed earlier has undoubtedly been helped by the proliferation of jib furling gears. Among the boats taking part in ARC 2001, 92 per cent had some kind of furling gear for their headsails and just over half (52 per cent) had in-mast furling mainsails. The percentages were almost as high in the SSCA 2000 Survey, with 84 per cent of the boats having furling headsails. In the SSCA Survey, the most common make was Profurl (36 per cent) which was rated second highest for performance and reliability, followed closely by Harken, which was almost as widespread (29 per cent) and was also highly rated. The top-rated FaMet was used on only 2 per cent of the boats. Several skippers interviewed in the Global Cruising Survey praised the versatility of their furling headsails, such

as Skip Novak: 'When sailing downwind in strong winds, I like the idea of dropping the main completely and winging out 60 per cent of a high-clewed 130 per cent headsail and all of the 100 per cent jib, both on rollers, and rigged to twin poles set on independent tracks on the mast and stowed vertically. Sail area can be adjusted by rolling in both to a minimal configuration, which makes the boat easy to steer and easy on the pilot as the centre of effort of both sails is well balanced.'

In Skip's case the genoa is of a high-clewed type, which usually is easier to furl than the normal deck-sweeping genoas. When sailing in tropical areas where squalls can be frequent and sudden, such large sails can be a nuisance. Also they are more difficult to pole out than a sail with a higher clew, so on *Aventura III* the yankee is in almost constant use and the 125 per cent genoa has been used only for one month in the last four years.

Whereas everyone seems to agree on the usefulness of headsail furling, opinions are still divided on furling mainsails, whether in-mast or in-boom furling. A possible explanation for this attitude was the fact that the survey was conducted at a time when there had been various press reports extolling the virtues of fully battened mainsails, lazy jacks and other rapid systems of mainsail reefing and stowing, which were being promoted as a better answer to mainsail reefing than the various systems of mainsail furling. My personal feeling is that, in spite of some misgivings, furling mainsails have certain attractions and are increasingly a regular feature on long distance cruising boats – as can be seen from the high proportion of ARC boats fitted with this system.

In-mast furling mainsails are the favourite solution for those interested primarily in easy sail handling. Ivan Cornell shows how a cameraman can get a better view of the boat under sail.

The ideal mainsail

There is no doubt that the main attraction of furling gear, both on headsails and mainsails, is the ability to reduce sail area quickly and with the minimum of effort, a particularly attractive feature for shorthanded or less muscular crews. Several skippers who had used this equipment extensively pointed out that they sailed their boats much more efficiently, because they always carried the right amount of sail for the situation. The subject of mainsail systems was examined in detail in the Global Cruising Survey, in which skippers were asked to comment both on the systems they were using at the moment and the kind of mainsail they would have on their ideal cruising yacht. Exactly half the skippers (20) mentioned a fully battened mainsail as their ideal choice, five of them also specifying that they would prefer an in-boom furling or stowing system. Eight skippers would opt for an in-mast furling mainsail, while a further seven were quite happy with a standard slab reefing main. One skipper could not decide between fully battened or in-mast furling whereas one skipper extolled the advantages of a junk rig. The fans of the various systems described the reasons very clearly why they preferred one system over the other, such as Javier Visiers, who has very firm views on the subject: 'Bearing in mind the profusion of mainsail furling systems, both in-mast and in-boom, I consider both to be an absurd solution. It is so much better to reduce the size of the mainsail by getting rid of the area that is not needed, while allowing the sail to maintain its shape. Without any doubt whatsoever, it's a fully battened mainsail for me!' Arthur Beiser fully agrees: 'A fully battened mainsail is so satisfactory that I would consider no other. In-boom furling can be used with such a mainsail and I might opt for it in a new boat, and maybe will even try it some day on *Ardent Spirit*. I have heard mixed reports from friends with in-boom furling, but the systems are improving.'

John Ellis has no doubts either: 'Fully battened mainsail with all encompassing lazy jacks system.' Clyff Huggett would go a little further: 'Fully battened main with in-boom furling and power hoisting and reefing.' Steve Dashew listed his own requirements: 'Fully battened, with lots of roach, conventional booms (if ketch), but these to be placed low so that it is easy to work on.' David Beauchamp shares the view that 'a fully battened sail provides so much more push that if you can afford it, it is well worth it. Especially if you can contain it with some form of in-boom furling. If you don't have in-boom furling, then the ability to take three reefs is essential. The occasion will come when just that little rag of mainsail to balance the boat will be so useful without having to rig the storm trysail.'

Don Babson agrees: 'I do like a fully battened mainsail, but if I were a little older I would consider in-boom furling. In the Millennium Odyssey, the boats with fully battened mains were noticeably faster than those with in-mast furling.' Matt Rollberg made the same point: '*Santana*'s fully battened main works well for us. We wouldn't have in-mast furling because of the potential for mechanical failure.' Zoltan Gyurko has different views: 'I prefer a standard mainsail, the most simple and easily replaceable thing is best.'

Giuseppe Italo disagrees: 'To choose a standard mainsail is to deny any progress in the 80 years since the Marconi rig appeared. Probably I would choose an in-mast or in-boom mainsail.' Bill Butler agrees: 'Hood mast furling or similar with

*The Deerfoot 62
Artemis shows
her perfectly
setting fully
battened sails.*

a battenless mainsail works wonders. An extra heavy leech helps it keep its shape, the loose-footed feature helps you recover from heavy weather gybes, and the ability to precisely tune the mainsail area to the wind is super-efficient.'

David Hersey feels that 'with a small crew it's hard to avoid a furling main of some sort. I have recently bought a new main with vertical battens, which certainly sets better and gives us more sail area.' Steve Spink, who has sailed extensively with David, does not fully agree: 'The in-mast furling system on *Company* is very convenient, but when it jams or a halyard breaks it can be a real problem, so I would opt for a fully battened slab reefed mainsail.' Skip Novak has no doubts either: 'With a good track system on the main, fully battened and a good reefing system (blocks on the leech), reefing a biggish mainsail should present no problems. In-mast and in-boom furling is not really necessary, is maintenance intensive, and prone to failure at the wrong time.'

Chris Harding takes the opposite view and has doubts about a fully battened mainsail, especially on the larger boats that he is used to sailing on: 'I would only ever consider having a standard slab reefed mainsail. Fully battened mainsails are very good as long as the sail construction and battens are of good quality. If going for full battens, ensure that the batten cars are from a quality manufacturer otherwise they have a tendency to break when going downwind. As for reefing, I have found that the easiest and most reliable system is a two-separate-line system run back into the cockpit. This way you have total control over the shape of the sail, and it is also possible to reef while running dead downwind.'

Volker Reinke would not consider anything but standard sails on his ideal schooner rig: 'Both mainsail and staysail should travel easily if provided with good-quality hardware. Furthermore, the advantage of a two-mast configuration is that one can always add more sail area between the masts, which can be easily dropped by a small crew if the winds increases.'

Conclusions

The choice of the ideal rig and the most suitable sails for a particular type of cruising are decisions that cannot be taken too lightly, and in the foregoing pages I have attempted to present as many opinions on the subject as possible. In my own case, the fact that I expected to sail most of the time shorthanded led inevitably to a cutter rig on *Aventura III*. As I pointed out, a staysail and high-cut genoa (yankee), both on the same size furling gears, are set in conjunction with a fully battened mainsail. All three spinnakers (one tri-radial and two asymmetric) are provided with dousers, and I use them frequently. My favourite downwind technique, which I learned many years ago from the Italian singlehander Mario Franchetti, is to set up the pole independently of the sail, so it is held firmly in position by topping lift, forward and aft guys – all three lines being led back to the cockpit. Regardless of whether I decide to pole out the yankee or the spinnaker, the sheet is led through the jaws of the pole, which is then hoisted in the desired place. Once the pole is in place, the sail can be unfurled, or the spinnaker douser pulled up. With the pole always kept independent of the sail, the latter can be furled partially or fully, or the spinnaker doused, without touching the pole. This is a great advantage when sail has to be shortened quickly, usually when threatened by a squall. When the squall has passed, as the pole is still in place the sail can be easily unfurled (or the spinnaker undoused). To simplify matters even more, *Aventura III* has two spinnaker poles rigged with permanent lines on either side of the boat.

3

Power to the People
DIESEL ENGINES, OPTIMUM POWER AND RELIABILITY

"As I get older the ability to hang upside down into a dark cavity to reach an oil filter is both more difficult and less fun."

ALASTAIR DUNCAN

No modern boat is complete without its 'iron staysail', and so diesel engines were examined in various surveys, when both the performance of individual makes and the availability of parts were discussed.

Optimum power

Most skippers taking part in the surveys agreed that a sufficiently powerful engine was essential on a cruising boat. This is particularly true in the Pacific where passes into lagoons are often subject to strong outflowing currents and, as most of the passes are quite narrow, tacking through them is often impossible. Optimum power was examined in an earlier survey in which the skippers were asked to indicate if their current engine was considered powerful enough both for the boat and the particular requirements of the cruise being undertaken. Although the majority considered their engines to be sufficiently powerful, or even in excess of their requirements, one-quarter of those interviewed stressed that their engine was not powerful enough as there had been many situations in which a more powerful engine would have been welcome. Looking at the figures closer, it became obvious that even skippers who were generally satisfied with their present engine power would have found a more powerful engine to be better suited to their needs. The main reason why most people would like to have a more powerful engine is not only to get them out of difficulty or potentially dangerous situations, but also to have more power, and therefore speed, in calms or light wind conditions.

The fact that most people regard a powerful diesel engine to be a desirable feature of a cruising boat was confirmed by the findings of the Global Cruising Survey. A trend towards more powerful engines was already detected among ARC boats, so the question of optimum engine power was examined in detail in the Global Cruising Survey. According to David Beauchamp: 'An engine on a sailboat is usually referred to as an auxiliary and should be just that. It does, however, need to be of sufficient capacity to do a good job when required. On at least three occasions I have been aboard a boat which had not been able to make any headway whatsoever against adverse sea and tide, simply because the engine was too small to do what was required of it. The old rule of thumb seems to work: at least 1 horsepower per foot of length. More than this size, together with the fuel to run it, is too much for the average boat to drag along under sail efficiently.'

Klaus Bartels and Arthur Beiser would use a different yardstick and allow 5 hp per ton of displacement. Skip Novak agrees: 'Ideal engine power is never enough. This is especially true if you cruise in high latitudes where there is either no wind, or storm conditions in channel sailing. If you want to be a purist then go with no engine, but if you have an engine, make it and the propeller a serious proposition (even sacrificing some sailing performance). For *Pelagic,* at 55 feet and 30 tonnes, 120 hp is adequate, but is the minimum. I wish I could turn a bigger screw!'

Javier Visiers, who plans to explore the same area in his new boat, fully agrees: 'It is essential to be able to have adequate speed under power. In 15 knots of wind from ahead and with waves to match one should be able to motor at the boat's designed hull speed. On my next 80-foot boat, it will be 250 hp.' John Ellis takes a similar view: 'Always get a more powerful engine than you think you need, because you will need it.' Thomas Wilm suggests that one should always fit an engine 50 per cent more powerful than the one recommended by the builder. Carlton DeHart sees this as 'another compromise. I feel that a boat should be able to power at least 2,000 miles on the fuel it carries in its tanks. On our Bowman 57 we had excellent service from an 85 hp Perkins, but even so it was not powerful enough when punching into strong winds and head seas.'

Bill Butler believes that 'for my ideal boat, of 38 to 43 feet, an engine of 40 to 50 hp will do. The engine should be water cooled, low speed, with a Velvet drive or similar transmission, a three-bladed fixed propeller, and a brake for the shaft.'

For Don Babson there is a very valid justification for having a more powerful engine: 'Bigger is better. We have a 65 hp, but sometimes 75 would have been better. In the Millennium Odyssey, we could have made it to the parties before all the goodies and grog were gone if we had had more horses.' Matt Rollberg, who sailed in the same rally, shares that view: 'We wouldn't do another round the world rally unless we had a bigger boat and a bigger engine.'

I was swayed by similar considerations when I tried to persuade the boatyard to fit a larger engine than the standard 50 hp on *Aventura III.* With hindsight, I am glad I was outvoted as the power is quite adequate for a nominal displacement of 8.5 tonnes. Also, a more powerful engine would have been heavier, taken up more space, and consumed more fuel. So my advice is to ensure you have adequate power without going over the top.

Some skippers would prefer two engines, such as Charles Gray: 'I'd prefer twin 77 hp for redundancy.' This is also what Luc Callebaut would choose: 'Ideally, I would like two engines capable to get us out of a bad situation: lee shore, strong current, etc.'

Tom Muller stressed the importance of having 'a simple, straight four-cylinder, no turbo engine of a well-known brand such as Yanmar, Perkins or Volvo, for

Adequate engine power is essential on a cruising boat. Pagan has to use full power against a 5-knot current in the pass at Rangiroa, in the Tuamotus.

which spares could be found and that could be repaired anywhere in the world.' Michael Frankel has other priorities: 'An electric motor equivalent to 40 hp. Sufficient fuel tankage for 750 miles at 5 knots.'

Fuel

In parallel with diesel engines, fuel capacity and range under power were also examined in the various surveys. In an earlier survey, the average fuel capacity was 400 litres (100 US gallons), although several skippers pointed out that additional fuel was taken in jerrycans for longer passages or when cruising in areas where diesel fuel was difficult to obtain. The average range under power, if motoring in calm conditions, was 750 miles per boat. Most skippers stressed the importance of adequate fuel capacity, and the optimum fuel-carrying capacity quoted was on average 110 US gallons (450 litres). It was interesting to notice that several of the skippers who had sailed around the world, such as Carlton DeHart, would ensure they had more generous tankage on their ideal boat, and therefore a longer range under power. As Steve Spink pointed out: 'Larger fuel tanks are both more economical and easier to provide at the designing/building stage. These need not be filled up to capacity when fuel is easily available, but would be highly appreciated when cruising off the beaten track.'

The amount of fuel carried by the boats in the various surveys varied in accordance with their needs and cruising area, although the majority left on longer passages with full tanks. In an earlier ARC survey, the average amount carried was 107 US gallons (484 litres), but this included several boats with very large fuel capacities. It was pointed out that in most cases more fuel was used to run the engine for battery charging rather than for propulsion. Although most boats leave for the Atlantic crossing with full tanks, most of the fuel is still there by the time they reach the Caribbean. However, the practice of leaving with full tanks on a long passage is highly recommended as the engine may have to be used for long periods in an emergency, such as a broken mast or a medical emergency that necessitates a speedy landfall.

For these reasons, fuel capacity and range under power were examined in a subsequent survey in which the average fuel capacity was 90 gallons (360 litres) per boat. The average range under power when motoring under calm conditions at medium revs was 750 miles per boat or an average consumption of half a gallon (2 litres) per hour. Asked about the minimum amount of fuel to be carried, some skippers suggested that when setting off on a long passage, one ought to have enough fuel to be able to motor between one-quarter and one-third of the entire distance should there be a serious emergency.

The Global Cruising Survey confirmed an earlier observation that in spite of many sailors' willingness to turn on the engine rather than wait for wind when becalmed, on most boats less fuel was used on passage for propulsion than for electricity-generating purposes. Consumption figures obtained for an earlier survey showed that on long ocean passages as much as 76 per cent of the fuel was consumed by the main engine while charging the batteries, and only 24 per cent while actually driving the boat. In the Millennium Odyssey the situation was more balanced, and fuel consumption was evenly split between propulsion and generation. Even so, there is little doubt that using the main engine to charge the batteries is a costly exercise, nor is it very efficient, particularly as most boats were equipped with powerful diesel engines.

Propellers

Various interesting suggestions concerning engines, apart from adequate power or sufficient fuel, were made in the Global Cruising Survey – such as the use of folding or feathering propellers to reduce drag. On the other hand, rather than eliminate propeller drag, some skippers would prefer to put it to good use by driving a shaft generator. The ideal solution suggested by one skipper was to fit a variable pitch propeller, which would ensure maximum efficiency both when used to propel the boat and when turning a generator attached to the shaft.

Folding or feathering propellers are increasingly used on cruising boats. Max-Prop is one of the most common makes.

As increasing numbers of cruising boats are fitted with folding or feathering propellers, the above suggestion is not feasible. This was confirmed in the SSCA Survey in which folding propellers were a common feature. The most common make was Max-Prop (75 per cent), followed by Martec (7 per cent) and Sailprop (5 per cent). Max-Prop was rated highest for performance and was narrowly beaten into second place for reliability, albeit by Autoprop, which was fitted on only 3 per cent of the boats surveyed. Having had a Max-Prop on both my previous and current boat, I can vouch for the quality of this well-engineered product whose performance will be enhanced and its life substantially extended if the propeller housing is filled with the recommended grease at regular intervals.

Reliability

The reliability of diesel engines was examined in several surveys, and some makes were rated consistently higher than others, which did not always reflect the better quality of the engine in question, but often the availability of spare parts or the quality of aftersales service. In the SSCA 2000 Survey the highest rated make was Yanmar both for performance and reliability. Yanmar was also the most common make (32 per cent) followed by Perkins (24 per cent), Westerbeke (11 per cent) and Volvo (8 per cent). Their ratings fell in the same order and show an interesting reversal, as in all my previous surveys Perkins used to be the brand that consistently came out on top. In the SSCA Survey Perkins continued to attract the most favourable comments, whereas interestingly enough, and in spite of the overall rating, Yanmar attracted several negative comments – mainly for its poor aftersales service. As to the comments concerning the availability of parts worldwide, it appears that the only one of the common brands for which spares were difficult to find was Westerbeke.

Because of spare parts being so difficult to find in some countries it was suggested that a selection of common spares should be acquired before a longer cruise. This should include at least one complete injector, a head gasket and other essential seals and gaskets, a belt for the alternator and impellers for all pumps. To this list I would add a spare seawater pump, or at least a repair kit, as on my own Volvo MD22 this had to be replaced four times in as many years. Carlton DeHart went so far as to also carry a spare alternator and starter motor, both of them individually sealed in vacuum packs. Just as important is to carry a set of tools for the engine, a workshop manual, a diagram showing all part numbers, and a list of agents worldwide for the particular make. Another useful suggestion, which had in fact been put into practice by several Millennium Odyssey skippers, was to attend an induction course covering the basic principles of maintenance and servicing of your boat's engine. The makers of some diesel engines run such courses for new owners, and from the comments made by skippers who had attended them they appear to be extremely valuable, particularly when you bear in mind that during a longer cruise the engine might break down hundreds of miles from the nearest repair facility.

Although diesel engines are considered to be one of the most reliable machines invented by man, their rate of failure on sailing boats is surprisingly high compared to diesel engines operating on land. Having once owned a car with a diesel engine for many years, I can vouch for their reliability and I am puzzled why their performance is so much less reliable on boats. There are various reasons for this, not least the fact that marine diesel engines operate in a corrosive environment, which takes its toll even on units that have been properly marinized, which is something that cannot be said for all engines installed in yachts. Another reason for the frequent breakages is the fact that on most yachts the engines are used irregularly and for short periods. When they are used, often they are not put under sufficient load, particularly when the main engine is used to charge the batteries.

I remember a long discussion on this subject with the skipper of *Honeymead*, Chester Lemon, an experienced diesel mechanic, who had left his farm in Queensland to travel the world by sea. Chester had complete faith in diesel engines, and as his livelihood as a farmer had depended on such engines, he knew both how to run them and how to put them right. The valuable point that he made, and that I have followed religiously ever since, both in cars and boats, is that diesel engines *must* be run under load. Running a powerful diesel engine just to turn a small alternator is simply not enough, and so, when underway, the propeller should always be engaged to put some load on the engine. Running the main engine just to charge the batteries is not recommended and a lot of problems may have their origin in this widespread practice. Just as bad is the practice of turning on the diesel engine to leave a dock or anchorage, but letting it run for only a few minutes and turning it off before it has had time to reach the recommended working temperature. Repeatedly submitting the engine to this kind of treatment will eventually take its toll on even the most reliable of engines.

The engine should be easily accessible from all sides for servicing, as on the Beneteau 51 Cacadu.

Breakages

Looking at the engine breakages that I have come across over the years, in most instances it is not the main engine that is faulty, but auxiliary equipment, such as water pumps, starter motors or alternators. One common source of serious failure is the inadequate provision made for the exhaust. On one boat, water found its way through the exhaust into the manifold causing the engine to seize up during an Atlantic crossing. The skipper managed to free the pistons by pouring a mixture of paraffin (kerosene) and oil into the cylinders and leaving it for three days. He then tapped the top of the pistons until they started moving, cleaned everything thoroughly, and the engine started first time. He advised other skippers to make sure that a one-way valve was fitted to the exhaust, or some kind of trap that does not allow water to siphon into the engine when sailing before large following seas. His point was extremely valid as in several other instances that have come to my attention the cause of engine failure was narrowed down to seawater ingression via a faulty exhaust system.

Another source of engine seizure also caused by seawater finding its way into the engine sometimes occurs on units having a direct cooling system. On such units, raw cooling water circulates around the engine block and any broken seal or gasket allows the water to find its way into the engine itself. Yet another cause of serious engine problems is dirty fuel, which can contain either impurities or water. Both of these should be separated out if the engine has been provided with an adequate filtering system, which many production boats do not possess. Some boats are not even provided with a separate water trap, while on others the filter element provided as standard can only cope with a small amount of dirt in the fuel.

The best way to avoid these problems is to install a large filter and water trap in addition to the fuel filter provided by the manufacturers. Both the filter and water trap should be in an easily accessible place where they can be inspected regularly. The fuel intake from the tanks should always be set sufficiently high above the level of any water and sludge accumulated in the bottom of the tank, which should be drained off regularly through a tap set in the lowest part of the tank, if this is at all practicable. Otherwise, the final filter should be provided with an adequate water trap. Most of the water that is found in fuel tanks has not got there with the fuel, but by condensation. On most boats, an overflow pipe from the engine returns excess fuel into the tank. Particularly on fibreglass boats, the warm returning fuel causes a certain amount of condensation, with the resulting water gathering in the bottom of the tank, from where it must be drained before it finds its way into the fuel system. Other problems can be caused by a little-known culprit, which can seriously damage injection pumps, or even block the fuel supply lines. This is a fungus that grows inside diesel tanks. A small amount of a special antifungal product (biocide) added occasionally to the tanks will keep the fungus under control, but not many people seem to be aware of this problem. One of the boats taking part in the ARC had to have its injection pump rebuilt at great cost after it had been seriously damaged by this fungus which had clogged up the entire fuel system.

On his ideal boat, Bill Butler would ensure that 'there are easily accessible oil filters in line for each fuel tank, allowing the fuel to be absorbed from, and returned to, any tank. The tanks to have inspection ports for cleaning. The fuel to always be treated with biocide.'

To avoid some of these problems, on all my boats I installed a day tank that is filled every few hours, and feeds the engine by gravity as it is mounted higher than the engine itself. The fuel is filtered both before and after this tank, and as the pre-filter has an easily inspected glass bowl, any water ingress can be dealt with promptly and easily.

Specific engine breakages that have occurred in various rallies are described in Chapter 13.

4

Gearing Up for a Blue Water Voyage
ANCILLARY EQUIPMENT FOR OFFSHORE CRUISING

"If you can't repair it, don't have it."   TOM MULLER

Autopilots

The increasing preference for autopilots as opposed to wind-operated self-steering gears can be seen by looking at the findings of the various cruising surveys. In the early surveys the majority of cruising boats had some kind of self-steering gear and less than half had autopilots. This tendency has now been reversed, mainly as a result of the development of reliable autopilots. The debate about the use of electronic autopilots as opposed to wind-operated gears in offshore cruising is of such importance that it was examined in particular detail in the Global Cruising Survey. Skippers were asked to comment on the use of autopilots, and to estimate their daily electricity consumption and how this affected their energy requirements generally. It is perhaps telling that several skippers were not able to indicate exactly the amount of electricity consumed by their pilots, except to complain that in most cases the consumption was much higher than had been anticipated. The average hourly consumption was estimated to have ranged from as little as 1 Ah (six boats) to 8 Ah (three boats), with the rest spread evenly between those two extremes. Based on all those figures, the overall average worked out at 3.9 Ah, which is quite close to what most manufacturers consider to be the hourly consumption of a standard autopilot steering a sailing yacht during an ocean passage. In most cases, the skippers pointed out that their existing battery capacity was able to cope with this demand, but on some boats the demands made by the autopilots were so high that they had to run their engines, or generators, once or twice a day to charge the batteries.

Several of those interviewed in the Global Cruising Survey found that the pilot used more electricity than the average quoted above would suggest. Carton DeHart was one of them: 'We had a Robertson autopilot with dual hydraulic rams. A small motor moved fluid from one ram to the other by reversing its direction. This used about 6 Ah when the boat was sailing along in a well-balanced condition in flat seas, but the consumption could easily double when the boat was steering in large quartering seas in rough conditions or when the sails were not balanced.' On Arthur Beiser's *Ardent Spirit*, 'the autopilot is always used when under way except in close quarters or in certain storm conditions. I never bothered to note its electricity consumption because it is small compared with the refrigeration load, which is the biggest user of energy.'

As can be expected, autopilots were used far less on the boats that also had wind-operated self-steering gears. In the Global Cruising Survey just over one-quarter of the boats had a windvane. All of these skippers pointed out that their autopilots were only used when motoring. However, David Beauchamp described a good system of reducing the power consumption of the autopilot: 'In light following winds I have worked out a method of using the autopilot connected directly to the Aries windvane. The pilot uses far less power and the solar panels are just about able to handle it.' This is what I also can do on *Aventura III* when I want to save power and don't want to use the main autopilot. A small autopilot is connected to the Windpilot windvane so that in effect the autopilot mimics the wind and the movement is transmitted to the servo-rudder. In this way, actual power to steer the boat is derived from the self-steering gear and electricity consumption is minimal.

The reliability of autopilots was examined in both the ARC 1999 and 2000 surveys conducted by *Yachting World* magazine. In the latter, of the 197 skippers surveyed, 136 rated their autopilot as the most popular piece of equipment on board. The most common make in ARC 2000 was Autohelm (now Raytheon), installed on 91 of the 136 boats surveyed, followed by Robertson (17), Brookes&Gatehouse (13), and a variety of other makes (15). The fact that there were only 20 failures reported during the Atlantic crossing shows that autopilots have greatly improved compared to previous ARCs when autopilot breakages were much more common. The most common failure reported on Autohelm's ST6000 and ST7000 were breakages of the linear drive units or of the bolts holding it to the quadrant. The latter could almost be described as an installation failure, which was a common feature to all makes and was also mentioned in the SSCA Survey. In this survey, Autohelm (Raytheon) was also by far the most popular make (48 per cent), followed by Alpha (11 per cent) and Navico (11 per cent). The rest of the sample was made up of a variety of other brands. Of the three most common makes, Alpha was rated the highest for reliability followed by Autohelm.

One oft-repeated comment by the ARC skippers who took part in the 2000 Survey was that their autopilots did not always appear to be powerful enough for the job, especially when there was a high sea running with winds to match. I have heard the same comment both in previous ARCs and in the various round the world rallies in which autopilot breakages have been a common occurrence. In all fairness to the manufacturers, it must be pointed out that in many cases the units were submitted to a lot more effort than they had been designed for. An autopilot that would be quite adequate to steer even a large boat when motoring in relatively calm seas would often give up the ghost if required to steer day after day in boisterous ocean conditions. This was particularly noticeable in the Millennium Odyssey, in which windvane self-steering gears were in the minority and most boats, many of which were shorthanded, were on autopilot all the time. Under such circumstances, what was surprising was not that a few autopilots broke, but that the majority performed so well. On *Aventura III* I have a Brookes&Gatehouse Hydra autopilot, and although the system worked well for a while, eventually the ram failed and had to be replaced. It was only then that the technician pointed out that for the kind of sailing I had been doing the standard ram was underpowered, and he suggested I had it upgraded to a larger, hydraulically operated system, which I did. To date, the new unit has covered some 6,000 miles and has functioned impeccably.

Windvanes

There used to be a time, not so long ago, when long distance cruising boats could be instantly identified from the windvanes mounted on their sterns. Yet among the yachts taking part in ARC 2001, out of a total of 219 boats only 41 were equipped with self-steering gears, compared to the 51 windvanes among the 235 yachts that had sailed in the previous year's ARC. This fact confirmed my conclusion from earlier surveys that the proportion of windvanes on cruising boats has been steadily declining. There are several explanations as to why so many offshore sailors choose autopilots instead of wind-operated self-steering devices, perhaps the most important reason being the fact that autopilots are regarded as more user-friendly. Indeed, it is much easier to set a course on the autopilot by the push of a button, than adjust the self-steering gear to the required course. However, once the windvane has been set, it does look after the boat without a continuous drain on the batteries.

Peter Förthmann, the manufacturer of Windpilot self-steering gears, describes the correct approach to these admittedly capricious devices: 'Any well-designed boat should steer a course without too much effort provided the sails are properly balanced. Otherwise the windvane will simply not cope. It is something that I keep telling owners, but often to no avail.' Indeed, as Carlton DeHart stressed, the sails must be properly trimmed and adjusted before handing over the steering to either autopilot or windvane.

In the ARC 2000 Survey, the most common make of windvane was Windpilot, which scored highest for reliability and won the *Yachting World* silver award for performance and reliability. The most common make in the SSCA 2000 Survey was Monitor (43 per cent), followed by Aries (22 per cent) and Sailomat (8 per cent), with the Aries topping the league table for product rating.

Many long distance sailors believe in the 'belt and braces' philosophy and are often equipped with both an automatic pilot and a wind-operated gear. Some boats even carry a second smaller autopilot as a standby in case the main unit fails. On the other hand, the few boats that have neither pilot nor windvane are usually skippered by keen racing enthusiasts who are prepared to steer by hand. In most cases, they also rely on larger crews.

This subject was also examined in the Ideal Boat Survey when the skippers were asked to rate the importance of having wind-operated self-steering and/or automatic pilot. On a point for point basis, autopilots scored higher than wind-operated devices, which is a reflection of the current attitude among many sailors who seem to have more faith in an electricity-hungry pilot than an energy-saving vane gear.

Outboard engines

A noticeable change that has occurred in recent years is the increased proportion of tenders equipped with an outboard engine. Compared to earlier surveys, most yachts now have an outboard engine, and sailors who row their dinghies are very much in the minority. The main reason for this change is the proliferation of inflatable dinghies, most of which are difficult to row. An outboard engine is almost essential for an inflatable dinghy, especially if used over longer distances. Especially for those planning to cruise in areas where one spends more time at anchor and commuting to the shore can sometimes be an expedition in itself, a reliable outboard engine is not just useful, but essential.

While spending some time in a popular anchorage in the Bahamas I noticed that the only time I saw anyone row a dinghy was when their outboard failed, which on a couple of occasions included myself. Some of the boats that I came across in the Bahamas, in addition to the standard dinghy, had plastic one-man kayaks that are easily paddled and are excellent for landing on difficult beaches with breaking surf.

Large inflatables are difficult to row and should be provided with a reliable outboard motor.

The reliability of outboard motors was examined in the SSCA 2000 Survey in which Yamaha was the most popular make (29 per cent), followed by Johnson (15 per cent), Nissan (12 per cent), Mercury and Evinrude (10 per cent each), Honda (7 per cent) and Mariner (4 per cent). Mariners were rated highest, with Yamaha close behind. Generally Yamaha attracted the most favourable comments, while

Johnson fared the worst. Honda was rated low for reliability and was also criticized for the shortage of qualified service agents, both in and outside the USA.

Having often been asked to arrange a tow for a boat whose main engine had failed to start, but that had a serviceable outboard engine, I decided to find a way to avoid such embarrassment on my present boat. I now have a specially adapted outboard bracket that can be quickly fixed to *Aventura's* stern so one of the two outboard motors that I carry on board can easily be used to push the boat should the main engine fail.

Amanda Neal has this piece of advice to anyone using an outboard engine: 'I grew up as a cruising kid with no outboard motor. We rowed and sailed everywhere, so here are two outboard lessons I learnt the hard way as an adult after having sailed 50,000 miles before ever using one. Learn how to drive an outboard motor, so on your first jetty landing you don't shred the inflatable to pieces on the oyster shells while out of control. Always lock your outboard onto the transom, so when you hit full throttle it won't fly off the back and sink, making you look stupid.'

Tenders

In an earlier survey I tried to find out whether a hard or a soft dinghy would make the ideal tender. Mostly because of the lack of space available to stow a hard dinghy, the majority of skippers are now opting for an inflatable tender, which does not mean that they regard inflatables as necessarily the best, but only that they are the most convenient. Several skippers explained their preference for hard dinghies by pointing out that they were both easier to row and stand up better to rough treatment such as landing on coral or rocky beaches. Hard dinghies also hold an outboard engine better, although it was mentioned that, precisely because they are easier to row, it is possible to dispense with an outboard engine altogether. On the other hand, the disadvantages of hard dinghies were also pointed out, such as the fact that they take up too much space, they can be a hazard in heavy weather when stowed on deck, can be swamped in big or breaking waves, are not much use for diving, and have the annoying tendency to bang against the boat or self-steering gear when at anchor.

When asked to describe their ideal dinghy, several skippers preferred one made of a rigid material and, being aware of the inherent stowage problems, their prospective owners specified that they would make sure that their ideal yacht was designed in such a way as to allow the stowage of a dinghy on deck. Some of those ideal dinghies would also be provided with a transparent bottom panel. Another desirable feature of a hard dinghy was the facility to convert it for sailing by providing it with a mast, centreboard and rudder. This option was mentioned not only by those who enjoyed the idea of having a sailing dinghy, but also by some who regarded the use of the dinghy as a lifeboat as a safety feature in case the yacht had to be abandoned. The suggestion of adapting the mast and sail of a windsurfer for dual use on a dinghy made a lot of sense.

Many of these suggestions concerning hard tenders will probably never be put into practice, as both in the ARC and in the round the world rallies the proportion of inflatable dinghies has by now risen to over 90 per cent as more and more people decide to acquire a one and only inflatable. As Don Babson pointed out: 'If we were cruising in the Bahamas or the Virgins, a RIB or large inflatable carried on powered davits would be great, but for a round the world voyage a dinghy that can be totally deflated and stowed away would be better.' A good set of davits, possibly powered, were listed by several skippers as a desirable feature on their ideal yacht. On his ideal yacht John Ellis would have 'a big comfortable dinghy that can transport six adults, with at least a 15 hp outboard. A big part of cruising is buzzing about in your dinghy.'

Arthur Beiser stressed another point: 'A very important and often overlooked subject is to have a place on deck to carry an inflated dinghy securely. Davits can be handy, but are not a good idea at sea except on a really big boat – and probably not even then. On *Ardent Spirit* we carry a 3.2-metre hard-bottom inflatable inverted in chocks on the forward deck where it is out of the way, and it has proved so great a convenience that we now think of it as a necessity.'

On *Aventura III* I have two Avon inflatables, both packed up and stowed in a locker when underway. The smaller one has an inflatable rigid floor, can be inflated in a few minutes, and is easily rowed. The larger one can carry up to six adults, has a folding rigid floor, and is a perfect tender for diving expeditions or trips ashore.

Tenders were examined in the SSCA Survey, in which the majority were either inflatables (43 per cent) or rigid inflatable boats (RIB) (42 per cent), with only 15 per cent being rigid dinghies. Among the inflatables, the most popular makes were Avon (52 per cent), followed by Zodiac and Achilles (15 per cent each), and a host of other brands. Among the most common makes, Avon was rated highest for reliability, followed by Achilles – a remarkable endorsement of their quality as both makes had an average age of over eight years. Among the RIBs, Caribe was leading the fleet both as the most common make (25 per cent) and also for having the highest rating for performance. Avon RIBs (20 per cent) were rated higher than Caribe for reliability, while the third most common make, AB (17 per cent), scored lower on both counts.

Ground tackle

As docking facilities in most ports outside Europe and North America are rather limited, cruising boats spend more time at anchor than alongside a dock or pontoon. The ground tackle on long distance cruising boats was examined in great detail in several surveys, when it was found that the majority of boats (85 per cent) used only chain with their main anchor. To qualify as 'only chain', the boat in question had to have at least 100 feet of chain for its main anchor alone, although in most cases boats carried twice that amount and sometimes even more. The insistence on more than adequate ground tackle shows the importance that long distance voyagers attach to being securely anchored under all conditions.

The skippers taking part in an earlier survey were asked to assess the performance of their main anchors, and by far the most common type in use was the plough. In the majority of cases, the anchors were genuine CQR, although a few skippers warned of poor imitations of this type. The average weight of the plough anchors on the boats over 40 feet LOA was 52 lbs (23.5 kg), while on the boats under 40 feet, the average was 45 lbs (20 kg). Most boats were equipped with anchors whose weight was in excess of what is considered to be adequate for a particular length of boat. This was equally true for the other types of anchors, as the average weight of Danforth anchors on boats over 40 feet was 65 lbs (29.5 kg) and 53 lbs (24 kg) for boats under 40 feet. The weight of Bruce anchors on boats under 40 feet averaged 37 lbs (17 kg). Several boats carried additional anchors of heavier weights (average 75 lbs/34 kg), to be used only in the case of severe storms or hurricanes. The majority of boats carried on average three anchors of different types and weights, and these did not include light folding anchors.

To cope with the heavy ground tackle, most boats surveyed in the Pacific were equipped with windlasses, either manual or electric. Several owners of manual windlasses complained that they were not powerful enough and were of little use in deep anchorages. Electric windlasses performed better overall and were recommended as being very useful by several skippers. In this respect, it is very telling that one-third of the skippers interviewed in the Global Cruising Survey listed an electric anchor windlass as one of the essential features they would have on their ideal boat. In fact, several pointed out that they already have an electric anchor windlass and stressed just how important it was to have a good, reliable system. As David Hersey underlined, 'a well-organized anchoring arrangement is essential'. Also mentioned as a very useful feature, when discussing anchoring generally, was a depth alarm, such as the one on the Brookes&Gatehouse Hydra system, which will trigger the alarm when either a pre-set minimum or maximum depth is reached. This can be a great help if the boat drags into deeper or shallower water, especially at night.

One common complaint was that non-calibrated chain tended to slip on the chain gypsy. One of the main reasons for this is that some US chains are slightly larger than European chains. An International Standard (ISO 4565) for yacht anchor chain aims to standardize sizes to 6, 8, 10 and 12 mm. The purpose of the standard is to achieve dimensional interchangeability of chain on windlass gypsies to ensure a proper fit. Although the manufacturers in Europe have adopted the new standard, US manufacturers may continue with non-metric dimensions, which means that there may never be interchangeability of chains made on the two sides of the Atlantic. The compatibility of chain and windlass gypsy should therefore be checked if they are bought separately, and especially if they have been bought in different countries.

Anchor types and ground tackle generally were investigated in the Global Cruising Survey in which the 40 skippers were asked to comment on their preferred anchor type. Just over half (22) indicated CQR, or plough type, anchors as their favourite, followed by Delta (6), Danforth/Brittany (5), Bruce (4), and one vote each for Fortress, Spade and Admiralty (Fisherman). Danforth-type anchors were the favourite back-up anchor, followed by CQR, Bruce and Delta.

John Ellis explained his preference: 'If I had to choose just one anchor for all conditions, it would be CQR. Because it's hinged, it won't necessarily break out when the boat swings with wind shifts. It's good under big loads and copes well on most bottoms. It also stores easily on the bow. What is also important is to have heavy-duty chain and lots of it.' David Beauchamp shares that view: 'Plough-type anchors seem to do a good job, especially if the weight of anchor is one or two sizes up from that specified by the manufacturers for the size of boat. On my CQR I use a lead weight, which slides down the anchor chain on a large shackle to lower the catenary – it works a treat! In my experience it seems that whatever type of anchor is chosen more depends on the person setting the gear than the gear used. It's the guy who can't wait to get below out of the inclement weather or the hot sun who disappears backwards across the bay when the breeze stiffens.'

Klaus Girzig agrees: 'I have often been amazed at just how lazy people are to re-anchor even if their anchor is obviously not holding well, or they have dropped it in the wrong place.' Indeed, as Don Babson quipped: 'Keeping your fingers crossed rarely works. After all, even the famous Moitessier lost at least one of his boats when he failed to re-anchor.'

Carlton DeHart always makes sure he is well anchored: 'During our circum-navigation we used a CQR 75-lb anchor with 100 metres of seven-sixteenth-inch chain with great success. We set the anchor, didn't just drop it, and never had to worry about it. The best advice is to put out the biggest anchor you can handle. The CQR is drop forged steel and will take a beating, especially when retrieving it out of rocks.'

Arthur Beiser has had 'personal experience only with Danforths, CQRs, and Fishermen. Of these, the CQR is the best all-round anchor, but the others can be better in special circumstances. For weight, I'd suggest at least 3 lbs per ton of displacement for CQR or Delta, but this depends a lot on windage as well as on the displacement of the boat. Certainly I would always go up one or two sizes from those recommended by the makers of the anchors.'

On Skip Novak's *Pelagic* 'we have a 105-lb CQR that is kept in the bow roller on 90 metres of half-inch chain. This is the best anchor all round, as it is easy to stow on the bow, and although it is not good for certain conditions, it is not worth changing your anchor every time you have a different bottom. I am not a fan of two anchors in tandem (on the same chain). This is a messy business. Better to have one big, oversize anchor and a heavy chain, and drop it once and keep things simple.'

Javier Visiers was among the skippers switching over to Delta anchors: 'After my latest round the world trip I have absolutely no doubts about the Delta. It is the best.' Chris Harding, who sailed in the same rally, agrees: 'Personally I have had very good results with the Delta anchor. Also the CQR has proven itself very good in nearly all types of seabeds.'

Bill Butler has other preferences: 'It is Danforth for me! I call my 40 pounder "old faithful". I also have a 40-lb Bruce and an even heavier CQR, as well as a 35-lb fold-able Navy seaplane anchor. All failed me at one time or another, except for "old faithful".' Luc Callebaut also likes flat-type anchors such as Brittany or Danforth: 'If you look at any commercial vessel, that's all you will see them use. I use a 75-lb anchor for our 46-foot trimaran. Good scope is essential. We try to put out 7 to 1 all three-eighth chain with a minimum of 125 feet of chain. Also, it is rare when we do not check our anchor with snorkelling gear or scuba. We used such an anchor on a 120-feet motor vessel during hurricane Luis in St Maarten after I placed it on the bottom with my scuba tank and we had the worse time getting it up afterwards! I had to use full engine power to break it out. If the bottom is hard, then nothing will dig in and you had better dive and make yourself a mooring using something big and heavy on the bottom. You will be amazed what you can find in popular anchorages!'

Don Babson knows what he wants: 'What is my preferred anchor? One that doesn't drag. We now put down two anchors regardless if staying overnight or going ashore. We deploy a 35-lb Danforth on a ¾-in nylon line with 20 feet chain lead, and a 45-lb Delta on five-sixteenth chain. We never have had both drag at the same time, but have had each drag if set alone. It is more work to deploy and haul aboard, but easier than dragging the boat off as it closes with a rocky shore! I do believe that one should have not only two anchors deployed, but they should be of different types. Some types are better in sand, some are better in mud or stones. None is good in kelp. Scope is perhaps the most important, both with chain and line. If anchoring with the latter, 5 to 1 is a minimum, and 7 to 1 is better if room allows.'

Antti Louhija is among those who prefer a Bruce anchor: 'Holding is good and there are no moving parts to get fingers squeezed.' Michelle LaMontagne, who always anchors with chain only, underlined one disadvantage of nylon rode in that it gets cut on coral.

ANCHORING TECHNIQUES

Although anchoring techniques as such were not investigated in any of the surveys, various comments and valuable suggestions were made when discussing ground tackle generally. One skipper pointed out that many people with little cruising experience seem to be unaware of the well-proven method of checking and setting the anchor by testing it with the engine astern. After the anchor has been dropped and the required scope paid out, and the anchor has had a chance to set, the engine is put into astern until it is felt that the anchor has bitten and is holding. This method is particularly recommended in exposed anchorages or where strong gusts of wind can be expected, such as those experienced in the lee of high hills. It is also a good idea to go through this procedure if the boat is going to be left unattended for any length of time. Checking a marina or harbour mooring in this way is also a good idea as either the mooring itself may be too light for your boat, or the mooring line may not stand up to the strain imposed by a strong gust of wind. It is surprising how often you will find that either your own anchor, or a mooring, will fail this simple test!

Other anchoring methods were also recommended for specific circumstances. Among these was the Bahamian moor, which is very useful when anchoring in tidal estuaries, tidal rivers, or where there is a strong current that changes its direction. Two anchors are used, both set from the bow, and the principle is to set one anchor forward and the other astern, so that the boat pivots in a relatively small arc to be held by either one or the other of the anchors, depending on the set of the current. Probably the easiest way to set this type of mooring without having to resort to the dinghy is to drop the secondary anchor first, then pay out sufficient scope so that one can go far enough forward to drop the main anchor in the desired place, the excess scope on the secondary anchor being taken in until the boat rests between the two anchors. As the tide changes, the boat will gradually swing into the opposite direction when the secondary anchor will become the primary one and vice versa.

Skip Novak's comments on the use of two anchors in tandem on the same chain took me by surprise as this was the method favoured by *Pelagic*'s skipper Hamish Laird when I accompanied him on a trip to Antarctica. I subsequently used this

Good ground tackle is essential when cruising in remote places. Aventura III at Port Circumcision off the Antarctic Peninsula.

system myself in doubtful anchorages – not just in Antarctica, but even in the Mediterranean when we left the boat unattended while travelling inshore. First I drop a 30-lb Fisherman on its own 10 metres of chain, which is shackled to the main anchor, and then a 45-lb Bruce, followed by enough scope of chain for that particular depth. The system works very well, it is relatively easy to retrieve, and we never dragged when we used it.

The usefulness of a stern anchor came up as a topic of conversation on many occasions, some people swearing by them, while others considered them a waste of time. Several skippers who were advocates of stern anchors suggested that permanent anchor stowage should be provided at the stern. If mounted on the stern rail, a Danforth-type anchor is preferable as it stows flat. For a plough anchor, a special fitting with a roller is more convenient, and in fact some production boats feature this arrangement as standard. Usually the stern anchor has only a short length of chain attached to it and the rest of the scope is made up of line, which ideally should be kept on a reel. On some boats the reel is mounted on the rail, while on others the reel is removable and stowed elsewhere on the boat. Stowing the spare anchor warp is not always easy, and a solution to this problem is to use one of various makes of flat polyester braid on their own reel that take up less space and are easier to handle. Personally I am not a great fan of stern anchors, and only use one in anchorages where there is a cross swell or current and I want to keep the boat pointing into the wind or swell. Otherwise I find stern anchors to be more trouble than they are worth as on a few occasions we ended up dragging the main anchor because of it.

Additional equipment

Various suggestions concerning ancillary equipment were made by the skippers equipping their ideal cruising boat. Various items were mentioned as desirable on an ideal boat, such as a provision for night lighting (preferably red), not just at the chart table but also in the saloon, toilet and galley. During a night watch, the watchkeeper might wish to make a cup of coffee or use the heads, and even a brief exposure to white light could spoil his or her night vision. Other features, some seemingly minor, that would make life on a longer cruise more comfortable and also much more enjoyable were also mentioned. On the entertainment side, a stereo installation with a compact disc player was mentioned by some skippers as being the kind of equipment that should be installed at the fitting-out stage as the wiring for the speakers, for instance, can be routed out of sight. Also in the audio field, a good-quality radio receiver in the short wave bands makes it possible to tune in to the long distance sailors' favourite, the BBC World Service. Television sets are also becoming more popular on sailing boats and, if tempted, you should make sure you buy a set that can receive in the various systems: PAL in the UK, most of Western Europe and Australia; SECAM in France and its dependencies in the Caribbean; NTSC in the USA, Canada and the English-speaking Caribbean islands. VCRs are no longer regarded as unusual on a boat and there are even some available that can run off 12 volts. Videotape swapping among cruising sailors is now as widespread as book swapping used to be in the past. DVD has recently gained popularity on cruising boats thanks to its versatility and smaller size.

Another consideration mentioned by skippers in regard to the ideal boat was the importance of having proper bottle stowage – not just a proper drinks cabinet, but the possibility of storing wine bottles. This reminded me of the results of my very first survey in which two skippers described their bottle openers as the most important instruments on board their boats! As in every other respect, it is a matter of priorities, and an ideal boat should reflect the owner's whims. It would be boring if all boats were the same. One skipper, obviously fond of his glass of wine, suggested installing a stainless steel tank, which would make it possible to buy wine in countries where it is cheap and easily available, and have an assured supply in places where wine is expensive or difficult to find.

5

Taking the Guessing out of Navigation
SATELLITE NAVIGATION, ELECTRONICS AND INSTRUMENTATION

"It seems to me criminal negligence to go offshore without at least a handheld GPS these days."
ARTHUR BEISER

Cruising boats used to lag far behind racing yachts in the range of instruments and equipment carried, but this is no longer the case and some of the most sophisticated gear can be seen on boats equipped for offshore cruising. Many of the ARC boats have the latest navigation devices and their range of instruments would put many a racer to shame. Tony Mark, the ARC safety inspector, confirmed this: 'The amount of electronic gadgetry on some of the ARC boats is truly amazing. The most sophisticated electronic navigation equipment is now found even on the smallest boats. But because of this proliferation, there is also a much higher percentage of breakages.'

Electronic equipment was examined in earlier surveys as well as the latest Global Cruising Survey. The range of instruments and electronic devices is now so wide, and changing so rapidly, that many of those surveyed admitted finding it increasingly difficult to keep up with the latest additions to a never-ending list of equipment.

Satellite navigation

There is no doubt that the single most important item that has contributed more than anything else to the expansion of offshore cruising is GPS (Global Positioning System). The greatly improved accuracy in navigation that has resulted from it has made a considerable contribution to safety generally. It is no wonder that GPS was rated as the most useful piece of equipment by the 197 skippers who took part in the ARC 2000 Survey. When the skippers were asked to assess the reliability of GPS, three different makes (Garmin, Leica and Trimble) were rated among the top performers. This demonstrates not only the unparalleled usefulness of GPS, but also its outstanding reliability. GPS received an even higher accolade in the ARC 1999 Survey, when it was voted the most popular piece of equipment on board, just ahead of autopilots. In both surveys, the reliability of GPS units was highly rated and the only criticism made was the difficulty of getting repairs done. This is probably the reason why most boats carry at least one back-up. The findings of the ARC surveys were confirmed by the SSCA Survey, in which the most popular make was Garmin, found on 49 per cent of the boats surveyed. Garmin was rated high both for performance and reliability. The second most common make was Magellan (18 per cent), which was rated much lower for performance, and was only one place above Micrologic (6 per cent of the sample), which came bottom of the table. Furuno (7 per cent) and Autohelm (6 per cent) fared better on both counts.

How much sailors rely on GPS nowadays was demonstrated by the findings of the Global Cruising Survey. The skippers were asked not only to comment on the usefulness of GPS, but also to indicate if they ever use astronavigation. Only six skippers admitted that they ever used their sextants, and the majority never fixed their position by traditional means. However, on every boat a sextant was kept for emergency purposes and most skippers stated that they were able to take a sight and work out a position should the need arise.

Arthur Beiser was among those who have absolutely no doubts about the value of GPS: 'I can't see any reason to put the desirability of GPS in question. It seems to me criminal negligence to go offshore without at least a handheld GPS these days.' John Ellis agrees: 'GPS is very safe. But I would carry at least two and have an additional one that is battery-powered and not reliant on the yacht's power. I don't think that people need to know astronavigation. What is important, and sadly lacking, are basic navigation skills such as navigating by dead reckoning, getting three point fixes, etc.' David Beauchamp feels that over-reliance on GPS makes it in fact unsafe: 'The main reason for considering GPS navigation to be unsafe seems to me that it makes going offshore possible for so many idiots. Apart from that, it is without doubt the greatest invention since Noah's Ark. I still check my astronavigation, but not so often as I should – which I suppose makes me one of those idiots!'

Carlton DeHart feels that astronavigation still has a role to play: 'I feel strongly that nothing replaces astronavigation. The first time I sailed around the world, I used only astronavigation. The discipline of taking morning and evening sights became a rhythm and made you feel part of the universe. The second time around, I used the old Transit satnav system, but still checked the satnav with astro-navigation because I didn't really trust it. The third time around, we used only GPS and dusted off the sextant once in a while, but relied on the radar to check the GPS. It's this complacency of depending on GPS that I feel is the hidden danger. The rhythm is gone, as well as the thrill of a landfall after many days at sea and seeing that all your calculations were correct. While sailing from the Marquesas to Tahiti through the Tuamotus at night, we knew exactly where we were and the radar confirmed our position. A lightning strike or the US military can take out your GPS at any time. You had better have your paper charts and sextant ready.'

This is exactly what happened to Antti Louhija: 'Twice my GPS screen went blank during my circumnavigation, and I had to navigate with a spare handheld GPS. It happened just as we were going through the Tuamotus! GPS navigation is accurate, but the charts are often not, and great caution must therefore be exercised.' This is good advice from Antti, who had the misfortune to lose his boat on an inaccurately charted reef while sailing at night in the Red Sea. The need for extra caution is also a point made by Chris Harding: 'On passage I generally trust the GPS 99 per cent. Obviously, all electronic instruments on a boat occasionally give strange results. As long as you understand the information that the GPS is giving you, and are not just blindly believing all it says, I think that the system is superb. Of course anything that relies on electricity has a weak point: if you lose your batteries, you no longer have your electronics. On ocean passages I regularly take sextant sights to confirm my position, also just to keep practising something that I consider very important.'

Don Babson also believes that 'GPS navigation is wonderful and we wouldn't have undertaken the round the world trip without it. Note should be taken that *no* form of navigation is the final answer. A case in point is while heading north in the Chilean canals our very accurate GPS showed us to be as much as 1 mile east of our actual position, and put us somewhere on land. The GPS was accurate, but the charts we were using were British Admiralty charts done in the early 1800s, which were of course done by sextant and therefore not too accurate.'

Among those who never used his sextant was Tom Muller: 'Never used astro and missed it about as much as hemp ropes in the year 2001.'

Several skippers stressed how important it was not just to have a sextant, and the relevant tables or at least the software on board, but also to occasionally brush up one's astro by working out a sight so as not to be totally reliant on GPS. Shortly before this book went to press, the European Union confirmed that its own, more advanced satellite navigation system, Galileo, will be fully operational before the end of the current decade, so the future of satellite navigation seems assured and will no longer be dependent on the US military.

Radar

Another navigation device originally developed for military use that is proving increasingly popular with cruising sailors is radar (Radio Detection and Rangefinding). Radars used to be seen only on the largest yachts and it took many years before the bulky scanner and the equally large set were brought down to a size that could be fitted on the average cruising boat. The only serious drawback is that in spite of all the improvements to the receiver and display unit, the antenna itself must remain between 2 and 3 feet long to obtain a good definition of the target, and therefore on smaller yachts the siting of the scanner is a major difficulty. This may not have been such a problem when many cruising boats were two-masted and the mizzen mast could be put to good use, but the present trend towards one-masted yachts complicates matters for those who wish to acquire radar. The solution is to site the scanner in front of the lower spreaders, or on one of the spreaders. The other alternative is to fit a pole at the stern, which on some yachts also doubles up as a support for a wind generator. It is also possible to suspend the scanner from the backstay with the help of a gimbaled mount, which has the advantage of allowing the scanner to see the whole horizon even when the boat is heeled over. Neither solution is ideal and this is probably the explanation why, in spite of its undoubted attractions, some cruising boats are not equipped with radar.

Radar was rated as one of the most reliable pieces of equipment in the ARC 2000 Survey, and this was shown by the fact that out of 116 units surveyed there were only two reported failures. Exactly half the units in the ARC Survey were Raytheon (58), followed by Furuno (33), with both makes attracting high ratings for performance and reliability. The situation was reversed in the SSCA 2000 Survey in which Furuno was the most popular make (on 52 per cent of the boats surveyed) followed by Raytheon (40 per cent). Raytheon scored slightly higher on reliability, and the two brands were rated almost equal on performance. The most interesting finding of the SSCA Survey was the fact that 76 per cent of the boats surveyed reported having radar, which is a much higher proportion than in any previous survey.

Several ARC skippers commented that they used the radar primarily for collision avoidance, and during the Atlantic crossing they also found it very useful for detecting tropical squalls. Radar can play a much wider role in navigation than that, though, particularly when cruising in difficult areas where charts are not accurate or reliable. Skip Novak, whose *Pelagic* is engaged in high-latitude cruising and exploration, pointed out that 'we rely on GPS when offshore, but inshore the radar is the primary tool for safe navigation'. David Hersey agrees: 'Radar is a boon in many situations. In practice our range is seldom more than 12 to 16 miles, but that is plenty in traffic or for making a landfall.'

The advantage of radar in collision avoidance became obvious to me personally on passage from Hawaii to Alaska on *Aventura III*. For several days, while crossing the western edge of the Pacific high, we passed through an area of thick fog with visibility rarely more than the boat's length. There was a large amount of shipping in the area, both cargo ships en route from Asia to North America, as well as many fishing vessels. We set a 6-mile guard zone on the radar, and every time a target entered the guard zone the alarm sounded. In this way we managed to continue sailing in complete security, although it was an eerie feeling to rush blindly into the milky nothingness.

Electronic charts and plotters

Another major innovation in recent years has been the development of electronic charts. Personally, I consider the main disadvantage of the electronic chart to be the need to peer at a screen whenever one has to refer to a chart. This can be irritating, particularly at night when one's night vision can be greatly affected by the need to use a bright screen rather than consult a chart lit by a red light. The use of electronic charts on yachts engaged in blue water cruising is less widespread than among those engaged in coastal navigation. Less than half the boats in the Millennium Odyssey used electronic charts, and even those that did also carried the essential paper charts as back-up.

Charles Gray was one of those who sailed in the Millennium Odyssey: 'GPS was both safe and convenient, particularly when used in conjunction with electronic charts. However, we always carry paper charts and also a sextant.' Luc

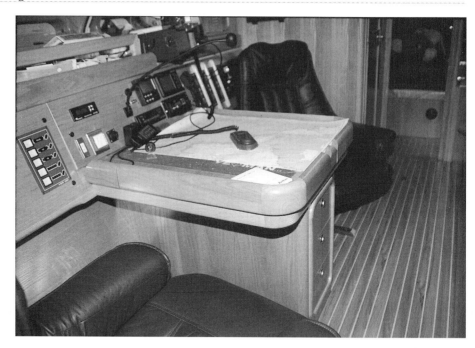

A Yeoman plotter is a good substitute for those who are not prepared to switch over to electronic charts.

Callebaut, who is based in French Polynesia and has cruised that area extensively, feels that 'the danger I see is that more and more cruisers rely blindly on GPS navigation, especially when they rely on electronic charts with GPS interface. These can be of very little use in places like the Tuamotus where one should never forget eyeball navigation, and other navigational aids like radar or depth sounder.'

Clyff Huggett warned against placing too much confidence in electronic charts, which can be just as inaccurate as paper charts: 'Now we tend to use paper charts and eyeball navigation when approaching an anchorage, ever since our electronic charts showed us sailing on land while approaching an anchorage. Unfortunately we do not have wheels!'

Michelle LaMontagne has good reasons for regarding electronic charts with some healthy scepticism: 'Having been struck by lightning four times altogether, of which three times were within a span of 17 days, I am a real advocate of using paper charts.' The risk of depending on electronic charts became all too real in my own case when my laptop computer crashed while cruising in the Bahamas, and could not be repaired. Suddenly all my detailed electronic charts could no longer be accessed and the computer could not be replaced for several months. Fortunately I had almost all the necessary paper charts on board and was able to order new ones for the areas to be visited later.

Chart plotters have gained in popularity as they combine all the advantages of the latest microprocessor-based position fixing systems with the accuracy of a conventional paper chart. Chart plotters were used on one-third (62) of the boats surveyed in ARC 2000, with Raytheon being the most common make (22), then Yeoman (7), and a variety of other brands. All makes performed well and there were no failures reported during the Atlantic crossing. Although not strictly a chart plotter in the electronic sense, the Yeoman plotter was praised for its versatility. It was, in fact, the highest rated of all equipment surveyed, and was voted best on performance, reliability and value for money. It is indeed a good compromise for those who are not sure about upgrading to electronic charts as it provides a paper chart with a valuable electronic function. The Yeoman is capable of working out latitude and longitude and to plot it on a regular chart, and can also plot ranges and bearings to and from any point on the chart in use. It also shows instantly the present position of the vessel if interfaced with a GPS. In coastal navigation its greatest advantage is that it makes dead reckoning extremely simple.

Chris Harding is not convinced of chart plotters generally: 'GPS coupled with a chart plotter is about as dangerous as things can get. Blind faith in these systems is very dangerous, for close-to-shore navigation I do not use or trust plotters and GPS, but use traditional means.'

Instrumentation

Whereas some of the navigation systems mentioned above, with the notable exception of GPS, may be regarded as optional, few people like to sail offshore without some basic instruments on board. This area has also witnessed tremendous advances, and today's instruments can be used either individually or as part of a fully integrated system. The amount of computed data being generated by wind, water and navigation instruments is put to more and more use, and virtually any information can now be obtained at the push of a button.

DEPTH SOUNDERS

Depth or echo sounders are probably one of the most useful instruments on a cruising boat. The basic sounder is a simple sonar device using ultrasonic waves emitted by a transducer mounted in the hull. The signal is reflected like an echo, which is picked up by the transducer and converted into an electrical impulse. When choosing a depth sounder, the most important question for the offshore navigator is to decide how deep the sounder should be able to read and also how many ancillary features are needed. The design of the hull will dictate the choice of one or two transducers.

The overall reliability of depth sounders can be gauged from the results of the SSCA Survey in which the most common makes were Datamarine (24 per cent), Raytheon (22 per cent), and Brookes&Gatehouse (13 per cent). They were rated in reverse order for performance, and Raytheon (Autohelm) depth sounders scored slightly better than the others when rated for reliability.

Luc Callebaut, who has explored the Tuamotus extensively, advised that 'I find a fishfinder to be less expensive and more useful than classical depth sounders.'

Far less common, but arguably quite useful in certain situations, are forward-looking depth sounders. Most of those who acquire them hope to be able to avoid collisions with submerged objects such as containers, or to get some early warning of an impending collision with a whale. While containers or large whales will probably show up on such a sounder, the time needed to take avoiding action is so short that their usefulness for this function is doubtful. They are, however, of more use when entering an anchorage and looking for the best place to drop the anchor.

SPEEDOMETERS

The majority of cruising boats use electronic speedometers, most of which are fairly simple devices. A paddlewheel mounted through the hull has a number of magnets embedded in its paddles. As they spin past a sensor, they create electric pulses, which are translated into nautical miles per hour to show either speed or the distance covered since the log was last checked. Although the majority of speedometers use paddlewheel transducers, there are several other types available, all of which have both advantages and disadvantages compared to the former. Some speedometers use solid-state transducers, which have no moving parts and can use either electromagnetic or sonic impulses.

In the SSCA Survey the same three makes as in the case of depth sounders dominated the scene: Datamarine (28 per cent), Raytheon (23 per cent) and Brookes&Gatehouse (14 per cent). They were rated in the same order for performance, with Raytheon scoring third for reliability. Standard, accounting for 6 per cent, was rated higher for both performance and reliability.

WIND INDICATORS

Most windspeed indicators work on the same principle as the basic speedometer in that the wind is measured at the top of the mast by a spinner, which sends an electric impulse to a counter at deck level. Most masthead units have a three-cup anemometer, on top of which sits a slender indicator or fly. Electro-mechanical windspeed indicators share some of the same problems as speedometers and they also suffer because of the fragility of the sensitive moving parts. They are gradually being replaced by solid-state masthead units.

In the SSCA Survey, Raytheon scored highest of all makes for performance and also outperformed the other two major makes for reliability. Raytheon accounted for 24 per cent of the boats surveyed, Datamarine for 27 per cent, and Brookes& Gatehouse for 17 per cent. The average age of the units was 11 years in the case of Datamarine, 8 years for Brookes&Gatehouse, and nearly 5 years for Raytheon.

INTEGRATED SYSTEMS

In a world of microchips and data processing, cruising yachts could not remain unaffected for long, and soon boats not equipped with their own computer will be the exception rather than the rule. The first area to be computerized has been data collection by various instruments. The navigator now has access to a whole range of information provided by a central processor to which all individual instruments are connected. The basic computed functions are true wind direction, true wind speed, and velocity made good (VMG). The latter is not only useful when racing around the marks, but also, for instance, when sailing downwind, as it shows instantly at what angle of wind the boat is making best speed. More complex data can be computed with the aid of inputs from other sources, such as GPS, the electronic compass, automatic pilot, etc.

The overall reliability of instruments was shown by the results of the ARC 2000 Survey, in which only integrated systems were rated, not individual instruments. By far the most popular makes were Raytheon (59 per cent) and Brookes& Gatehouse (27 per cent). The systems worked almost faultlessly during the Atlantic crossing, and the only problem encountered was the difficulty of interfacing the instruments with other equipment such as autopilots.

*Brookes&
Gatehouse
instruments have
a good reputation
for aftersales
service. Here,
a Brookes&
Gatehouse
technician is
servicing the
equipment on an
ARC boat.*

Conclusions

Because of the wide choice available, a logical first step for anyone fitting out a boat for offshore cruising is to draw up a realistic list of priorities before actually buying anything. It is also essential that instruments and equipment requirements are matched to the area where you intend to cruise. This is also where the old adage 'only rich people can afford to buy cheap things' has an undoubted validity, as in the long run it will probably pay to choose instruments made by reputable firms, some of whom give a worldwide guarantee valid for several years.

The impression that I gained from being in close contact with thousands of offshore sailors is that an increasing number expect their equipment to do everything for them. This results in some people becoming virtual slaves of their hardware, which can take a lot of the pleasure out of cruising. A certain push-button mentality is also becoming prevalent among today's seafarers, as shown by the increasing number of cruising boats using autopilots in preference to wind-operated self-steering gears. The main drawback is the constant need to generate electricity to keep the autopilot going.

It was interesting that several experienced skippers stressed the need of keeping things as simple as possible or, as David Beauchamp praised, 'simplicity at all cost'. Tom Muller made this very clear: 'The more electronics one has, the more problems, and if something goes wrong at sea with this type of equipment, there is little one can do about it. Cruising boats should be self-sufficient in every respect and what cannot be put right with your own means must not be regarded as an essential piece of equipment.' Another valid point made by several skippers was that no matter how much equipment you pile on a boat, it is the skill of the crew that is ultimately the guarantee of a safe voyage.

6

Keeping in Touch
E-MAIL, RADIO AND
SATELLITE COMMUNICATIONS

*"Global communications have added a wonderful dimension to offshore
cruising. The ability to keep in touch with family and business has been a
tremendous liberating factor."*　　　　　　　　　　　　　KLAUS GIRZIG

L ong distance cruising is being revolutionized by communications just as
much as is the day-to-day life of those living on land. It wasn't all that long
ago that a yacht setting off across an ocean was completely out of touch
until landfall. For many, that was the attraction of sailing, and there are still some
who feel that modern communications have robbed them of much that was so
special about blue water sailing.

Marine radios

Until fairly recently, HF radio transceivers were the only long range communication systems on board cruising boats, but in recent years their importance has
been seriously undermined by satellite communications. Nowhere is this more
obvious than in the ARC, in which until very recently almost every boat had an
HF radio on board. In ARC 2001, for the first time there were almost as many
satellite telephones in the fleet as HF radios. There is no denying the usefulness of
a satellite telephone, but there are still a few areas in which HF radios continue to
be very useful on cruising boats. The most important ones are the ability to
communicate at no cost with other boats over long distances, to report your
position, obtain weather forecasts, keep in contact with various radio nets, to send
and receive e-mails, and to receive weatherfax images.

Single side band radios (SSB) have, in theory at least, a worldwide range. Under
certain conditions the 2 to 23 MHz bands, which have been allocated for marine
use, comprise frequencies that can reach any point in the world. Depending on the
frequency used, the ground waves bend over the horizon for up to 150 miles, while
the sky waves are reflected off the ionosphere and bounce back to earth thousands
of miles from their source. The knack of long range communication is to know

exactly which frequencies to use to ensure optimum propagation at certain times of day or night, and under which conditions. The antenna no longer needs to be tuned manually to the frequency used as the automatic antenna tuner or coupler does all this at a press of a button.

The operator's task has been made much easier by advances in radio design and frequencies are now selected digitally rather than by twisting a dial. Just as on VHF radios, frequencies are now synthesized and there is a wide choice of channels, which are pre-set by the manufacturer. Most of the set frequencies are International Telephone Union channels, which continue to be used for making calls through the international telephone system. However, as the demand for this service has been seriously undermined by the wide use of satellite telephones, many well-known land-based stations have been forced to close down.

In ARC 2001, out of 219 boats, 155 had an HF radio. This is the equivalent of 71 per cent of the entire fleet, which is a fairly high proportion bearing in mind the equally high number of boats equipped with satellite telephones (144). This shows that there were several boats that had both, and there were only three boats that had neither. The above figures demonstrate that HF radio is far from defunct. Over half the radios in the ARC 2001 Survey were ICOM (61 per cent), which was highly rated by most operators. Almost all problems reported were due to poor installation.

The proportion of HF marine radios was also high in the SSCA Survey, in which this type of radio was reported on 62 per cent of the boats surveyed. ICOM had the largest share (54 per cent), followed by SGC (27 per cent), SEA (10 per cent), and Kenwood (5 per cent). ICOM fared well both on performance and reliability, although Kenwood was rated the highest.

Amateur radios

An alternative preferred by many cruising sailors for long range communication is amateur radio, which is a global communications system with a clearly defined purpose. The frequency bands allocated to amateur operators are interspersed with those used by the SSB marine radio system, as both of them use the same type of transmission and even the sets are very similar. The major difference is in the price, with an amateur set costing half of its marine equivalent. This cost factor, and the feeling that in an emergency an amateur will always be able to raise another amateur somewhere in the world, has persuaded many sailors to equip their boats with an amateur set. One serious impediment, however, is the requirement to have a full licence in order to operate an amateur set legally. The practical examination – which in some countries requires proficiency in morse code as well as technical know-how – is quite stringent, and as a result many owners of amateur sets do not possess a licence. As most of them had acquired the sets only for safety reasons, they often listen but do not transmit, and those who try to do so without being licensed are quickly detected by other operators who usually tell them to get off the air. However, I have not heard of any case of a real emergency where the amateur fraternity refused to help a sailor in distress. Should there be a serious emergency involving a yacht with an unlicensed set on board, there is no doubt

SSB radios continue to be the most convenient means of communication between cruising boats.

that amateur operators would do their best to help. However, those who really intend to work the amateur frequencies and are attracted by the many attractions of the worldwide nets should make the effort to obtain a proper licence.

The large proportion of amateur radios on US cruising boats is probably explained by the fact that it is somewhat easier to obtain an amateur licence in the USA than in some European countries. Regulations concerning the use of amateur radio in many countries, particularly in Europe, are more stringent. Another significant difference is that in the USA it is possible to patch into the telephone system via an amateur radio contact. Usually the marine operator chooses a contact near to the person that he wishes to call. The land-based radio amateur is then asked to patch the caller from the yacht into the telephone system, which often means that a call can be made home from the middle of the ocean for little more than the price of a local telephone call. Many US yachts use this facility to talk regularly with their family and friends back home while cruising anywhere in the world. This facility to use the amateur radio as a telephone is illegal in most other countries, but if it were allowed, there is no doubt that many more non-US yachts would carry this equipment.

The performance of amateur radios was examined in the SSCA Survey, in which about half of the boats reported having such a radio on board. The most common makes were ICOM (42 per cent), Kenwood (29 per cent), SGC (14 per cent), and Yaesu (11 per cent), with Kenwood being rated highest.

AMATEUR VERSUS MARINE RADIO

As far as long range radio communications are concerned, the ultimate choice of a marine SSB or an amateur set will depend on each user's individual priorities. SSB radio has two clear advantages over amateur radio. First, it can be operated legally with little more trouble than is involved in obtaining a VHF operator's licence. Second, although the amateur fraternity operates a huge number of nets run by shore-based enthusiasts, a proper 24-hour safety net is only operated on certain marine frequencies. Apart from that, to communicate with shore-based parties who are not amateurs themselves can only be done via SSB radio. Another advantage of SSB radio is the ability to receive weather information, which can be printed out on a weather facsimile printer. Finally, most SSB sets can also be used to listen in on the amateur frequencies. If, after having taken all these matters into consideration, amateur radio continues to be more attractive, then the only solution is to acquire one and also the proper licence to go with it. What is certainly wrong is to regard amateur radio as the poor man's SSB, which it is not. The concept of amateur radio is fundamentally different, and some marine users of amateur radio seem unaware of the basic tenets that motivated the early hams and led to the creation of this truly international association. Founded at the dawn of radio communications, its basic function was, and still is, to enable amateur enthusiasts to communicate with each other over the airwaves. The amateur radio maritime nets that have grown up all over the world play a vital role in enhancing the safety of those who sail offshore, and I believe that the easing of the licensing laws would bring about an increase in the number of yachts carrying this type of radio legally.

E-mail

Electronic mail has become the favourite method for global communications on board sailing boats, and as new systems are becoming available the situation is constantly improving. At the moment there is a variety of ways to send and receive e-mails on board. The fastest way is via one of the satellite systems described below: Inmarsat M and C, or to use a satellite telephone such as Iridium. Close to land one can use cellular telephones. The system that has gained rapid popularity among cruising sailors is one of the HF radio-based systems such as PinOak, SeaMail or SailMail. Because of its better global coverage, SailMail is now the most popular, whereas amateur radio operators use the Winlink system.

Once on land, there are now internet outlets where you can check your e-mail in many marinas and ports frequented by cruising sailors. As Michelle LaMontagne put it, 'There is now an internet café on every rock.' One e-mail system that can be used over the public telephone network is Pocketmail. This system uses a free number in the USA, but is more costly to use outside that country.

E-mail, and the advantage of having this system on board, was discussed in detail with the skippers in the Global Cruising Survey. Among the 33 skippers surveyed who were cruising at the time, 21 had e-mail on board, and with few exceptions the various systems that were used worked well. The majority used Inmarsat C while sailing offshore, while two skippers cruising in the Mediterranean used their mobile phones, and a third one used his VHF radio. Two of the dedicated Magellan systems failed to live up to the owners' expectations. Eduardo Gallardo was one of them: 'I used the GSC 100 coming across the Atlantic, but it didn't work, so I sold it. While cruising in the Med I find cyber cafés to be much easier.'

Among the 12 cruising skippers who did not have e-mail, there were some who made it very clear why they did not, such as Bill Butler: 'Never! The reason to cruise is to try to escape from the vicissitudes of life. It is OK to connect from shore to send and receive e-mail, but to sail away being continuously plugged into a shore line, no way.' Richard Walker fully agrees: 'No thanks, it is bad enough that we can be contacted when in port!'

Don Babson took the opposite view: 'We do have e-mail on board via Inmarsat C, and it is great, and if you can keep it short and accessible to family only, then it is not expensive. We do most of our e-mail while in port at internet cafés, which can be found almost anywhere.'

As a professional skipper, Chris Harding is fully aware of the advantages: 'We are using the Mini M system which, while expensive, is generally very reliable. This service makes a huge difference to the running of the boat – just the fact that clear and precise messages can be sent without the problems involved with making a telephone call and all the misunderstandings. Parts can be ordered quickly and they will be sent to the correct address.'

The skippers were also asked whether they'd prefer e-mail to a satellite telephone, and those who didn't have either were asked whether they would consider having an e-mail facility on their ideal boat. Most specified that they would definitely consider having e-mail on their next boat but there were also five exceptions who preferred to stay incommunicado. Antti Louhija was not among them: 'I do not have e-mail on board. Nowadays there are e-mail facilities in almost every harbour, even in remote places, where you can collect and send your mail, which I usually prepare beforehand on my computer on board. Rather than e-mail, on my next boat I would acquire a satellite phone.'

The internet

This unlimited source of information will undoubtedly revolutionize offshore cruising once the internet becomes more easily accessible when sailing offshore. Although connections tend to be quite costly, boats equipped with Inmarsat A, B and occasionally M are now able to connect to the internet from anywhere in the world and thus have an inexhaustible source of information, as well as access to a host of weather and other essential services. Some of the best sources of information are those provided by US government agencies, such as NOAA, which are also used as raw data by the forecasters providing individualized weather routing.

Most long distance cruising boats have a weatherfax on board.

All this information is freely available on the internet, from tropical storm warnings to satellite images of the Gulf Stream, and weather forecasts for any location on the world's oceans. The main obstacle to being able to access the internet via one of the existing satellite systems is the size of the antenna. Because of the distance to the satellites, and also the continuous movement of the boat, the antenna needs to be quite large, which makes this impractical for smaller boats. The situation may change once a new generation of communication satellites is launched into low orbit.

Satellite communications

One of the most remarkable changes that have occurred in recent years is in the field of satellite communications. Nowhere is this more obvious than in the ARC fleet, and even if it could be argued that the yachts sailing in the ARC are not necessarily representative of the current cruising scene, past experience has shown that whatever happens in the ARC (or similar offshore rallies) sooner or later percolates down to most other offshore cruising yachts. The most commonly used systems on cruising boats are described briefly below.

INMARSAT M

This is a digital system that can also carry facsimile and low-speed data. It uses the geostationary Inmarsat satellites and provides near-global coverage. The Mini M version has a smaller antenna and is therefore more suitable for sailing yachts.

IRIDIUM

This system uses a constellation of 66 satellites that ensure global coverage. The handset is somewhat larger and heavier than an ordinary cellular telephone. It handles voice communications and slow data transfer, so it is suitable for e-mail but for the time being it is too slow for the internet. Various other satellite telephone systems, with more limited coverage than either Inmarsat M or Iridium, are in use, while new ones are being developed; therefore the situation is changing rapidly.

INMARSAT C

This is a text-only system that can connect to the international telex network, facsimile or e-mail. The terminals have an in-built GPS that can send a pre-recorded distress message automatically to a land-based co-ordination centre, indicating the vessel's latest position. Global coverage, small antenna and low power consumption are its main attractions.

The 219 yachts in ARC 2001 boasted the entire array of satellite communications: 78 had Inmarsat M, 40 Inmarsat C, and 8 Inmarsat D. The latter is a tracking system. It was also interesting that although Iridium telephones had only been back on stream for a relatively short time, after the original operator had gone out of business, 66 ARC skippers had put their faith in this revitalized system. Together with the owners of the 78 Inmarsat M units, it meant that 144 ARC boats had a satellite telephone on board. This probably explains why 64 skippers decided not to invest in an SSB radio as well, so that – as mentioned earlier – only 155 boats were equipped with an HF radio. Over half the ARC boats had e-mail on board, with the majority (112) being over the satellite system, while an additional 14 used their SSB radios to link to one of the HF e-mail systems. Although 126 ARC boats (56 per cent) had some form of e-mail on board, there was still a large number without this facility. This situation is expected to change significantly in the future as other e-mail systems become available. The slow speed of data transfer provided by the existing systems means that internet access is still slow, unreliable and very expensive, but this is another area in which significant changes are expected in the near future.

Regarding reliability, by far the best results in the ARC Survey were shown by the Inmarsat C units, with no breakages reported. The main advantage of this text-only system is that the units consume very little power and therefore can be left on all the time. They are also a useful and reliable back-up for e-mail, although more expensive than other systems. The yachts sailing in the Millennium Odyssey were equipped with the whole array of satellite communications. Every boat had either Inmarsat C or M, and two had Iridium phones as well. Matt Rollberg was satisfied with the system he used: 'We have Inmarsat C which we initially bought for e-mail. However, over the years we've become dependent on the weather reports and safety messages, so that Inmarsat is now indispensable. We tried an e-mail system using the HF radio before buying Inmarsat C, but decided against it.'

Carlton DeHart agrees: 'E-mail is a great method to tell the folks back home that everything is all right and you are safe and sound. We had both Inmarsat C and SailMail. The former was expensive and the latter was not dependable.' Bob Hall had the same experience: 'We found Inmarsat C e-mail to be expensive, but worth it. We also have the capability of using ham radio e-mail, although it is more dependent on weather conditions.'

Charles Gray advises 'any blue water sailor to consider adding Inmarsat C, not only for e-mail but for safety purposes. Knowing that by pushing the two distress buttons you instantly tell, via satellite, all those who might help that you are sinking or in dire distress, and that you can transmit your exact co-ordinates by virtue of the built-in GPS, is comforting.' Skip Novak fully agrees: 'I feel that Inmarsat C is the best solution for e-mail. It is efficient, has no moving parts, easy to keep track of the cost, and non-intrusive – unlike a telephone.'

The Inmarsat M units, and especially the Mini M version, also scored very high for reliability. In the ARC 2000 Survey, over half the units were made by Thrane & Thrane, with only one breakage reported. Klaus Girzig used his Mini M extensively both as a phone and fax during the Millennium Odyssey: 'Although relatively expensive, the system worked impeccably throughout the two years of our circumnavigation.'

Iridium did not fare too well in ARC 2001 as several malfunctions were reported. Satellite coverage was also not as good as advertised. Several ARC boats used their Iridium phones to send and receive e-mails, and the quality of this service was uneven. I made the same observation during an Atlantic crossing late in 2001when we lost coverage during the last week before reaching St Lucia. In spite of contacting the technical service at Iridium, the source of the problem could not be diagnosed. It meant going back to the reliable Inmarsat C system, which worked faultlessly.

HF-based e-mail systems are gaining popularity among cruising sailors, mainly because it is much more cost effective. Tom Muller gives the system full marks: 'I have been using SeaMail since 1995, and lately SailMail, and the system works perfectly for me. I could not be without it.'

Luc Callebaut shares that view: 'I have been a ham operator for 12 years and was lucky to be involved with the Winlink system from the beginning. This is a radio/e-mail interface for radio amateurs, and the new WL2K system with Airmail software works very well. I recommend getting a Pactor 2 modem, as Pactor 1 modems are slow and not working well in poor propagation. Once you have the gear – laptop, SSB radio and modem – you need to connect to a shore system to handle your e-mails. Ham operators can use WL2K, others can subscribe to SailMail or SeaMail, to name the main ones.'

I leave the last word on the subject to Michael Frankel: 'For me, e-mail has revolutionized long ocean passages. It ranks right up there with GPS as a technological marvel. I have crossed the Atlantic without GPS, but I have never been able to communicate reliably with the world while being far out at sea. Too many magazine articles on the subject of Inmarsat communications have focused on the high cost of this system. Not enough has been said about safety messages, news broadcasts, family peace of mind, and the psychic rewards of instant communication.'

Cellular telephones

Originally developed for land use, cellular telephones are now widely used on boats. There are various systems in operation and some are still incompatible. Both analogue and digital systems are in use in the USA, whereas in Europe the system has been standardized with the introduction of GSM (Global System for Mobile communications). Digital GSM now covers all of Europe, as well as large areas of the Middle East, Asia, Australia and New Zealand. More operators in the USA and South America are gradually joining this system. Three main frequencies are used by GSM operators: 900 and 1800 MHz in Europe and most of Asia, 1900 MHz in most of the USA. While these various frequencies continue to be used, it is advisable to acquire a tri-band telephone capable of using any of those frequencies. A different frequency is used in some of the Caribbean islands, so most telephones in use in the USA or Europe are not compatible with the local system. The exception is the French islands in the Caribbean, which use the European GSM system. Coastal coverage in most countries is generally good, so mobile phones can be used when coastal cruising not only for voice communications but also e-mail, text messages and increasingly for internet access.

Conclusions

Taking the right decision concerning offshore communications, or advising anyone on the best equipment to acquire, is not easy – mainly because everyone has different requirements. As mentioned earlier, an HF radio, whether amateur or marine SSB, still has many uses and I would urge anyone setting off on a longer voyage to have one, as for many years to come radio will continue to be a useful means of communication. For those who wish to be able to stay in touch while sailing offshore, e-mail is highly recommended. One of the satellite systems, either voice or text, are preferable – although many cruisers seem to be quite happy with one of the e-mail systems using HF radios. An HF-based e-mail system such as SailMail would probably suit those who intend to use e-mail infrequently, while larger users should consider one of the satellite phone systems.

For those who don't have e-mail on board, being dependent on internet outlets ashore is a mixed blessing. In some places they are widely available and reasonably priced, in others they are difficult to find and very expensive. I was quite amazed to find early in 2002 that a busy place such as George Town in the Bahamas had only one public internet access place, which was slow, often out of order, and terribly expensive ($30 per hour). For over two years, Michael Frankel used public internet outlets in many countries as he sailed around the world with the Millennium Odyssey, and very often he found the experience extremely frustrating: 'The bad news is that there are many excuses why the facility is down or slow when you want to use it. With only one or two working computers, there is frequently a long line of yachties waiting to get on the computer. Each one can take upwards of an hour to read and send all their messages.' However, Michael also reminds us that 'we quickly forget that a few years ago none of this technology was available or even dreamt of'.

7

Dancing in the Moonlight
OFFSHORE ROUTINES – WATCHKEEPING, ELECTRICITY GENERATION AND CONSUMPTION

"Never used astro and missed it about as much as hemp ropes in the year 2001."
TOM MULLER

I have often been taken aback at cruising seminars or lectures by the naivety of questions asked by some coastal sailors who seem to have great difficulty in imagining life on board during a long passage. Often they seem surprised when I try to explain that most voyagers lead a normal life, with regular meals and the occasional sundowner, even if the nights are interrupted by the unavoidable watches. Although routine might sound like the wrong term to describe life at sea, of necessity the daily activities of any well-run ship have an element of routine about them.

Watchkeeping

Offshore routines were investigated in a number of surveys and every aspect that makes up a day on the high seas was discussed with the skippers and crews. Keeping watches is undoubtedly a demanding chore, and the fellow who once asked me if we went to sleep every night was not entirely misguided, as a few people do indeed turn in for the night and leave their boat to be looked after by its self-steering and God above. However, these are the minority, and on most boats somebody is usually awake to keep an eye on things.

Watchkeeping varies enormously from boat to boat, from a few who do not keep regular watches at all, to those who run their yachts along Navy lines. Two of the factors that influence watchkeeping are the availability of an automatic pilot or windvane, and the size of the crew. In an earlier survey carried out in the Pacific among 100 long distance cruising boats, I found that on most boats where watches were kept as a matter of routine, a fixed system of watches only operated at night. On boats with a crew of two, the night was usually split into four three-hour periods, with two watch and two rest periods. A similar arrangement operated on boats with a crew of three, so that on any given night only one crew member had to take two watches. Boats with larger crews generally kept two-hour watches, especially those steered by hand. In most instances older children also took watches, although they were usually spared night watches.

Watchkeeping was also investigated in a subsequent survey conducted among sailors who had just completed an Atlantic crossing. Trying to put their vigilance to the test, I asked every skipper how many ships he and his crew had seen during the crossing, once they were well clear of the Canary Islands. The average number of sightings was almost four per boat, but looking at the answers more closely, it was perhaps not surprising that there were many more sightings on boats where watches were kept than on those where the crew admitted that they only kept the occasional lookout. Three singlehanders did not see any ships at all, whereas in contrast, on a boat that was hand-steered all the way, there were 14 sightings. The sightings included about an equal proportion of large ships and yachts. As scores of yachts cross the Atlantic at about the same time, such encounters in mid-ocean tend to be the norm rather than the exception, even if this pleasure is sometimes one-sided. Several skippers described having close encounters at night with yachts that were showing no lights and no sign of life. In both cases the yachts ghosted by about 100 feet away, kept on course by their self-steering gears. As could be expected, before long there were indeed some mid-ocean collisions in the ARC, but only one was in fact reported to the organizers. In the other instances both boats were obviously at fault, and as no serious damage had occurred their crews clearly decided on discretion.

Encounters with larger ships were usually limited to the airwaves, some skippers trying to contact passing ships on VHF. Such calls were not always returned, and one yacht had to take avoiding action as the ship he was trying to contact bore down on him, with no one on the bridge and apparently no radio watch being kept either. The old assumption among yacht skippers that the keeping of watches or the showing of lights is less crucial when one is out of the shipping lanes must be reconsidered, especially as the practice of weather routing can take ships all over the oceans away from traditional shipping lanes. I have been in near-collision situations on many occasions and can vouch for the fact that many ships do not have anyone on either visual or radar watch in mid-ocean. Even in such a busy area as that off Cape Finisterre (north-west Spain), we were nearly run down one night by a large freighter while sailing *Aventura III* from the Isle of Wight to Porto in the Millennium Odyssey. The ship was overtaking us on our starboard side and seemed to be passing safely on a parallel course a few hundred metres from us. Suddenly it altered course by about 30 degrees and pointed its bows straight at us. As we were sailing wing and wing, we barely had time to gybe the mainsail and bear away as the giant ship passed by so frighteningly close that we could see the faces of the crew working, unaware, on the deck above us. We called them on the VHF but there was no reply, so we presumed that the ship was on automatic pilot and had altered course automatically when it had reached the next waypoint on its pre-programmed route.

This incident shows just how important it is to have someone on watch at all times, and certainly where there is shipping around or in coastal waters. In fact, all skippers questioned pointed out that discipline became stricter on nearing land or when sailing close to known shipping lanes. At such times, watches were usually kept even on boats that did not take watchkeeping too seriously in mid-ocean. This is certainly a wise precaution as my investigation into the loss of 50 cruising boats in various parts of the world had shown that the single most common cause for the losses had been poor watchkeeping. Over half the disasters probably could have been avoided if somebody had been on watch.

Keeping a good lookout at all times can undoubtedly play a major part in reducing the risks, and even if a navigational mistake has been made, a good pair of eyes can still avoid disaster. The fact that modern ships equipped with the latest instruments are still wrecked shows that even the most sophisticated gadgetry does not make a good lookout obsolete. One-quarter of the boats whose loss I investigated were lost on reefs, and at least half of them could have been saved if avoiding action had been taken in time. Although reefs do not show up well on radar screens, those on the windward side of islands always break, except in the calmest of weather, and are thus visible and audible even on the darkest night. Even on the lee side of an island, reefs are often visible, especially if there is some swell.

Another cause of small boats being lost at sea is collision with ships. The days are gone when power gave way to sail as a matter of course. Not only are a large number of ships reluctant to alter course, but larger vessels are unable to do so quickly even if they wanted to. Therefore it is safer to assume that any ship on a converging course is not going to give way and to take whatever avoiding action is necessary in good time. If the decision is made to alter course, the new course should differ by at least 30 degrees so as to leave no doubt about your intentions.

Watchkeeping should not be neglected even when off known shipping lanes, as the most deserted areas of the ocean can be crossed by fishing boats, naval ships, research vessels, submarines and, of course, other yachts. In one particular incident, two cruising yachts did collide at night off Tonga, fortunately at low speed and without causing serious damage to each other. Both skippers were convinced that the area was so deserted that it was not necessary to keep someone on watch, nor was either of them showing any lights. When the skippers had got over the shock of the mild collision, they had the pleasant surprise of realizing that they knew each other and had not met since leaving California.

The tendency not to keep watches during an offshore passage is not necessarily a sign of lack of experience, as there are plenty of experienced skippers who admit to going to sleep at night, some of them following the practice since earlier days when yachts or ships outside of the shipping lanes were a rarity. Nor is the wrecking of boats the prerequisite of inexperienced sailors, for the skippers of well over half the boats whose loss I investigated had sailed many thousands of miles before disaster struck.

It was therefore not entirely surprising that many of the sailors who saw fewer yachts during the Atlantic crossing also took a more lackadaisical approach to watchkeeping. It underlined the truth of a statement made by a skipper interviewed in a previous survey who commented: 'It is only people who don't keep watches who never see ships at sea; we seem to meet them all the time.' This is a telling comment from a skipper who decided to sail around the world without self-steering gear for the precise reason of ensuring that someone would be in the cockpit at all times.

The system of watches was examined in the latest Sailing Women Survey primarily to find out what systems are used on passage on shorthanded boats. On all boats sailed by a couple, watches were shared equally, although occasionally the skipper took a longer watch at night as Saundra Gray explained: 'When sailing alone we share watches equally, but Charlie is on more at night and in bad weather. If we have qualified sailors aboard we set up a more formal watch schedule. Fatigue is one of the drawbacks for me on long passages. Even with others aboard, if the weather is bad no one gets much rest.'

A similar system was used on *Mariposa*, as described by Dorothy Walker: 'Basically we take four-hour watches during the night, but during the day it depends who feels up to doing more hours. I do not mind night watches as long as the weather is benign, as I can sleep in daytime more readily than Richard, so watches may be unbalanced because of that.' As Glynn Beauchamp pointed out, this may not be such a good idea: 'We've learned that any unfair distribution of watches tends to tire out one or the other, so that the other one has to pick up the slack. It is therefore advantageous to keep equal watches as far as possible, so that both can remain equally alert. We've found that on passage the three hours on, three hours off, works best for us.'

Jody DeHart explained that: 'On *Miss Muffet* we share watches equally with a six-hour watch on either side of noon and three-hour watches during the night. This allows for a good sleep during the day. This watch system has worked well for thousands of miles.'

Keeping regular watches when there are only two on board is not easy, so various systems are used to suit people's sleep pattern, as Jackie Lee explains: 'When the weather is stable, our night routine is for Luc to take a four-hour watch until midnight, followed by me until 8 am. Luc then takes the morning watch until noon, with both of us sharing the rest. We do this because Luc cannot sleep during the day, but I can sleep anywhere, anytime.' Lois Babson mentioned that on *Que Sera Sera*: 'Don does six hours from 2100 hours to 0300 and I take the next six hours. During the day we are both on watch unless one or the other is napping.'

Such long night watches are not to everyone's taste, so on *Kaprys*, as Lucy Misayat explains, 'watches are shared equally at night, with two hours on and two hours off. There are no formal watchkeeping arrangements during the day.' Judy Hally pointed out that on *Hornblower*, 'when we sail as a couple, watches are shared equally. When we have crew, the males take night watches while I take the majority of watch time during the day while they nap.'

Ann Harsh prefers a fixed system: 'We find four hours on and four hours off works best for us. We do not like rotating watch schedules, so even if we have three persons on board the schedules are kept the same every day, ie noon to four every day. We find that the passage of longitude provides enough variation.'

Obviously a different system is used with larger crews, as Amanda Neal describes the routine on *Mahina Tiare*: 'Because we teach offshore navigation, we always have two people on watch, one steering and one on lookout. They are on watch for two hours and switch at the helm every half-hour. John has no set watch as he is always available for making decisions.'

Watchkeeping on my boats has always been strict, but having both an efficient windvane system and a powerful autopilot means being on watch on *Aventura III* is not too strenuous for the crew. Even so, on my latest Atlantic crossing in the winter of 2001, my crew was surprised by my insistence on keeping proper watches even in mid-ocean. My caution was justified a few days after we left the Canaries when we met, in broad daylight, a sailing yacht of around 50 feet that crossed closely astern of us without any sign of life on board, nor did anyone answer our calls on channel 16. After that, watches were kept willingly for the rest of the crossing, on which we met nine ships altogether, but only one other sailing yacht.

Lights at night

The showing of lights at night is another subject of varying opinion and practice. Half of the skippers surveyed in the Pacific stated that when on passage and well offshore their boats showed no lights at all, mainly in order to save electricity. A number of skippers specified that they did keep their navigation lights on when sailing in known shipping lanes, but not otherwise. Over one-third of the boats showed some kind of light from the masthead at all times, either the regulation tricolour navigation light or an all-round white light. On the remaining boats, a storm lantern was hung in the rigging at night, although one skipper noticed that the low light disturbed his night vision so he reverted to showing a masthead light.

Bill Butler described his system: 'We show only a masthead light at night. Ships can't see most running lights, which we turn on only when there is traffic. My secret weapon is a rotating amber light as used by utility company vehicles, marinized and mounted high on a block of wood with a long electric line that plugs into a car lighter-type plug. I use it when sailing on my own and asleep, or when closing with traffic that fails to see me either on radar or visually.'

The showing of lights is related both to watchkeeping practice and electricity consumption, so in both the Atlantic and Global Cruising Survey these aspects were examined in relation to each other. The main reason people fail to show lights at night is primarily the desire to conserve electricity, and not that they do not wish to be seen, although this practice is now an accepted precaution in areas known to be prone to piracy attacks. The concern with saving electricity was not limited to boats with high consumption, as out of a total of 50 boats surveyed in the Atlantic, 17 skippers admitted that they rarely showed lights offshore, while an additional 9 skippers specified that they only switched on their lights if they saw another vessel. Several skippers complained about the powerful bulbs in some tricolour masthead lights, which on small boats can flatten an average battery in two or three nights. This was one of the main reasons why many skippers eventually decided to switch off their lights altogether.

Electricity consumption and generation

One of the main conclusions of the earlier surveys was that the consumption of electricity was causing many skippers serious concern, and often the only solution they could think of was to turn off the power-hungry item. Automatic pilots are one of the pieces of equipment that can raise the consumption of electricity dramatically, and several skippers were annoyed that their autopilots consumed more than they had been led to believe. This may be explained by the fact that the pilots had to work much harder to keep a yacht on course in the vigorous downwind sailing of an ocean passage, when compared to the smaller swell met with during most coastal cruising.

DIESEL GENERATORS

A high proportion of cruising boats are now equipped with diesel generators independent of the main engine. The increasing need for an additional source of electricity generation is virtually unavoidable on most cruising boats, bearing in mind the many power-hungry accessories that most sailors now regard as essential: autopilots, watermakers, freezers, as well as certain luxuries that normally run off AC such as television sets, video recorders, washing machines, dishwashers, microwave ovens, breadmakers, etc. The problems reported in earlier surveys, in which diesel generators were often mentioned as the most unreliable equipment on board, only appear to have got worse as so many more boats now have one of these units. Among the boats surveyed in ARC 2000, as many as 40 per cent had a generator; and the problems seem to be just as bad as in the past, as one in eight gensets failed during the Atlantic crossing. This is an appalling record, bearing in mind that the survey covers a period of only three weeks or even less. In many cases the problems were due to poor installation, and as many of the boats were relatively new, time had been too short to sort out any teething problems. The most common faults were related to water pumps, fuel injection pumps and starter motors. In the ARC Survey the most common brand was Fischer Panda (22 per cent), followed by Westerbeke (10 per cent), Onan (9 per cent), Northern Lights and Dolphin (5 per cent each). Their performance ratings followed roughly the same order, although there had been a marked improvement among the Fischer Panda gensets, which in the previous ARC had suffered a host of breakages, but seem to have sorted out some of those problems in the meantime. Even so, of the 17 units in ARC 2000, there were three reported failures during the crossing. Generally, gensets in the ARC seem to be so prone to breakdown that they are now firmly established at the bottom of the reliability table.

The situation was much more encouraging among the boats taking part in the SSCA Survey, in which 22 per cent of the boats reported having a separate diesel generator. The most common makes were Westerbeke (28 per cent), Northern Lights (23 per cent), Kubota (14 per cent), Onan and Kohler (7 per cent each). Northern Lights was rated highest for both performance and reliability, followed by Westerbeke and Kubota. As this survey covered a much larger span than the ARC, its results are more significant. Many owners gave their tried and tested units high marks for reliability, which is probably explained by the average age of the units as none of the better-rated makes were older than five years. The average breakdown per unit works out at about once every 1,000 hours of use, which is equivalent to one serious failure every five or six years. Several boats in the SSCA Survey (11 per cent) also carried a gasoline (petrol) generator, primarily as a back-up. By far the most common make was Honda (74 per cent).

As electricity consumption is a cause of so much concern for those planning an ocean voyage, I asked each skipper for suggestions based on his personal experience.

Some of the skippers interviewed in earlier surveys stressed that rather than be obsessed with the need to produce more electricity, one should rather try to save. It was thus repeatedly pointed out that it was a mistake to rely solely on an automatic pilot, and many skippers stressed the advantage of a wind-operated self-steering gear on long passages. Indeed, as can be seen from the results of the Global Cruising Survey, most boats on which autopilots were used most of the time had to run either their engines or generators at frequent intervals to charge their batteries. Don Babson described the procedure on his boat: 'We have a 7 hp Yanmar genset with a 200-amp alternator to provide charging for our four 6-volt Rolls batteries. When not using the main engine, we ran the genset at least five – often seven – hours in every 24 hours when at sea.' This was considerably more than on Klaus Girzig's *Alparena*: 'Although we had sufficient battery capacity, on all ocean passages we ran the generator for about one hour every day to make up for the electricity consumed by the autopilot.'

One immediate observation in this latest survey was the steep increase in energy consumption compared to earlier surveys. Among the 40 skippers interviewed in the Global Cruising Survey, 36 were able to give fairly accurate figures for their daily electricity consumption. The average consumption for a 24-hour period while on passage was as follows: 12 boats consumed less than 100 amps, 10 boats consumed between 100 and 200 amps, 7 boats between 200 and 300 amps, 3 boats between 300 and 400 amps, and 4 boats over 400 amps. Narrowing down that consumption to the estimated hourly consumption of the autopilots, the skippers of 12 boats indicated that their autopilot used less than 2 Ah, on a further 12 boats the autopilot used between 3 and 5 Ah, on 7 boats between 5 and 8 Ah, and on 5 boats the autopilot used over 8 Ah. Four skippers could not give any figures as they only used the autopilots when the main engine was running.

Bill Butler was one of the latter: 'I use the self-steering gear most of the time, with the autopilot only used when we are under power. To conserve electricity, even the GPS only gets turned on briefly two or three times a day.' Carlton DeHart was at the other extreme: 'All theory seems to go out of the window when you are cruising and running all your equipment 24 hours a day. You find you use much more power than you had planned on using. While sailing in the open ocean, we charged our batteries twice a day, at 6 am and 6 pm for one hour. We had 1000 Ah of 24-volt battery capacity with a 120 amp alternator. The autopilot, radar and inverter ran continuously as well as all instruments. We tried to charge the batteries at dinner and breakfast time, as well as charge the freezers and fridge at the same time. My advice is to install the most battery power you can handle and a very large alternator. It is always nice to have a little reserve in case you can't charge on schedule because of bad weather.'

Don Babson kept a close eye on his consumption: 'We consumed around 140 amps per 24 hours when sailing in warm weather, as we use a lot of ice in our drinks, plus we are running the autopilot all the time. While in Patagonia our consumption dropped to 65 amps per day as the fridge didn't run much as it was so cold, we didn't require ice cubes for our cocktails, plus we spent a lot of time hand-steering.'

Several skippers who depended on their main engine as their primary source of charging stressed the importance of having a good charging system, ideally with the alternator being provided with a smart regulator. All these points were repeated when the skippers commented on the electrical system they would have on their ideal yacht. The point was also made that alternative means of generating electricity, besides the main engine, should be a priority. Indeed, this view was shared by most skippers, who agreed on the advantages of wind and water generators, or solar panels if deck space was available.

WIND AND WATER GENERATORS

A large number of cruising yachts are equipped with alternative means of generating electricity, the most popular being wind generators. Although wind generators would seem to be the most attractive alternative source of energy, they didn't fare well in the surveys. Nearly one-third of the boats in ARC 2000 had wind generators, which were rated the least useful equipment on board, but this is probably explained by the fact that the winds reported during the Atlantic crossing had been unusually light. The majority of the units were mounted permanently and, as most of these boats were single-masted, the generator was usually fitted on its own pole installed at the stern. In some instances the same pole was also used as a mount for the radar scanner. In spite of the negative comments, most skippers were satisfied with the performance of their wind generators in keeping the batteries topped up both in port and at sea, although it was pointed out that when running downwind the apparent wind was often too light to produce a reasonable charge. On the other hand, in very strong winds, especially at anchor, some generators had to be disengaged either because they tended to burn out the diodes or, more often, because of the irritating vibration transmitted to the entire boat. By contrast, water generators attracted generally positive comments for reliability and were praised for producing a good charge. Even so, some owners had reservations about them, mainly because of the drag – which they estimated reduced their speed by between ½ and 1 knot depending on the size of boat. It was also pointed out that at higher speeds it was very difficult to haul in the generator. Another disadvantage of towing a generator is that you cannot tow a fishing line at the same time. This can be a serious consideration as fresh fish makes a welcome addition to the menu on a long passage. One skipper praised this unit, which he had used extensively until he lost two propellers in quick succession, probably bitten off by a hungry fish.

Both wind and water generators were examined in the SSCA 2000 Survey, in which 52 per cent of the boats surveyed had a wind generator, which is a substantial increase from the 38 per cent reported in the 1996 Survey. The most common wind generator makes were Fourwinds (27 per cent), Air Marine (26 per cent), Ampair (12 per cent), Wind Bugger (9 per cent), Aerogen (8 per cent) and Hamilton Ferris (6 per cent). Among these makes, Aerogen was rated highest for performance, while Ampair got the highest ratings for reliability. Most makes attracted critical comments caused by poor manufacturing standards or unsatisfactory after-sales service. Fourwinds attracted some negative comments because of parts that rusted and the unit not being waterproof. Some makes were described as noisy (Air Marine), or not coping with high winds when breakages of the blades or shaft were reported (Wind Bugger). Water generators fared much better and were praised as a good back-up. However, they were less common, with only 17

units in the SSCA sample. The most popular make was Hamilton Ferris (41 per cent) and the comments were generally favourable.

SOLAR PANELS

Solar panels are gaining in popularity, and over a quarter of the ARC boats now use them. However, they are much more common among long distance cruising boats, for in the SSCA Survey solar panels were found on 55 per cent of the boats. Among them, just over half were made by Siemens (51 per cent), followed by Kyocera (12 per cent) and Solarex (11 per cent), with Kyocera rated highest for both performance and reliability. Among both ARC and SSCA boats, the main complaint was that the electricity produced by the panels falls far short of the claims made by the manufacturers. However, while solar panels were used in the ARC mostly as a back-up, several SSCA skippers relied on them as a prime source of energy. In order to obtain the desired results, the boats had to have a minimum of four 50-watt panels.

BATTERIES

Battery performance was examined in the SSCA Survey, in which the average capacity was 550 Ah per boat. The rating given to individual makes is hardly relevant as there were over a dozen separate brands, and the sample contained both wet and gel types. Some skippers complained about the high cost of some makes of battery and suggested that there was much better value in 6-volt golf cart batteries.

The two wind generators on the Italian catamaran Cush *take care of most energy needs.*

THE IDEAL SYSTEM

The skippers taking part in the Global Cruising Survey were asked to comment on the generating system they would have on their ideal yacht. With only two exceptions, all skippers agreed that some kind of additional source of electricity generation was not only desirable, but essential. Twenty-seven of these 40 ideal yachts would be provided with a diesel generator. Most skippers would also have additional sources of energy, among which the most popular were solar panels (28), followed by wind generators (20), and water generators (5).

Bill Butler made his views quite clear: 'Electricity is the *heart* of your boat; it keeps everything ticking. Lots of battery storage capacity is essential. If you never let the batteries run down, they'll last four years and more. All banks should be isolated through battery transfer switches. All loads should be made to work off any one of the banks, which should be regularly charged. Murphy always hovers nearby. You should always have a secondary way to charge. Wind generators are reliable. Solar power works. A compact Honda genset will bring a dead battery back to life. Some sort of back-up is 100 per cent essential.'

Carlton DeHart does not agree: 'Except for diesel generators, all other sources do not provide enough power to run a yacht full of equipment on a full-time basis and the cost is high compared with the service they provide. My only other choice would be solar panels for when the boat is left unattended for a long period of time, the freezers might be kept cold and batteries kept charged. Wind generators only work effectively at anchor. Towing and shaft generators are very noisy, and only work when sailing at near hull speed. All passive generators are expensive, usually claim to produce twice the power they deliver, and are very temperamental. It's better to have one good, dependable generator and not spend the money on gadgets.'

Luc Callebaut takes a different view: 'You need alternative energy sources, even if just for back-up. We would not be happy to have to run the main engine every day to charge the batteries. The noise, the wear on the engine, the fact that you cannot leave the boat unattended, are all serious deterrents. On *Sloepmouche* we have nine solar panels (about 450 watts) that work flawlessly as long as you get sunlight or even enough light. Those, under good conditions, provide all the power we need at anchor. We have a Fourwinds generator that helps during grey days. We have a shaft alternator that helps a lot during passages if we make at least 5 knots. I prefer that option to a towing generator, which may get fouled in the prop during unexpected manoeuvring. We also have a portable gas generator on deck that comes in handy to run big power tools. So we are quite self-sufficient.'

On his ideal yacht, Chris Harding 'would be unhappy to rely only on one source of generating electricity. As a second source I would use a diesel generator. The only other practical source would be a wind generator, but unfortunately they are noisy, dangerous, and when running downwind (as on most long passages) they are not very efficient due to low apparent wind.' John Ellis fully agrees: 'Even though they *always* break down, I would have a genny. The modern yacht is usually very power hungry, so wind or solar generation may not be sufficient.' On his ideal catamaran, Clyff Huggett would have 'more solar panels. Also a larger genset of 6 kW. I would not use my main engines to charge batteries unless they were running for some other reason. But I would have larger alternators fitted, say

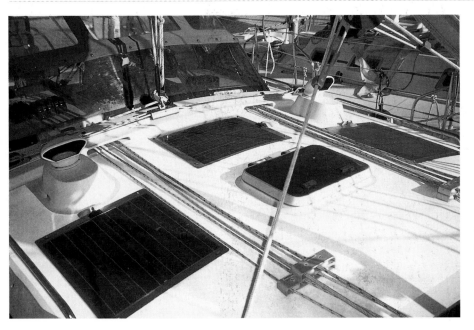

Flexible solar panels can be fitted to any free deck area to supplement other generating sources.

100 amp, just in case my genset failed. I would also use a wind generator in case I go back to the Caribbean where there is always wind.'

Antti Louhija summed it all up: 'On a future boat I would not be happy with only the main engine as the sole source of electricity. During ocean crossings in the trade wind belt my towing generator worked satisfactorily. The same unit could be converted to a wind generator in windy anchorages. Solar panels take too much deck space on a small boat when sailing, but they are good when leaving a boat during inland excursions. I would seriously consider a diesel generator in order not to need to use the main engine for charging when not needed for propulsion.' Matt Rollberg agrees with every point except one: 'We wouldn't have a wind generator since we've met people who have lost fingers trying to stop them in high winds.'

There were, however, two skippers who seem to be quite happy to use only the main engine for charging and would use the same system on a future boat too. Skip Novak said: 'For our purposes, the main engine charging is all we need as we motor a lot. The other charging solutions would not really enhance life on board, and in some cases their paydown time is not cost effective.' Steve Dashew agrees: 'We used to have a generator but removed it as it did not get enough hours (about 150 per year) to be worth the weight and space.'

Personally, I had come to the same conclusion that, depending on one's cruising area, there is no real need for an additional diesel generator. I found that even when not going far, but just moving from one anchorage to another, the engine is used enough to charge up the batteries for another one or two days. I was very fortunate in having Wilhelm Greiff, who is an electrical engineer, advise me on the charging arrangements on *Aventura III*. A second alternator of the same type as the one supplied with the engine, and fitted with a smart regulator developed by Wilhelm, was added to the main engine. The two alternators are backed up by a Rutland 913 wind generator and three 40-watt solar panels. The system is efficient and covers my energy needs adequately. On ocean passages I usually have to run the engine for one hour every day. The two alternators running in tandem charge at a rate of around 90 amps, which is what we normally use over a 24-hour period.

Wilhelm Greiff knew exactly the kind of system he would have on his ideal yacht: 'A WhisperGen, solar panels, as well as two alternators on the main engine, at least one of them fitted with a smart regulator.'

Conclusions

With the possible exception of a separate diesel generator, I fully share Wilhelm's view; and after more than two decades of investigating various aspects of offshore cruising, I consider the problems associated with electricity consumption and generation to be among the most serious faced by long distance sailors. This observation is borne out by the fact that electricity generation and the problems associated with it was the most common cause of complaint among participants in the ARC. Although it would be impossible to draw one overall conclusion from all suggestions and observations made by the hundreds of skippers who contributed to the various surveys, there appears to be a consensus regarding electricity consumption, namely that it is a problem that must be tackled long before leaving on a voyage. This is exactly the point made by Wilhelm Greiff when interviewed in the Global Cruising Survey: 'I continue to be amazed at how many people do not pay this matter the attention it deserves.'

The first requirement is to make a realistic assessment of one's projected daily needs and then double that figure for good measure. The battery capacity should be at least twice that amount, and the batteries should be in separate banks – one for general consumption, and one dedicated to engine starting. The two banks should be separated by a diode. Consumption and battery capacity should dictate the size of the alternator, as often the standard alternator provided with the engine is not powerful enough. On *Aventura III* the domestic bank is made up of six heavy-duty batteries with a total capacity of 720 amps. An additional battery, separated by a diode, is dedicated to engine starting.

Some kind of auxiliary charging system is almost indispensable on boats with heavy demands, and the various options are described above. A separate diesel generator is probably the best answer on boats with a consumption of over 200 amps per day. On yachts equipped with a freezer whose compressor is driven by the main engine, a good solution is to charge the batteries while running the engine for the freezer. Otherwise, on boats with a modest consumption, water generators appear to provide the better solution on passage, and wind generators in port. Provided you have sufficient deck space, solar panels might be able to cover most needs, although the demands on boats that have room to accommodate them usually surpass the modest output of the panels. On some boats that do not have sufficient space for the panels to be mounted permanently on deck, the panels are displayed temporarily when at anchor or in port. Solar panels are also useful on boats that are left unattended as they continue to trickle charge the batteries, thus keeping them in optimum condition.

8

Give Us Our Daily Bread
PROVISIONING, REFRIGERATION
AND WATER

"Never forget that you are an intruder on the oceans of the world. Respect all life forms for whom the sea is their home." BILL BUTLER

Napoleon certainly did not have transatlantic sailors in mind when he said that an army marches on its stomach, but the sentiment is equally valid, for feeding the crew well is a crucial factor in running a happy boat.

Provisioning

Meals are always a welcome interruption on a long passage, and provisioning was a major preoccupation of the crews whom I interviewed on both sides of the Atlantic before and after the Atlantic crossing. Fresh fruit and vegetables purchased in the Canaries lasted well, especially when carefully selected by hand at a fresh produce market and not from a supermarket where all produce is normally chilled. Cucumbers, cabbages, pumpkins, oranges and lemons were items mentioned by several crews as good buys, while hand-picked green tomatoes carefully stored lasted for four weeks on one boat. The storage of fresh produce is crucial, and several people recommended storing vegetables and fruit suspended in netting. A similar recommendation was that vegetables such as potatoes and onions kept better when stored in a dark place. Bananas should be kept well away from any other fruit or vegetables, as an enzyme found in bananas will fasten the ripening process. Conversely, if one wants certain fruits to ripen quickly, they should be stored close to a bunch of bananas. Regular inspection and the consumption of fruit as it ripened were also advocated. By far the most popular purchase in the Canaries was oranges, which lasted extremely well, and several crews regretted that they had not bought more. Many people advised that one should be generous with the fruit and vegetable allowance when planning a transatlantic or other long passage so as to be able to dispose of any items that look doubtful and may spoil the others. It was suggested that rice and similar dry goods should be bought in small quantities because of the possible presence of weevils and moths. Storing these items in airtight plastic containers prevents cross-infestation of stores if any of these small beasts do appear.

Unrefrigerated fruit and vegetables will last well on any ocean passage – but not on deck!

For making cooking easier on passage, one crew followed the practice of cooking large meals before leaving, then dividing these into smaller portions and storing them in the freezer to be reheated as required. If you have a freezer, this is a good standby for use in rough weather, or, as Jody DeHart explained: 'I have a big problem with seasickness so I do all the cooking while in port, where the boat is steady and it's so much easier to prepare all meals than when it's very rough. With all the major cooking done, the meals are placed in the freezer. On passage, they are heated in the microwave and served. This allows me to escape from the galley, but, as my husband says, I turn $2000 worth of groceries into leftovers before we even leave the dock.'

Another experienced voyager recommended carrying plenty of cans of ready-made soup in liquid form, as being the easiest, quickest and most nourishing meal to serve in rough conditions. Another cook swore by the type of food sealed in a bag, such as rice, which can be boiled in salt water to conserve water supplies. Because of the difficulty of cooking in a continuously rolling boat, it was also suggested that sufficient snacks and light meals be carried on longer passages. Several people were doubtful about the merits of dehydrated foods, as extra water had to be carried to reconstitute them.

In spite of the improvement in refrigeration equipment, many voyagers still prefer to do without a freezer, mainly to avoid the daily chore of running the engine or generator to keep it going. Therefore there are still many boats on which frozen foods are not used, and for long-term storage canned, dried and vacuum packed foods continued to make up the major proportion of the stores. Freeze-dried goods are also gaining popularity, and most boats carry a balanced mixture of all types of stores. In all surveys, only a minority relied on all their stores being in the freezer, which is not such a bad idea as I know of several instances when a broken freezer in mid-ocean had left the crew almost without food for the rest of the passage. It is also worth bearing in mind that some countries, the USA and Australia in particular, confiscate all frozen meats on board, so you should try and arrive there with an empty freezer. In fact, these countries confiscate other food-stuffs as well, such as eggs, smoked meats, and all fresh fruit and vegetables, so it may be wise to plan on arriving with a fairly empty larder.

The usual period for which people provisioned is from one to three months, most trying to buy larger quantities in countries where certain goods were cheaper or of better quality. It is also wise to stock up with certain items that are not available everywhere, such as bread or pancake mix, tinned butter, dried eggs, etc. Nor should one forget certain luxuries or special goods that may be unobtainable in less-developed countries. Last but not least, one should attempt to stock up with duty-free spirits wherever these are readily available or cost little. Wine is another item that was recommended to be bought in sufficient quantities before sailing to remote areas, as the cost of wine in some countries can be prohibitive.

Provisioning is another aspect of cruising that has seen a considerable improvement in recent years. There is now a much better selection and availability in most areas visited by cruising yachts, and basic supplies are available almost everywhere.

BAKING BREAD

The staff of life, one's daily bread, is one aspect of provisioning that was examined in one of the earlier surveys. Bread was baked on two-thirds of the boats during the Atlantic passage, varying from every day to once a week, but it was usually every two or three days. A variety of methods were used, with the majority of cooks baking bread the classic way in the oven using dried yeast, although one cook found soda bread an easier solution by substituting baking powder for yeast. The few who used the instant bread mixes highly recommended this simpler method. On several boats the bread was baked in the pressure cooker, a method highly recommended by those using it, whereas several of the Scandinavian sailors used a special bread tin that goes on top of the stove and produces a bread in the shape of a ring. As microwave ovens become more common on cruising boats, an

Bread on passage: shortly before setting off across the Atlantic, Nina and Antti Louhija are given a loaf of bread baked specially for the American 500 participants.

increasing number of cooks use them for baking bread. Bread-making machines are also gaining in popularity, although they tend to use a lot of electricity, so most cruising boats seem to do without them.

From what I was told, and also based on my own not very successful experience in the field, baking bread is not everyone's favourite occupation. It is therefore not surprising that on many boats bread is only baked as a last resort, with one crew lamenting that their bread was as hard as stone and inedible – and they ended up making pancakes instead. Another crew who tried various methods without great success, suggested that it might be useful to practise baking before leaving home if one lacked experience in that direction. On a large proportion of boats there was no attempt at all to bake bread. Those with freezers often stored bread in them, others carried long-lasting bread – such as German rye bread – while others solved the daily bread problem with a different-style menu, either by making scones or by replacing bread with biscuits, crispbread or hard tack. The problem is no longer as bad as in the past as long-life bread is now available in many places and, if stored well, will keep for several weeks.

Water and watermakers

No other aspect of life on board an offshore cruising boat has seen such a radical change in recent years as that of water and its availability. As a result of the arrival of compact, reasonably priced watermakers, one major concern has been taken off the mind of the cruising sailor. Before the advent of watermakers, most boats setting off on a long passage tried to leave port with full tanks and a few additional jerrycans on deck that could be taken off the boat in an emergency. In an earlier survey, the average amount of water carried was 45 US gallons (180 litres) per person. In that same survey, the average consumption of water per person was 25 US gallons (98 litres) per person, which is close to a daily consumption of just over 1 gallon per person per day. Invariably more water was used on boats equipped with showers and pressurized water systems. A low consumption of water usually occurred on boats where people drank liquids in other forms, such as beer or fruit juices.

A valuable tip given by an ARC participant may well be valid in other parts of the world as well in Las Palmas. As the taste of the water is not too good, the crew of most boats also bought large plastic bottles of drinking water, which are available from all supermarkets. This suggestion, as well as the practice of taking a few additional jerrycans of water, is highly recommended, as it is a mistake to have all drinking water in only one tank in case it becomes contaminated while on passage.

Fresh water capacity varied widely on the boats surveyed, although most boats designed for cruising had a minimum capacity of 100 gallons, usually in one tank, which may not be the best solution for the reasons mentioned above. Either to supplement the existing capacity or to provide an alternative source of water, several boats had been fitted with extra tanks, some of them of the collapsible type. Usually these were smaller production boats whose fresh water capacity was considered too small for an extended cruise. The average water capacity in permanently installed tanks was 105 US gallons (420 litres), which was considered adequate by most skippers.

In line with the general trend to electrify everything on board, most boats have a pressurized water system, which on most production boats is now standard. However, some skippers pointed out that they preferred to pump water manually (or pedal-operated if fitted with a foot pump) while on passage and only revert to the pressure system where there was plenty of water available. 'My water consumption dropped to less than half once I turned off the electric pump and the crew had to use the foot pump instead,' commented one skipper. Hot water and showers are also becoming more common, and the proportion of boats having them more than doubled compared to earlier surveys. In most cases, hot water is provided by a calorifier that is connected to the cooling system of the main engine. Usually the hot water tank is also fitted with an electric immersion heater, which can be used when the boat is connected to shore power.

Some cruising boats have portable deck showers, often used in conjunction with special water bags. These black plastic bags have a capacity of approximately 2 gallons, and when left in the sun provide a most efficient way to heat up water. Hooked to the boom they make an excellent hot water shower over the cockpit, while on one boat the hot water was poured into a large insecticide sprayer mounted in the shower room, an ingenious way of providing a pressurized hot shower without electricity.

One way to stop worrying about water consumption is to equip the boat with a watermaker, and in the ARC 2000 Survey 39 per cent of the boats had a watermaker. The most common makes were Spectra (37 per cent), PUR (18 per cent), Seafresh (14 per cent), Sea Recovery (7 per cent) and HRO (5 per cent). In spite of their popularity, Spectra watermakers were rated very badly for both performance and reliability, and the angry comments made by their owners reflected their frustration. In many cases the fault may have been caused by poor installation, usually by authorized Spectra dealers. The other makes received much better ratings, with no failures reported during the ARC. It was interesting that the situation was completely reversed in the SSCA Survey in which Spectra attracted the highest ratings. In the SSCA sample, 54 per cent of the boats had a watermaker and, among these, the most common make was PUR (50 per cent), followed by Village Marine (15 per cent), Spectra (11 per cent), AquaMarine (9 per cent) and HRO (3 per cent). Overall, the reliability of the units was quite disappointing, with an annual failure rate of one in four units reported. PUR scored low on both performance and reliability, although it must be pointed out that the average age of the PUR units was nearly five years, whereas that of the Spectra units was only 15 months.

Apparently the new generation of reverse osmosis watermakers promises to eliminate some of the recurrent problems experienced with older models. Notwithstanding some of the problems mentioned, watermakers can make a huge difference to the quality and comfort of life on board, which is shown by the large number of skippers who listed watermakers as one of the essential features to have on their ideal yacht. As to current users, several of those who have them stressed that they would never again sail without one. Carlton DeHart made this very clear: 'A large-capacity watermaker is an absolute must as the quality of life aboard is directly proportional to the amount of water available. We had a unit that made 52 gallons of water per hour, with the generator burning half a gallon of diesel per hour. That meant we could make 104 gallons of water for every gallon of fuel we burned. That was a good ratio.' David Hersey fully agrees: 'We had a three-phase watermaker which churned out 210 litres per hour. It never let us down and there was always plenty of water for the washing machine and unlimited showers.'

Such high-capacity units may not suit everyone's requirements unless you have very high water consumption, as in the case of David Hersey's *Company*, on which even the toilets were flushed with fresh water. A few skippers mentioned the high consumption of electricity needed by the watermakers, but this did not seem to be too big a problem as most boats that had watermakers also had diesel generators, which covered all their energy needs. Perhaps the best reasons for having an adequate supply of water is to be sure of having a healthy crew as well as harmony on board, because, according to Michelle LaMontagne, 'ample water keeps you from getting sick; daily showers keep couples from fighting because they feel yucky'.

Refrigeration

Although the number of boats having refrigeration is steadily increasing and most people agree on the usefulness of a refrigerator, a high proportion of those surveyed appeared less inclined to give their approval to freezers. It is probably significant that many of those who were against freezers had been cruising for longer periods, and had reached their decision either because they had learned to live without freezers or because they had lost faith in their reliability. Asked to rate the usefulness of their refrigerators, most owners considered them to be very useful – and only a few had doubts about their usefulness. They all stressed that even if not essential, a fridge can make life very pleasant, and a cool drink is greatly appreciated on a hot day in the tropics. It was also pointed out that a fridge can be particularly useful for keeping butter or margarine chilled or to preserve the contents of tins or milk cartons after opening. On some boats, fridges had been installed independent of the main energy supply by hooking them up either to solar panels or wind generators.

Asked about the usefulness of freezers, most skippers of the boats that had them stressed their usefulness on a long passage, both to preserve food and to store freshly caught fish that cannot be consumed all at once. The main drawback of a freezer is that it consumes a lot of energy, and the engine – or a separate generator – has to be run about once a day to keep the freezer going. David Beauchamp didn't mince his words when he vented his frustration: 'We use about 65 amp-hours per day. This is broken down into 50 for the damned freezer and the remaining 15 for everything else!'

In some instances the insufficient insulation provided by the boatbuilders was criticized by owners who felt that this aspect has not been given the attention it deserves. This general attitude was reflected in the ARC 2000 Survey, in which freezers were in a distinct minority, although nearly half the boats (46 per cent of the total surveyed) had some sort of refrigeration. The most common makes were Isotherm (30 per cent), Frigoboat (13 per cent) and Grunert (3 per cent), with the remainder made up of a variety of makes. The first two makes are now fitted as standard on many European production boats. Overall, the units functioned well and there were hardly any failures reported during the Atlantic crossing. In the SSCA Survey, Adler Barbour was by far the most common manufacturer among

Two lambs hanging in the rigging. Who needs a freezer in Antarctica?

refrigerators (40 per cent), followed by Isotherm and Norcold (7 per cent each), Grunert and Technautics (6 per cent each), Sea Frost (5 per cent), and a host of other makes. With an average age of nearly eight years, Adler Barbour scored high on both performance and reliability. Generally, reports of breakages were fairly rare among refrigerators, making them one of the most reliable units on board cruising boats. Adler Barbour was also the most common make among freezers (18 per cent), followed by Grunert (14 per cent) and Technautics (10 per cent), with their ratings following the same order.

Cooking fuel

In spite of many people's continuing dislike of having gas on board, propane or butane appear to be firmly established as the most common cooking fuels. The majority of boats use domestic-type propane or butane tanks, although many European-built production boats are equipped with the smaller Camping Gaz containers. Until not so long ago, Camping Gaz was almost unheard of outside of Europe, but the containers are now accepted at filling stations in the Caribbean and most Pacific islands.

The difficulty of obtaining cooking fuel was investigated in one of the earlier surveys. As far as ordinary gas tanks were concerned, most crews had no great problem filling them either in the Mediterranean or the Caribbean, although valve fittings vary between countries. Some US-type tanks could not be filled in Europe, and their owners solved this by acquiring local tanks instead. Unfortunately there is no international standard for the valve fittings, and because of this, some cautious skippers carry the necessary adaptors, as most filling stations do not have them, being only equipped to service their own types, which sometimes vary even within the same country.

One problem that was pointed out is that in countries where butane is not available, gas containers are filled with propane. The switching over from butane to propane is not a recommended practice and can lead to unexpected problems. Propane gas is normally used in tropical countries and can damage burners designed for use with butane gas. The burners tend to burn out and have to be replaced more frequently. More dangerous is the fact that the two types of gas have different expansion rates and there is therefore a risk of gas leaks from full containers when moving from cold to warm climates. If changing from butane to propane, it is recommended to also change the regulator or at least have its rating checked. Another suggestion, made by skippers who had their Camping Gaz containers refilled in the Canaries, was to check their weight on the premises as often they are not filled properly. Two of these skippers ran out of gas during the Atlantic crossing and one crew had only cold meals for the last week before landfall, except for some canned soup that they managed to heat up on the engine – not the most efficient way of cooking a meal at sea!

Diving

One common pastime that combines safety with pleasure is diving, and in two earlier surveys I found that most boats had snorkelling equipment on board, and about 10 per cent also had diving tanks as well as a diving compressor. There is no doubt that the ability to dive is a major safety feature – as I can vouch myself. On several occasions I have had to don a mask and snorkel to untangle a line from the propeller, to escape the clutches of a lobster pot, to free a fouled anchor, to check if the anchor had set properly, or even to set the anchor by hand if it did not look as if it was going to hold. Retrieving objects that have been lost overboard is another use for diving tanks, as is the ability to give the hull a scrub before a long passage – not to mention the more pleasurable pastime of scuba diving. There is much one can do even without scuba gear, such as shell collecting and spear fishing, or just being part of the aquatic environment by enjoying the beauty of the underwater scenery.

Concerning spear fishing it must be pointed out that in an increasing number of countries the use, or even possession, of spear guns is prohibited. In some of these countries, such as the Bahamas, restrictions only apply to visitors. Stringent restrictions also apply to scuba diving. In most countries, only properly qualified divers are allowed to use such gear, and often only if accompanied by a local licensed instructor. Valid diving qualifications or permits are usually requested. Also, when filling one's own tanks at shore stations the test certificate of the tanks may have to be produced.

Fishing

In spite of statements that indicate that stocks of fish in some areas are nearing extinction, those who bother to equip themselves with the necessary implements will find that trolling a line will provide them with a constant source of protein while on passage. To catch fish during an ocean crossing can hardly be described as a difficult skill, and the speed of the average sailing boat seems to be just about right for this kind of activity. Those who want to be more sporty can invest in a rod, but for most of those who are only interested in fishing for food, all that is needed is a line and a selection of lures. A reel, mounted at the stern, can be a great help – not just to reel in the fish, but also to sound the alarm when a fish has bitten. Having landed – and lost – many fish by trying to land the catch in a centre cockpit, I can now vouch for the great advantage of having a stern platform, as on my present boat. One thing to remember when bringing the fish close to the boat is to keep the line under tension all the time and not to let the fish break the surface. Ideally the boat speed should be reduced when hauling in the fish, but not below 3 or 4 knots. Once the fish is close to the boat, quick uninterrupted action is necessary to gaff it behind the gills and bring it on board.

Photography

The ability to record the highlights of your voyage can greatly enhance a cruise, and most boats nowadays have a camera of some sort on board. For standard photography, a waterproof, or at least showerproof, lightweight camera is highly recommended. Those with in-built zooms are the best. As space is restricted on boats, the wider the lens angle the better. Digital cameras work well, especially if you have a colour printer on board, which makes it possible to print out the photos to hand them to people you may have met ashore. In many remote parts of the world, a gift of a photograph is greatly appreciated, especially by local children, and this is why in the past some people took Polaroid cameras along. Needless to say, that wherever you sail, local customs must be respected, and taking photographs or filming people without prior permission is often frowned upon and should be avoided.

Results given by underwater cameras, whether still or video, are often very disappointing, not so much because of the quality of the camera itself, but the skill – or lack of it – of the operator. All equipment should be stored in a dry place, and film will keep best for long periods in the fridge.

9

Better Safe than Sorry
Piracy, Firearms, Collisions, Abandoning Ship

"For world cruising, self-reliance is the key and part of the pleasure. There are too many rescues being called out unnecessarily." Skip Novak

Ever since man first pushed out from shore in some kind of floating craft, his main concern has been to arrive safely. This concern for safety is still most sailors' main priority, although – as mentioned in earlier chapters – developments in both yachts and equipment have made cruising potentially safer than ever before. None the less, many people continue to regard the seas as a dangerous environment in which one's life is at constant risk. The fact that in the last 50 years more lives have been lost in virtually any other leisure activity than in sailing cuts no ice with most of them, nor will they accept that one is much more in control of one's destiny on a well-found boat than in most other situations.

Most sailors, however, have complete faith in their boats. Tony Mark, the ARC safety inspector, confirmed this when he pointed out that 'people are much more interested in safety than they used to be. It is quite noticeable how much more safety conscious and demanding people are. They want to know that their boat is perfect and are prepared to do everything that is necessary to bring it up to the highest standard. This is particularly evident among the owners of small- and middle-size boats who want to get it right. It is those on the largest boats that are quite nonchalant and believe they'll get away with anything.'

This concern with safety is reflected in the large number of questions about the subject I am asked at lectures and seminars, so this chapter will try to find out if such concerns are justified. One of the most frequently asked questions is how dangerous is it to cruise in foreign waters? Invariably my reply is that cruising is far less dangerous than living and working in a big city, and that ocean sailing itself is far less dangerous than driving home from work or after a cruising seminar.

The unknown

Fear of the unknown affects many sailors, and I doubt if there is anyone who at some point or other has not felt apprehension whether approaching an unknown shore at night, navigating among reefs, having a large ship pass too close, or sailing through an area where boats had recently been attacked. Fear was the main subject of discussion after a lecture I gave at the annual convention of the Western Trauma Association in the USA. It was quite significant that so many of those hardened surgeons and physicians expressed the keenest interest in this subject, which underscored their day-to-day activities. Shortly afterwards, at another lecture, the same subject was brought up again. This time the audience was made up entirely of sailors, and the most common fear described was not the fear of something specific, of an identifiable danger, but simply the fear of being on a small boat in the middle of the ocean. Indeed this is something that I have witnessed among some of my own crew, and the most telling example involved a close friend, who was a certified ship's captain, but had little experience of sailing on a yacht. I had no reason to suspect any sort of problem, so we shared the night watches equally among the three of us on board. It was only after we had arrived at our destination that my friend took me aside and said that he had an embarrassing confession to make. One dark night, while we were sailing about 30 miles south of Puerto Rico, he was overcome by a profound fear bordering on panic. The feeling of terror was so overwhelming that he was on the point of activating our EPIRB, knowing that it would alert the search and rescue authorities in Puerto Rico. All he wanted was to be taken off the boat. Fortunately he managed to control himself and finish his watch. His experience taught me to be more careful with fresh crew, especially when left to do a night watch on their own. My niece, who sailed with me from Tahiti to Hawaii, expressed the same kind of feeling and admitted that she was sick with fear when sitting alone in the cockpit at night, being overcome by the vastness of the surrounding ocean and the immensity of the starry sky above. Gwenda shares this general anxiety when she is sailing offshore, and it is this basic fear that probably explains her dislike of long passages, rather than the complaint about the boredom of spending so many long days at sea.

I find it quite strange to be frightened like this when, for me, this is the most exhilarating part of offshore sailing – the feeling of being all on your own on a small boat, far away from humanity and the restrictions of a land-based life, and in total control of your own fate. Having witnessed many voyages that came to an end because of such fears, often (although not always) expressed by the women on board, I decided to investigate this subject in more depth in the Sailing Women Survey. It must be stressed that all the 20 women who took part in this survey have cruised, or are cruising, with their partners for long periods. It was therefore quite surprising that when asked to describe their greatest fear, only eight of them mentioned losing the man overboard as their greatest fear. For Alison Wicks, the greatest fear was simply 'the sea', while Germaine Beiser could not specify any specific fear besides a general anxiety. This was also the reason why Annelie Rollfing disliked long passages. Severe weather was the next most common source of concern, followed by that of a serious medical emergency. Some women went to great lengths to describe their concerns, such as Saundra Gray: 'I am not normally a fearful person. I dislike bad weather, consequently I am much more tense when we are being knocked around. The possibility of one of us going overboard is a concern, especially at night and in bad weather. The awareness of the slim chances of a rescue at sea of someone handling a boat singlehanded, in a storm, are sobering. Collisions at sea are much more of a possibility than most people think. I know it is a big ocean, but often large ships seem to gravitate to the spot where my small sailboat is. Fatigue is a bad companion, and not being able to rest puts one into jeopardy for injury, bad decisions and cross tempers.'

Jody DeHart shares those feelings: 'When conditions get really bad, my husband stands very long watches as my seasickness leaves me a useless lump in the bunk. My greatest fear is that he might get washed overboard and I would have to deal with trying to get him back. Because of this fear, we take every precaution possible to prevent it from happening.'

Glynn Beauchamp described the difficulties of being left to cope on her own if, for example, David had to be evacuated: 'As we are so much a team I would need to have someone else put on the boat to help me get to port. I would be very worried about Dave and not be able to concentrate as well. Having someone to help me would enable me to get the boat to safety.' Ann Harsh, who is the skipper of *Harmonie*, has different concerns: 'I don't have one main concern – probably fire on board, a medical emergency, or the anchor dragging.' Dorothy Walker's main fear is 'hitting something at night while sailing at some speed'.

I leave the last word on the subject to Anna Huggett, who took me by surprise when she pointed out that her greatest fear is 'that the anchorages will become too crowded, polluted or too expensive, and we will be forced to give up this life'.

It was quite surprising and, at the same time, revealing, that not one of those 20 women mentioned piracy, robberies or physical violence as one of their main concerns. Maybe these are subjects that are more worrying for the men.

Piracy

In spite of the reassuring comments at the beginning of this chapter, there is little doubt that no other hazard has marred the beauty of cruising more than the threat of piracy, whether on the high seas or in coastal waters. It is a risk that mariners have had to confront for thousands of years, and the good news is that as far as attacks on pleasure boats are concerned incidents in recent years have been relatively few in numbers. The situation is very different when it comes to big ships, which have seen a steady increase in piracy incidents in recent years. Hot spots for reported piracy attacks on any kind of shipping are well known, and undoubtedly the main reason why there have been so few victims among cruising sailors is that they have heeded the warnings and avoided such notorious areas as the Sulu Sea and other troubled areas in both the Philippines and Indonesia, the coast of Somalia, or the vicinity of Socotra Island. Unfortunately the maritime authorities are more concerned with attacks on commercial shipping and do not regard attacks on pleasure craft as a high priority, or even to be their responsibility. This is reflected in the absence of hard information about attacks on yachts on most internet sites dealing with piracy. A number of recent incidents are listed on www.noonsite.com.

Having organized several rallies, which passed through known danger areas in recent years, every conceivable precautionary measure was taken to ensure the safety of the participants and the risks were thus kept to a minimum. One yacht

sailing in the Millennium Odyssey successfully repelled an attack off Somalia, the incident demonstrating the advantage of sailing in the company of other boats through known danger areas. The basic rules are as follows:

Safety in numbers. When crossing a dangerous area it is preferable to sail in the company of other boats.

- Try to form a convoy of between three and six boats of similar speed whose crew are prepared to remain in close contact and, if necessary, slow down or help the slower boats.
- Maintain visual contact in daytime, and find a way to keep in contact at night (ideally by radar) without showing masthead lights or any other lights that can be seen from beyond the range of the convoy.
- Maintain radio silence on the standard VHF channels, which can be easily monitored by other parties by scanning all channels, but keep permanently open an SSB channel on a frequency agreed and available to all other boats in the convoy.
- Have a crew member on permanent listening watch on the agreed SSB frequency, and/or have the SSB radio connected to a speaker in the cockpit.
- Monitor the immediate area on radar and, if anything suspicious approaches, alert the others immediately. Even if the suspected vessel is still out of visual range, but it appears to be on an intercepting course, the convoy should close ranks.
- At least one boat in the convoy should be equipped with a satellite telephone, and have the numbers available of any maritime or naval authority in the neighbouring countries so that they could be contacted promptly in an emergency.
- Make sure that a responsible person ashore receives regular position reports from the convoy and can promptly contact the relevant authorities in an emergency.
- If the worst comes to the worst, do not resist the attackers, keep calm, hand over all valuables, and follow their instructions. In all known recent cases, when the crew being attacked offered no resistance, the pirates appeared satisfied with just robbing the boat but refrained from killing anyone.

Onboard safety

The previous section has tried to limit the debate to true cases of piracy against cruising boats. The term piracy describes attacks against a vessel by another vessel on the high seas, and in this respect many recent incidents involving yachts should not be attributed to piracy. The death of Peter Blake was the result of a violent robbery, and while this type of crime involving cruising sailors has increased, cases of actual piracy involving cruising yachts are still quite infrequent. The areas where piracy is a real threat to yachts are well known and should be avoided. Theft and robberies from yachts are, on the other hand, much more widespread geographically, and the best way to deal with them is to take certain precautionary measures – which are not very different from those one would take in a similar situation when travelling on land or living in a big city.

The subject of personal safety was examined in the Global Cruising Survey, and skippers were asked to describe the precautions they take especially while cruising in remote areas. Among the 40 skippers, 6 stated that they rarely lock their boats, while 2 never felt that locking the boat was necessary. Skip Novak commented: 'My philosophy is that if this becomes an issue, then I would rather not be there with a boat in the first place – as the boat becomes like an albatross around your neck.' Michael Frankel agrees: 'If I felt that locking the boat and having an alarm were necessary, it would greatly diminish the cruising experience.'

Most other skippers took a somewhat different view and described a variety of precautionary measures, although several pointed out that they were not paranoid about safety and that their security measures depended entirely on the area they were in. Nine boats had alarm systems, although several of them were never set. Mirek Misayat eventually gave up using his: 'The forced entry system kept setting itself off for no reason and upsetting the neighbours, so much so that one broke into the boat to disconnect it.' Steve Spink described his method: 'In remote anchorages we lock the boat, but leave lights and radio on so it looks as if there is someone on board.' Indeed, as Javier Visiers pointed out, no locking system is entirely secure, and if someone is determined to break into a boat he will succeed. In spite of that, the number of such robberies reported in any of the round the world rallies was surprisingly low. John Ellis would have been the first to hear about any theft and he commented: 'Dinghy theft seems to be more prevalent rather than theft from inside the yachts. I advise everyone to use a combination padlock on a steel cable to secure the dinghy motor and the tank, both when going ashore but also at night when the dinghy is tied to the boat. A combination lock is also recommended on the boat itself so there is no key to be lost.'

Several skippers recommended bringing the tender and outboard on deck for the night, especially in certain areas such as parts of the Caribbean. This was a wise precaution almost everywhere as on many occasions dinghies and outboards were in fact stolen not by locals, but sailors from other boats.

The skippers were also asked how they approached the matter of security while on board in a remote anchorage. Seven mentioned that in high-risk areas they locked the hatches and companionway from the inside, while on three boats the alarm was set. A more primitive, but probably more effective, system was used by Don Babson and Volker Reinke, who copied Joshua Slocum's example and spread tacks on their decks when in remote anchorages – 'provided you remember to gather them *all* in the following morning,' quipped Don. Marc Labaume used a different system: 'On our catamaran we stretched a nylon thread across the open sliding door. Should anybody enter, it released a piece of wood that made quite a noise. The device was conceived by my son Xavier, then aged eight.'

Luc Callebaut has a sophisticated system on his boat: 'The alarm activates a horn inside the boat, another horn on top of the mast to alert neighbours, and a deck light. We also have a schipperke dog and joke that the alarm system is there to wake up the dog!' For those who are not keen to cruise with a pet, Zoltan Gyurko recommended getting 'one of those fake barking dogs'.

David Beauchamp said: 'In remote anchorages we sometimes set the alarm, which has a flashing red light. This works well in keeping friends from calling too late at night or too early in the morning, so presumably works to dissuade more unwelcome callers as well.' Arthur Beiser comments: 'We try to avoid remote, uninhabited anchorages unless we are really sure they are OK.' Bill Butler feels the same: 'Avoid remote anchorages, and never stay more than a night or two when in one. Always keep a lookout for strange boats. Keep moving if you are the lone boat. A motion detector connected to an alarm or a bright light will buy time and scare away amateurs. For others, grab the Mossberg.' Whether to have a gun or not will be discussed below.

While ashore, most stressed the need to use one's commonsense. John Neal commented: 'We don't wear flashy clothes or jewellery. We carry a hidden wallet, and always take a known taxi driver in an unfamiliar area.' Terence Brownrigg was not too concerned: 'I never felt threatened at anchor and consider it more likely to be mugged while ashore. Just be sensible and don't antagonize the locals.' Michelle LaMontagne, who as a woman often travels alone, has the following advice to give: 'Don't flaunt money, overpay, or overtip as in most Third World countries people will only feel that you don't care about money. Be fair, but keep within the local custom of costs and tipping. Many cruisers have ruined local economies by trying to *improve* the lifestyle of local people.'

Firearms

Regulations concerning firearms vary enormously from country to country and their presence on board a cruising boat can cause certain difficulties because of the formalities involved. In some countries firearms are bonded on board, but more often they are removed for the duration of the boat's sojourn in a particular port or even country. The return of the firearms on the eve of departure can sometimes lead to complications and it is advisable to make the necessary arrangements in this respect when surrendering the weapons on arrival.

Of 100 skippers questioned on the subject in an earlier survey conducted in the Caribbean and South Pacific, 38 had firearms on board and many of them were in two minds about the advisability of carrying a gun while cruising. All skippers taking part in the survey, both those with guns and those without, were asked their opinion on this subject and were encouraged to comment and make suggestions. The majority of skippers were firmly against the idea, and this included both those who had a gun and also some of those who did not. Only 11 skippers considered firearms to be essential for their protection. Six skippers who were reluctant to carry arms nevertheless stressed that their possession might be justified in certain parts of the world, even if not in the South Pacific, where the interviews took place. For some skippers who did not wish to carry guns, the solution to this problem was to avoid areas with a bad reputation.

Several owners described their guns as a deterrent and not an offensive weapon. The most unexpected condemnation of guns on boats came from a retired officer in the French Gendarmerie, who refused to have guns on board his boat as he considered them to be more trouble than they were worth. Because of the various disadvantages of having firearms on board, several people had acquired tear gas or pepper spray containers which were regarded as an acceptable alternative for self-defence. As one skipper put it, 'It's far better to have a potential robber crying his eyes out in the cockpit, than to discover you have shot dead the cousin of the local police chief.'

Similar feelings were expressed by the skippers in a survey conducted in the Atlantic, in which the proportion of yachts equipped with guns was considerably lower. Less than one-fifth of the boats had firearms on board and it was pointed out on several occasions, when firearms were discussed, that it was foolish not to declare the guns when clearing into a country just to avoid a few formalities, as the complications can indeed be severe if the authorities discover that guns have been hidden.

The Global Cruising Survey provided the perfect opportunity to sound out a number of experienced sailors on this controversial subject. The proportion of armed boats was even lower than in the previous surveys, as of the 40 boats, only five carried firearms, and three of them were in fact hunting rifles. Some of the skippers who used to carry arms declared themselves firmly against them, and even two of those who have them had now changed their opinion. The most adamant supporter of armed power was Bill Butler: 'A 12 gauge stainless steel Mossberg shotgun is the ticket. Holds eight or nine shots of different types, and does not raise eyebrows as a pistol will do, is harder to have stolen, and you do not have to spend time at target practice. Just aim at the bad guys and fire.'

Skip Novak now carries only hunting rifles on board: 'We have a shotgun and a rifle, but these are for hunting. In our area we do not worry about piracy, but I have sailed in the Far East and Red Sea, and personally I would feel safer with some arms in those areas. You may save yourself, and I would have no doubts about using them when the time came. Judging that time, of course, is the difficult part.'

Arthur Beiser has obviously considered the matter thoroughly: 'I have no moral scruples about carrying firearms or using them if necessary, but the situations in which they might be of use are so limited as it is a big mistake to even show them when outgunned or when it's not imperative to do so. Also, the legal complications are daunting. Should they be declared? If you don't and are caught, what then? These are the reasons why I have not thus far taken any. But I do take a few canisters of pepper spray, which I think is more useful against burglars and amateur intruders, which are more common than pirates, at least where we cruise. I doubt I would knowingly go to a region where a couple of Uzis and a rocket launcher would be needed.'

Bill Butler is among those who feel safer by having firearms on board.

Carlton DeHart feels the same way: 'Up until the Europa round the world rally we always carried firearms on our boat. After all, it would be un-American not to be well armed. After a long talk with the organizers of the rally on this topic, we left all firearms at home and have done so ever since, and will do so in the future. A gun is not enough if you meet up with pirates. You will need missiles and grenades to keep them at bay or take them out. If you are not prepared to do this, it's better to not have a gun and not to start shooting. As for robbers, a gun does no good as you can't start shooting inside your boat. We did carry a 55 mm ship's flare gun and three cans of grisly bear spray, a type of super mace that shoots 40 feet, used by hunters in the northern woods. We never had any reason to use either. Being unarmed puts you in a different frame of mind and you work hard at not getting into trouble rather than figuring out how to shoot your way out.'

Clyff Huggett agrees: 'Our policy is: no smoking, no drugs, no firearms. And no drinking while the sails are up. If you are boarded by armed men, the chances are you will be outnumbered and the gun you carry may incite the pirates to use theirs. If you think you are going to be rammed by another vessel, try firing a flare at the other vessel.'

Several skippers recommended flare guns, or preferably pistols, as a good alternative to firearms. Don Babson was among them: 'I know how to use firearms well, but have never shot another human so am reluctant to pull out a gun never to be fired. I did threaten a fisherman off the coast of India in a small boat, who kept trying to come aboard, with my big flare gun. It did work for he jumped overboard from his own boat. I don't think I would have blasted him, but he quickly made up his mind not to get shot, and over the side he went.' At close quarters, Michelle LaMontagne recommended using 'a hot, unopened glass bottle of soda, well shaken which explodes like a hand grenade on impact'.

Luc Callebaut described the dilemma faced by those who might consider having firearms: 'If you take them out when threatened, you may scare the aggressors away or, more likely, you may encourage them to fire at you! You don't always know in advance. If taken by surprise you may not have time to get your gun, and you cannot have it ready every time you meet someone you don't know.'

This is exactly what went through my mind when sailing from Panama to Ecuador in March 2002. One dawn I was approached by a large whaler-type boat with three men on board. They looked quite menacing as they came at great speed towards *Aventura*, only to slow down a few feet away to shout instructions as to how to avoid their nearby long lines. If I had been armed, I should have had my gun ready to fire before they got too close. Fortunately I was not armed so what turned out to be an entirely innocent incident could have had tragic consequences. Like myself, most sailors must have given the subject of firearms a great deal of thought, and decided that arms and yachts are not a good combination. This is shown by the results of the three surveys on this subject mentioned above, in which the proportion of boats carrying firearms has fallen from 38 per cent in the early 1980s, to 18 per cent in the late 1980s, and to 10 per cent or less in the latest Global Cruising Survey.

Collisions

The single most common cause of yachts being lost offshore is collision, whether with ships, whales, containers, tree trunks and a whole range of unidentified debris, of which there seems to be plenty floating in the world's oceans. Some boats have disappeared without trace while on passage, and the reasons for their disappearance will never be known. Some collisions can be avoided and the prudent skipper who insists on a proper lookout being kept at all times can narrow down the risk to a minimum. In spite of the dangers posed to yachts by all manner of unidentified objects, the main hazard continues to be the possibility of colliding or, more likely, of being run down by a ship. No one will ever know how many small boats have been sunk by large ships and this may be the most plausible explanation for some mysterious disappearances over the years. In a few cases, the shipwrecked crew were rescued by the very ship that caused the sinking, but in most instances the unfortunate yacht disappeared without a trace. Usually the crew of the large ship are not even aware that they have struck something, as witnessed by the story of the tanker that arrived in New York with the remains of a fibreglass yacht wrapped around its bulb. The only way to avoid this danger is to keep a permanent watch and to treat ships with the respect they deserve.

Unfortunately even the greatest vigilance cannot avoid every type of collision, especially at night, and this is where a strong hull comes into its own. However, even the strongest hull may not be able to withstand the violent impact of certain collisions, and the obvious example that comes to mind is the possibility of being struck by a submarine surfacing or cruising at periscope depth. Several collisions with unidentified objects seem to point to this possibility, such as the loss of a yacht that sank after colliding with something while on passage from the Caribbean to Bermuda. The skipper heard a strange ringing sound from outside the boat. As he went on deck to investigate, the boat struck something hard and started filling with water. He barely had time to launch the liferaft before the boat sank. Another mysterious collision caused the sinking of two boats on transatlantic passages from the Canaries. Both boats struck underwater obstructions in mid-Atlantic, and in both cases the damage was so grave that the yachts sank almost immediately.

A similar unexplained collision happened to the yacht *Traigh* while on its way to join the ARC in the Canary Islands. In broad daylight with the crew on deck, a loud bang was the first indication that an underwater object had been hit. The impact was severe enough to sheer the rudder and seriously damage the keel, causing the boat to have to be towed into port by a local lifeboat. This happened in the Irish Sea, where there have been several documented incidents involving fishing boats and submarines. Submarines can only detect the presence of surface vessels by noise, so it may be advisable to motorsail when passing through an area known to be used by submarines, or if ringing sounds are heard in the water, the engine should be turned on immediately to announce one's presence.

Similar sinkings after collision with an unidentified object occurred in the South Pacific but the crew managed to take to the liferaft, from which they were rescued and could tell the tale of their disaster. However, there are several cases of yachts that have disappeared without trace while on passage, and the cause of such sinkings will always remain a matter of speculation. From Joshua Slocum to Alain Colas, sailors and their boats have vanished at sea without explanation. Although structural defects or gas explosions cannot be ruled out in some cases, collision remains the prime suspect. Even when the crew has been rescued, as in the cases mentioned above, the real cause is rarely known, as the majority of these unexplained collisions happened at night.

Many more examples have come to my knowledge, fortunately not all with disastrous consequences. One involved an ARC boat that was caught up in, and brought to a complete standstill by, a huge fishing net drifting in mid-Atlantic, which was kept afloat by several plastic floats. The yacht became so enmeshed that the crew were unable to free the yacht themselves. Their calls for help on the VHF radio were finally answered by a large motor yacht on its way to the Caribbean, whose crew came to their assistance. It took the combined efforts of two divers to cut the yacht free.

Collisions with whales are another hazard and there have been several involving boats sailing in the ARC or round the world rallies. The number of whales has increased dramatically in recent years due to the international moratorium on the

A friendly encounter with a whale in Antarctica, but bumping into such a giant in mid-ocean could spell disaster.

hunting of whales. While some may enjoy seeing these creatures in the middle of the ocean, most skippers share the view that yachts and whales do not mix and prefer to keep their distance from the leviathans. In the past, mysterious collisions have often been blamed on whales, due mainly to their habit of sleeping on the surface, oblivious to everything around them, especially a sailing boat moving through the water with little noise. Deliberate or accidental, the possibility of a collision with a whale causes considerable concern to many sailors. Those who have had close encounters with whales advise that it is never too early to take avoiding action, such as to alter course away from them as soon as they are sighted. If a whale does approach a vessel and certainly if it shows any interest in the yacht, everything possible should be done to discourage it, such as running the engine or pouring oil, diesel or paraffin in the water around the vessel. It has also been suggested that certain light colours of antifouling, such as white, should not be used as this may make the boat resemble the underbelly of a large whale, which could lead to an attack by killer whales.

Two yachts sailing with the Millennium Odyssey from Chile to Easter Island decided to make a detour from the direct route to visit the island where Alexander Selkirk was a castaway, and which inspired Daniel Defoe's adventures of Robinson Crusoe. *Risque*, a Swan 57 sailed by the Morgan family, came dangerously close to sharing that same fate of being shipwrecked in the South Pacific as they were surrounded by a pod of about ten pilot whales. After swimming with the yacht for a few minutes, the whales started attacking it, hitting the hull violently several times. Fortunately the well-built yacht suffered no serious damage, but the incident was very similar to other such incidents that have occurred in the South Pacific, where it is known that at least three yachts have been sunk by whales – and in the case of Bill Butler's *Siboney*, by similar pilot whales. Being only some 60 miles from *Risque* when the attack occurred, I advised the other Millennium yachts to prepare a jerrycan of diesel to be ready to pour into the sea if similarly threatened. The idea had come to me while sailing in Fijian waters on the first *Aventura* when we were surrounded by a group of killer whales who kept close company for a long time. After a while I became concerned that the whales showed no sign of going away, so I got a can of kerosene and poured some overboard. The film spread quickly, the kerosene got into their blowholes, and within seconds the whales were gone. This may have worked in *Risque*'s case too, but having just been together to Antarctica, where on countless occasions we had gone deliberately out of our way to get close to whales, shooing them away was not the crew's first reaction.

Abandoning ship

Alexander Selkirk was marooned on the island that today bears his name, and his fate was incomparably better than that suffered by anyone forced to abandon a sinking yacht in a liferaft. This may be one of the reasons for a tendency among a few skippers to leave on an ocean passage without a liferaft, but to make other arrangements to keep afloat and alive. This subject was first investigated in the South Pacific, and re-examined in later surveys. The skippers of the boats without liferafts were asked the reasons why they chose to sail without rafts and also what provisions they had made for abandoning ship. Several stated that they had decided to leave without liferafts because they had lost confidence in them after reading reports about liferafts capsizing in heavy weather, or not inflating when needed. Other reasons mentioned were the difficulty of having rafts regularly serviced when cruising, or their inability to be steered or sailed in a certain direction – this latter reason causing some people to look for an alternative to self-inflating rafts. Some skippers gave the reason of having complete faith in their yachts as the main one for not having a liferaft, and in three cases no provision at all had been made for abandoning ship. Two of these boats were made of steel, the third was a plywood catamaran, described by its owner as unsinkable.

Although the number of boats cruising without a liferaft is very much in the minority, I consider it to be a dangerous tendency. In spite of their drawbacks, liferafts have saved many lives in recent years – some such instances being mentioned in the previous section on collisions – and the few failures have been exaggerated out of all proportion. In some countries the presence of a regularly serviced liferaft is compulsory on every ocean-going yacht, but in countries where the decision to carry a liferaft is left to the skipper, the possibility must be faced that a situation might arise when the yacht has to be abandoned to save one's life. Fire could be such an occasion when even an otherwise unsinkable boat may have to be abandoned in a very short time. A self-inflating raft can make the difference between life and death.

LIFERAFTS

The seriousness of this matter prompted me to carry out a special investigation concerning liferafts and their main features. One of the first conclusions I drew was that some people were prepared to buy unsuitable liferafts for their size of boat, often because the price was right. Occasionally the rafts were larger than necessary, and this could turn out to be counterproductive as a liferaft that is not loaded to its designed capacity may capsize in rough weather. The occupants of a liferaft act as its ballast, and a large raft that is only half full may be too light in strong winds. On the other hand, during a simulated survival test, it was observed that a liferaft filled to capacity rapidly became very uncomfortable as there was not enough space for all the occupants to rest properly at the same time. Bearing this in mind, the sensible solution would seem to be to have a liferaft that has two spare places above the standard crew, ie a six-man raft for a crew of four, or an eight-man raft for a crew of six.

During the same survey it also became obvious that many owners had very little knowledge about the features of their raft, such as what kind of floor they had or the type of emergency pack it contained. Most skippers had no idea if their rafts had a single or double floor and only a few seemed to know the reasons for having a double floor. Nor did the majority know the contents of their emergency pack, or even if their liferaft contained one. The main advantages of a double floor are increased strength, improved comfort, and particularly in cold climates, enhanced insulation. As far as the emergency packs are concerned, the test mentioned above established that the rations provided in the standard pack would barely sustain a normal person for the nominal three days, which is the time inside which liferaft manufacturers assume a shipwrecked crew will be rescued. Most manufacturers offer the option of a more complete emergency pack, but even the most comprehensive of these is only calculated to last for a few days. Because by necessity liferafts must be compact, emergency packs cannot take up too much space and the amount of water provided is especially small. The only solution is to make provision for additional water to be available in case the boat has to be abandoned. Just as important is to supplement the emergency pack by preparing a well-equipped panic bag, the contents of which are discussed on pages 109–10.

Another factor that should be taken into consideration when making provision for abandoning ship is the likelihood of most or even all the crew members becoming seasick, even those who are not usually seasick on board a yacht. It has been recommended that every person should take some preventative medication before boarding the raft. Obviously this is not possible when a boat has to be abandoned rapidly, but if there is some prior indication of this possibility, each crew member should take some anti-seasickness precautions. Most liferaft manufacturers include anti-seasickness medication in their standard pack.

One of the difficulties mentioned was that regular servicing of liferafts was often a major problem. In many places it is difficult to find a reputable service station, and in some cases the liferafts could not be serviced. Several owners complained about poor service and this may be the reason why some skippers had started inspecting and servicing liferafts themselves. As with every other specialized service, this DIY approach should not be taken too lightly and, if at all possible, the servicing should be left to those trained and equipped to carry it out.

The skippers were also asked if they had ever used a liferaft: only one skipper had ever used one in an emergency, although a few others had used one as part of a course on survival techniques. Several skippers praised the usefulness of such survival courses, at which one is trained in launching, righting and boarding a raft. Another valuable comment praised those service agents who encouraged owners to be present during the opening of rafts, and who actually let them pull the release lanyard to see for themselves what happened. Emergency sessions are held with participants in both the ARC and round the world rallies when a simulated rescue operation is staged.

The location of the liferafts was examined in the same survey and it was found that the majority were kept on deck, either mounted on the coachroof, aft or fore decks, or stored in a more protected place somewhere near the cockpit. Because the valise-packed rafts especially are not always fully waterproof, some people prefer to keep them in a protected, easily accessible place near the cockpit. This is certainly advisable considering the limited time one might have in which to launch the raft if the boat was badly holed and sinking rapidly. Some production boats are equipped with special liferaft lockers in or near the cockpit, and it was pointed out that in an emergency it may be difficult to lift a heavy canister out of a deep locker, particularly by somebody who is not strong or is injured. On some boats the problem has been solved by providing a special pulley system that allows even the weakest member of the crew to launch the raft in an emergency. On boats without such special provisions, a launch session should be held in port to see if every member of the crew is able to launch the raft should the boat need to be abandoned.

PANIC BAG

While discussing the question of abandoning ship, I asked the skippers, both those with liferafts and those without, if they had prepared a bag or container to be grabbed if the boat had to be left in an emergency. Only about half the people had actually prepared such a panic bag, and on several occasions my questions on emergency preparations prompted those who had neglected this aspect to consider putting together such a bag. The question was often turned around, as those interviewed tried to find out from me what other people put in their bags or what should be the most essential items to include. From the contents of bags that had been prepared, it was obvious that what was regarded essential by some people, was superfluous to others. Although undertaking a long offshore passage, many of the less experienced crews had retained the attitude of people who are within range of quick and efficient rescue services and expect to be saved in a short time. Therefore they had only concentrated on saving themselves. In contrast to this attitude, among those with considerable offshore experience, who had given this subject a lot of thought, the main priority was to be able to look after themselves and survive for long periods without outside help.

Looking at the contents of such a great variety of bags, some containing a bare minimum, with others being able to support the crew for several weeks, I drew up the following list of the best ideas and most common suggestions:

- *Food*: a mixture of dry and concentrated food, not all of which has to be reconstituted with water; food in self-heating tins; chocolate; glucose.
- *Medicine*: first aid kit; vitamins; laxatives; sunblock preparations; painkillers; anti-seasickness medication; any personal medication.
- *Safety*: EPIRB, battery-operated GPS, satellite telephone (if available) with spare battery; flares (in separate waterproof container) or flare pistol; portable VHF radio with spare batteries and aerial; dye marker; torch and batteries; signalling mirror; spare sea anchor; survival handbook.

- *Miscellaneous*: hand-operated watermaker; knife (pocket knife with various blades); drinking cup; spoon; plastic plate(s); fishing gear; can opener; sponge; repair kit with patches and adhesive; assorted plastic bags.
- *Personal*: passports; money; paper and pencil; reading matter; playing cards; dice.
- *Comfort*: survival suits or blankets (aluminium); spare clothing; sunhats; sunglasses; folding umbrella (can be used to shelter from rain or sun, catch rainwater and even as a sail if strong enough).
- *Navigation*: compass; plastic sextant; almanac or navigational computer; routeing chart(s).

The above list is based on the contents of a great variety of panic bags, several skippers having made valuable suggestions on this subject. Thus one skipper, who keeps two plastic drums with all essential survival items on his aft deck, changes the routeing chart contained in one of them every month, to know what winds and currents to expect should he be forced to take to his liferaft. The skipper of an off-shore charter yacht holds a 'panic' session with the crew before each passage, assigning precise tasks to everyone. Two people would be responsible for the launching of the raft, two would launch the inflatable dinghy and water containers, while the radio operator would broadcast a Mayday on the radio and activate the EPIRB.

The usefulness of a satellite telephone cannot be emphasized enough, as help can be summoned by calling one of the international rescue organizations. A spare fully charged battery should always be stored in the panic bag. Similarly, a handheld VHF radio was mentioned by several skippers as being better than flares in attracting the attention of a passing ship. Its batteries should always be kept fully charged and spare ones should also be packed among the items prepared for abandoning ship.

Most of the panic bags were rigid plastic containers, those with a wide mouth and screw top being considered the best. They must obviously float, be waterproof, and should have a point of attachment and lanyard to make fast to the liferaft. On most boats, the containers were kept close to the companionway. Also in an accessible position were a few water containers, as only rarely did the panic bag or emergency pack itself contain water. The practice of keeping a few jerrycans of water lashed on deck has much to recommend it if the boat had to be abandoned. The water containers should not be completely full, so that they would float if thrown overboard. Undoubtedly the most important item is a hand-operated watermaker, but even if one is available some additional water should also be carried.

Among all the subjects I have examined in the various surveys, abandoning one's ship is the least popular topic of conversation. And yet I found that those who had given the matter serious thought were quite happy to talk about their preparations, whereas those who were reluctant to confront such an eventuality – and were obviously of the attitude that such things only happened to other people – had made little or no preparations. My questioning sometimes got them thinking, and on several occasions I could detect a change of attitude. Most memorable was one skipper who proudly showed me how he had made his boat unsinkable by providing it with several buoyancy bags hooked up to compressed air diving tanks.

A well-prepared panic container could make the difference between life and death.

'It's all very impressive,' I said, 'but what are you going to do if you have a fire?' His face fell in disappointment, as it was an eventuality that he had never envisaged when he decided to set off without a liferaft.

Most sailors are firm believers in the belts and braces philosophy. When one's own life might be involved, it may not be such a bad idea to also carry a piece of string.

Conclusions

The tragic death of Peter Blake, who was shot by robbers who had boarded his yacht while anchored off Macapu, in the Amazon delta, has focused attention on the subject of safety generally, and especially on the wisdom of carrying guns on a cruising boat. This terrible incident proved the long-held belief that violence begets violence. It is now sadly possible to speculate that if Peter Blake had not appeared with a gun, he would have survived the attack. In any case, it would be interesting to know how many of those who were in favour of carrying guns in the past may have changed their mind in the light of this tragedy.

Personally, I share the view of Skip Novak or Michael Frankel, and would avoid sailing to areas with a bad reputation. After all, I wouldn't go as a land tourist to certain disreputable places, so going to a risky area on my own yacht is simply asking for trouble. Often when sailors start avoiding certain areas, the local authorities and businesses get the message and do something about putting things right. This is what happened in the Rio Dulce area of Guatemala where a spate of robberies from yachts was reported during 2001. Other cruising boats started avoiding the area until the marina operators got together and put pressure on the authorities to sort things out, which they did.

The safety of the crew when cruising in remote places is something to be considered carefully, and many valuable suggestions were made in the foregoing pages. As several skippers pointed out, an efficient alarm system is a good idea both as a deterrent when the boat is left unattended and as an early warning system when the crew is on board. For personal protection, guns are, in my view, difficult to justify, but non-lethal means should be considered – such as pepper spray or tear gas canisters. However, one must be aware that these are illegal in many countries, so they should be acquired where legally available and kept on board in a safe place.

The safety of the boat itself if left unattended in an anchorage was mentioned in Chapter 4, and this is a matter of serious concern to most sailors as trips ashore are such an intrinsic part of cruising. Some people take every conceivable precaution before leaving the boat, while others never leave the boat out of sight unless securely docked in a marina. For Giuseppe Italo Masotti, this is the only option: 'I would not leave the boat at anchor, no matter where I am. In Elba this is a serious offence punishable by a hefty fine.'

The structural safety of the boat was discussed in Chapter 1, when many skippers expressed their preference for a strong, seaworthy hull. A collision with a floating container or a whale concerns most sailors, and although such incidents are extremely rare, some of the suggestions made in that chapter, such as the provision of a collision bulkhead forward, or at least a sacrificial crumple zone, should be seriously considered in the building stages of the boat.

If the worst comes to the worst, a good-quality liferaft, regularly serviced, should be a main priority. A well-thought-out panic bag should also be prepared. In my view, the most important items to go in that emergency container are a hand-operated watermaker, a satellite phone, and a portable GPS. The relevant phone numbers of the US Coast Guard stations, or similar, should be written in indelible marker pen on the container. I can well imagine a situation in which a shipwrecked sailor is sitting in the liferaft calling the search and rescue authorities to indicate the exact position from a handheld GPS.

Finally, if one cannot avoid sailing through a known danger area, there is always safety in numbers and one would be well advised to do it in company with other boats, or possibly join a rally. One of the aims of the website www.noonsite.com is to assist in co-ordinating the movements of cruising boats through a known piracy area, especially those planning to head for the Red Sea, so anyone wishing to form or join a convoy should contact www.noonsite.com.

10

Only the Wind Is Free
THE PRACTICAL SIDE OF THE CRUISING LIFE

"The cost of cruising? It's something that I've been afraid to really find out!"
DAVID HERSEY

Finances

There is nothing that can undermine the enjoyment of cruising more than the lack of adequate funds. Many a dream voyage comes to a sad end because of an empty kitty, and in most cases this is not caused by an unforeseen emergency or huge repair bill, but by leaving home without adequate reserves in the hope that things will work out somehow. Sometimes they do, but more often they don't – and a drop in currency exchange rates or higher than allowed-for costs can spell the end of a voyage.

To find out how much it costs to cruise, and hopefully pick up some useful tips for anyone planning a similar voyage in the future, a survey was conducted among the crews of the 40 boats taking part in the Expo'98 round the world rally. This was followed up by a similar survey conducted in the final stages of the Millennium Odyssey. Virtually all costs were quoted to me in US dollars as this is the currency used by most sailors, even those who are not American, so any costs mentioned in this chaper will use this same currency.

Sailing around the world, whether in an organized event or on an individual basis, can be a costly business and I am grateful that most participants in both rallies were prepared to discuss their financial and budgetary arrangements. This allowed me to draw some conclusions, which should be of interest to anyone planning to set off on a world voyage. Although one may be tempted to believe that sailing in a rally is going to cost more, this was not necessarily the case – as was pointed out by Margaret Reichenbach of *Santana*: 'We didn't spend any more doing a rally than cruising on our own; in fact, being in a rally has allowed us more time for inland travel. Besides boat maintenance and capital expenses, travel is probably our second biggest expense.'

Obviously the greatest expense is preparing the boat for the actual voyage and many costs are incurred before the voyage has even started. In the Millennium Odyssey there were a number of new boats that had been bought and equipped specifically for this voyage, but there were also several older boats that had to be extensively refitted. Duke Marx of *Distant Drum* estimated that he had spent around $140,000 to get his 20-year-old boat ready for a circumnavigation. His friend Bob Hall of *Hornblower* reckons that he spent about $40,000, mostly on new equipment, with the overall cost being kept down by the skipper and crew doing most of the installation work themselves.

MAINTENANCE AND REPAIR

As several skippers pointed out, once under way the largest single expense is that of maintenance, repair and spare parts. The highest figure was quoted by Lou Morgan, whose new Swan 57 *Risque* cost an average $2,000 per month to maintain – or an estimated total of $45,000 for the duration of the rally. Stu and Julie Conway estimate that their Swan 53 *Stampede* swallowed up $40,000 in repair and maintenance costs over the two years. This is almost the same as the $42,650 spent by Ann Harsh and Ralph Nehrig of the Amel Super Maramu *Harmonie*. As they are both accountants by profession, it is perhaps not surprising that they could provide me with itemized figures for all the expenses during their circumnavigation, down to the $1,600 spent on Ralph's cigarettes! Their travels ashore, including one flight to the USA, totalled $12,000. *Stampede*'s crew spent twice as much on travel ($25,000), which is the same amount as the one mentioned by Klaus Girzig of *Alparena*, in whose case most of that money was spent on flights for the family to join the boat in several places around the world. In *Alparena*'s case, the estimated cost of boat maintenance was $25,000 for the duration of the rally. Michael Frankel, who sailed as crew on *Hornblower*, did an ad hoc survey among 36 Millennium boats in Tahiti and came up with the lower average figure of $15,000 per boat. This is probably a better reflection of the true cost as it took into account the maintenance budget and replacement expenses for all boats in the rally.

The crew of *Santana* have kept accurate records of all their cruising expenses, both before and during the Millennium Odyssey, and came up with a total figure of approximately $30,000 per annum, which includes all boat expenditure, living costs, as well as travel expenses. Compared to this, the crew of *Harmonie* spent about $60,000 per annum, or approximately $2,750 per person per month.

Compared to the figures quoted by owners, it was interesting to look also at what some of their crews were spending. Not surprising these figures were much lower, and ranged from between $600 and $800 per month in the case of one young man sailing with his father, to $500 per month by a young man sailing as a paid hand on one of the yachts taking on charter guests. Among the shore expenses quoted were photography, meals ashore, souvenirs (described by one crew as trinkets and trash) and, the highest expense, the cost of internet access from various cyber cafés.

Michael Frankel, who was one of the crews who shared expenses with the owners, estimated his total costs for the rally at $19,900 (or $1,200 per month), itemized as follows: his share of the rally fee $1,600, food and fuel share $2,100, communications $3,200, mail forwarding $900, and shore activities $12,300. In Michael's view it was money well spent: 'I think my expenses were reasonable. It was much cheaper than living on land for 16 months, and a lot more fun!'

SHARING COSTS

The Expo'98 Survey was primarily concerned with the running expenses of the boats, and the way the crew shared in those costs was closely examined. On two-thirds of the boats, the owner expected the crew to pay a share of all running costs. In most cases, this went only as far as contributing to the cost of food; but on 40 per cent of the boats the crew were also asked to contribute to the cost of diesel fuel, while on 20 per cent of the boats, the owner also asked the crew to make a contribution to the general cost of the voyage – which, on a few occasions, also included unexpected repair bills. One owner, who was paying all bills, including those for food, commented rather bitterly:

'With hindsight it would have been wiser to have asked my crew for some contribution, but this is not in my nature. However, having guests for over one year, and some of them hungry young men, can be an expensive business!'

On another boat, where similarly the crew were not asked to contribute to any costs, the owner explained: 'We consider our crew as guests for as long as they are on board. They all pick up the tab when we eat ashore, buy drinks for the boat, and also do some provisioning. We don't even have to ask, so it seems to work out very well.'

Although the price of food can vary considerably from country to country, if one looks at the cost of provisioning over a longer period, the average cost of provisioning during a world voyage is fairly close to prices in Western Europe or the USA. Most Millennium skippers gave separate figures for provisioning, which averaged out at about $2,500 per person per annum, or slightly more than $200 per month. By comparison, the average monthly cost of provisions for the Expo'98 participants was considerably higher – at $310 per crew member. As can be expected from such a mixed fleet of large and small boats, containing both some very wealthy people as well as crews on limited budgets, average figures may not be significant and there were indeed wide fluctuations, from a modest personal monthly allowance of $100 to a rather generous $600 per crew. Most estimates, however, were close to the average spent by the crews of the two rallies ($250 per month), which is a reasonable amount to allow for when planning cruising finances.

Although most people, in both rallies, were on a fixed income, whether from savings, pensions or other sources, only 60 per cent kept a strict monthly or annual cruising budget. 'We unfortunately know only too well how far we can go,' commented one of the skippers cruising on a limited budget.

UNFORESEEN EXPENSES

Unfortunately disaster can strike at any time, as was shown in the second leg of the Expo'98 rally, when two boats were dismasted between Madeira and Gran Canaria. Luckily both were insured, and in both cases the rig was replaced in record time so that the boats managed to catch up with the others in Panama. It was the first and only time in any of our round the world rallies that a boat had been dismasted.

Another expensive repair bill faced by the insurers occurred during the Atlantic crossing when the aluminium-hulled *Allegra B* collided with a whale. It was presumed that the whale surfaced under the boat and the damage was caused by the whale hitting out with its tail after the initial collision and seriously damaging

A major repair bill, such as having to replace the keel bolts of this boat during a round the world rally, could seriously affect one's finances.

the propeller shaft and rudder. The boat continued to St Lucia for repairs, but could not be repaired in time to catch up with the rest, so the owner decided to resume his voyage with the Millennium Odyssey.

Most skippers in both rallies were able to provide exact figures for any unforeseen expenses, which averaged $4,700 per boat for the entire circumnavigation. Whether by chance or divine Providence, in every instance the major repair bills occurred on the boats whose owners had a generous maintenance budget. The skippers were also asked to indicate an average amount that had been earmarked for repairs or unforeseen expenses. This kind of provision was in operation only on some of the larger yachts, and in those cases the average annual allowance worked out at just over $9,000 per boat, which was overspent in one instance only. 'It is good to have a budget, but a substantial reserve of money is also essential to cover the cost of non-budgeted repairs and other expenses. In conclusion, work out a budget and then add 50 per cent to it.' This was sound advice from David Batten of *Allegra B*, a banker by profession.

Although one would expect newer boats to have lower repair bills, in fact this was seldom the case and often brand-new yachts in the ARC have had a lot of things go wrong during their first year. The new yachts in the round the world rallies were no exception. Among the boats surveyed, the lowest maintenance budgets were those of yachts between three and five years old, whereas repair and maintenance costs were higher than average on new, untried boats and also on those over five years old.

Looking at the cost of yacht repair over the last two decades, it is quite obvious that in real terms the costs have risen out of proportion to inflation. With the increase in the number of cruising yachts, in many foreign ports local engineers regard yachtsmen as a soft touch, especially when they are called to a job in a marina. Therefore it is sometimes better to dismantle the faulty equipment and take it to a repair shop, rather than call the engineer to the yacht. 'Allow more money for boat wear and tear than expected,' stressed one disgruntled skipper.

Fuel costs were itemized in both surveys and the Millennium boats spent on average $3,500 per annum on fuel. This average is, however, misleading as some boats used a lot more fuel than others to run generators or diving compressors, besides their main engines. Among the smaller boats the average cost of fuel was as little as $1,000 per year. The average monthly fuel bill for the entire Expo'98 fleet was similar to the Millennium Odyssey and came out at $3,960 per annum. This is much more than most cruising boats would spend, but it must be borne in mind that this round the world rally was relatively fast paced and the engine was used more frequently during a circumnavigation that took only 17 months to complete.

The actual price of diesel fuel varies a lot from country to country, but Lou Morgan of *Risque* estimated that during their world voyage they paid an average 75 US cents per litre.

INSURANCE

Another cost that must be vectored into the cruising budget is insurance, both for the boat as well as personal and medical insurance for each crew member. Matt Rollberg explained that *Santana*'s annual policy cost $2,900 when ocean crossings were included, but it was reduced to $1,400 per annum when the boat reached the Mediterranean. In *Harmonie*'s case the annual insurance premium was about $5,000. Michael Frankel estimated that the average premium per boat for the duration of the Millennium Odyssey was $7,000, but this figure took into account all boats, from the largest to the smallest. The individual cost of insurance was also examined among the Expo'98 boats and, with all boats being insured, the annual premium came out at an average of $4,800. Several owners had benefited from a special rate provided to rally participants, and so in most cases the premium was only slightly higher than 1 per cent of the value of the boat, which is very reasonable.

Personal and medical insurance was more difficult to assess in both rallies as there was a wide variety and range of options. Everyone, however, had some kind of long-term medical insurance. In the Expo'98 rally, only one-quarter of those surveyed quoted comprehensive health insurance figures, although most mentioned that they had some kind of travel insurance. Health insurance premiums varied greatly and were often incorporated in a wider insurance scheme. In one case this also included life and home insurance, and the annual premium came to $10,000 for a couple in their sixties. Alison Wicks urges anyone setting off on a world voyage to take personal health matters just as seriously as the preparations of the boat: 'Everyone should have a thorough medical check-up before leaving, monitor their health throughout the voyage, and get the best international health insurance available – that way you probably won't need it!'

Whereas all boats in both rallies were insured, in a previous survey I came across several cases of uninsured boats. Sometimes this was dictated by financial constraints, while in some instances the boats were uninsurable as they did not have the required minimum of three experienced crew for an ocean crossing. This is a stipulation that used to be made by some insurance companies and it hit hardest some experienced couples, who had been cruising together for years. Some cruising couples were forced to take on additional crew for an ocean passage, while others decided to sail without insurance, but intended to renew their policies on arrival. Sometimes the renewal of a lapsed policy can lead to complications as some insurance companies insist that the vessel is resurveyed before renewal, probably to make sure that it actually got there. Some insurance companies, however, are prepared to revalidate the policy on receiving a formal letter from the owner stating that the boat had completed the ocean passage safely and was now engaged in cruising.

Insurance is another aspect of cruising where a radical change has occurred in recent years, and most boats are now insured compared to two or three decades ago when many boats were uninsured. I must admit that we too were not insured during the six-year voyage on the first *Aventura*, simply because we could not afford it. Luc Callebaut feels this is wrong: 'Some people say they cannot afford insurance; I say we cannot afford losing our boat without insurance.'

COMMUNICATIONS

Other expenses that should be allowed for when cruising are communications, eating out, as well as entertainment ashore – such as rental cars, excursions, going to museums or buying souvenirs. Most skippers were able to quote exact figures for these costs, which, in the case of eating out, worked out at a weekly average of $140 per person.

In order to help other sailors with their own budgeting, participants in both rallies were asked to indicate the weekly sum that they considered to be a reasonable amount to be allowed for eating out. Interestingly, the average of $140 per person per week quoted earlier was exactly the same as the one currently spent, which can only mean that those surveyed did not believe in denying themselves the pleasure of an evening out.

Several skippers pointed out that among the higher than expected costs were communications. Indeed, keeping in regular contact with family and friends can be costly, especially as telephone calls are much higher in countries outside of Western Europe and the USA. In both rallies, most boats had Inmarsat C, which was highly praised for its usefulness even if not for its cost.

Among the Millennium participants a large proportion of the budget was spent on communications. In the case of *Harmonie* the total amounted to $4,000, while at the other extreme *Stampede*'s crew spent $25,000 on communications. The high figure is explained by the crew of *Stampede* having to maintain regular business communications as well as the high cost of internet access from the boat. *Alparena*'s satellite telephone costs alone came to about $10,000 but, as Klaus Girzig explained, this was money well spent: 'It was really the price of my freedom, as thanks to my Mini M I could have a chat almost every evening with my wife Renate, who had to stay behind with our young son and also look after the family business, so she could only join me during school vacations. Life would have been much more difficult for both of us without this marvellous telephone.'

EXPECTATIONS

Having found out how much people spend both on themselves and on their boats, it was interesting to find out if they discovered that the voyage cost them more than they had expected. The opinions were fairly evenly divided between those who stated that the voyage had cost them as much as they had expected (42 per cent), and those who felt they had spent more than planned (47 per cent). One skipper declared that he had spent more due to some major repair jobs; another one felt that he and his wife were spending more ashore; while another skipper blamed the high costs caused by shaking down his new boat. Only one skipper stressed that he had spent less than expected – the owner of one of the larger boats that was joined occasionally by paying guests. Is this perhaps the answer?

As to how people spent their money, more (48 per cent) paid their shore expenses by credit card than in cash (28 per cent), while the remaining ones used both methods. In a few cases debit cards were also used and, in most cases, their owners had made arrangements with their banks to have regular payments made into their accounts. Visa cards proved the most common (76 per cent), followed by American Express (28 per cent) and MasterCard. Several skippers had two or even three different types. Asked if they had encountered any problems having their cards accepted, it was pointed out that only Visa cards are accepted by Citibank when paying the Panama Canal transit, whereas MasterCard may be more useful in the South Pacific as this appears to be the preferred card in Ecuador, Galapagos and some Pacific islands. The majority, however, stated that they did not have any problems paying by either credit or debit card in any of the places visited. This also applied to obtaining cash by card, and among those who did this regularly, which comprised almost the entire fleet, 83 per cent stated that this was done easily everywhere. Only a few described it as occasionally difficult, and none as impossible. One problem mentioned was the fact that sometimes the magnetic strip on the card failed to work. This is perhaps caused by moisture, and is another good reason why one should carry more than one card.

The use of credit cards is now so widespread that on only two Expo'98 boats were all expenses paid in cash, which was the only reserve carried on board. These were also two of the boats operating on the lowest budgets, and, as one of their skippers stressed, 'There is no better way to budget your finances than by paying cash. We always know the balance!'

At the conclusion of each survey, the skippers were asked if they were to undertake such a voyage again, what financial recommendations would contribute to the overall success of the voyage. One skipper, who had spent his annual maintenance allowance six months into his circumnavigation, suggested that 'any improvements or upgrades to the boat should be done at home, where it is cheaper and easier than once the voyage has started. Also, have on board all essential spares: pumps, engine parts, spares for the automatic pilot, as they cost a lot more along the way.' 'Win a major lottery prize first' was the wry comment of the only skipper who felt that the voyage was in fact costing him *less* than expected. In similar vein, another skipper suggested 'start with a lot of money and expect to spend it all!'

The irrepressible Fabio Colapinto of *Taratoo* summed it all up at the closing ceremony in Rome when he said 'the Millennium Odyssey proved that rich people can sail around the world'. 'Less affluent people can do it too!' retorted Michael Frankel, who pointed out, 'Coincidentally, my monthly crew expenses were about the same as my monthly Social Security pension, proving that the not-so-rich can also sail around the world.'

Cruising in stages

Whereas in the early days of cruising most people set off on a voyage and stayed with the boat until its successful completion, nowadays the availability of safe places where you can leave the boat for longer periods encourages people to break up their voyage into several stages. One major element that has contributed to this new way of cruising is the wish to avoid certain areas during the tropical storm seasons. In fact, many insurance companies now stipulate that cruising in tropical areas is limited to the safe season, so unless prepared to sail out of the tropics, most owners prefer to leave their boat in a safe place. The choice of a suitable place to leave the boat is part of long term planning, so various factors should be taken into consideration. Naturally the route and voyage requirements should be foremost among them so as to ensure most favourable sailing conditions. Other considerations are the existence of a safe marina and reliable yard for maintenance and repair work, the quality of local labour and its costs, the proximity of an international airport, etc. Trinidad, and to a lesser extent Venezuela, fit most of those requirements and can be easily included in the cruising plans of those sailing in the Eastern Caribbean. Most boats arrive there by early December, cruise the islands until May, and by the time the safe sailing season has come to an end, the boat can be in either of those places. Trinidad is now the most popular summer destination, with good availability of hard standing areas where boats are hauled out for the duration of the off season (June to November). Five or six months later, the voyage can be resumed at the start of the new season.

A similar role is played by New Zealand for boats cruising in the South Pacific, where there is a wide range of boatyards doing refitting work during the period when most boats are laid up (mid-November to April). A long stopover in New Zealand fits perfectly into long term cruising plans, as normally boats plan their arrival in French Polynesia at the start of the safe season (early April) which gives them six months to sail westward before heading for New Zealand as the safe season draws to a close (early November). New Zealand can be left in time for the next season, when one will have another six full months of safe cruising in the tropical South Pacific.

Other cruising areas where boats are stored between seasons are Mexico, the Bahamas, Venezuela, Guatemala, Honduras, Costa Rica and Panama. Only some of these countries are outside the tropical storm area, so this fact should be borne in mind when choosing such a place. Several countries bordering on the Mediterranean offer special deals during the European winter season (November to April) and this is a particularly attractive option for boats that fly the flags of non-EU countries, whose presence in the EU is now limited to 18 months. There are several Mediterranean countries that do not belong to the EU (Malta, Turkey, Cyprus, Israel, Croatia, Tunisia) that have good marinas where a boat can be stored between seasons. Wherever the boat is left, customs should be informed of the circumstances as in some countries the boat must be put in bond for the duration of its stay. In some places the formalities are carried out by the marina or boatyard, in others by the skipper, but everywhere the onus is on the owner of the vessel to ensure that local regulations are complied with.

Amanda Neal sees this type of cruising as getting increasingly popular with future sailors: 'I think that cheaper travel and more places to leave your boat safely for the season has made cruising more enjoyable as it's now possible to return home more frequently when leaving on a voyage of several years.'

Pets

The restrictions applied to pets are similar to those concerning firearms and there are a few countries where importing a pet illegally is considered no lesser crime than trying to hide a gun from customs. Regulations concerning cruising pets are extremely stringent in some countries, and this is the main reason why the number of cruising boats with pets has decreased over the years. To have or not to have a pet is a difficult question and anyone considering having a pet should think very carefully before setting off on a long voyage.

The subject was examined in two surveys, in which three-quarters of those interviewed rated the idea of having a pet on board a cruising boat with a resounding zero. Many of those interviewed pointed out that although they were fond of animals, they considered it cruel to keep an animal in the confined space of a sailing boat. Ilse Gieseking admitted that having a dog with them during their voyage around the world had been a major mistake, mainly because their freedom of movement had been severely restricted in many countries. In some ports they were not even allowed to come alongside a dock, while in others they were frequently inspected by health officials who wanted to make sure that the dog had not been taken ashore.

It is not a view shared by Jackie Lee, who is sailing with a schipperke dog on the trimaran *Sloepmouche*: 'He weighs about 7 kg, is not too big for the boat, but big enough to be a watchdog, and he is one of our greatest sources of enjoyment on board. Our excursions and explorations are always enhanced by his enthusiasm for discovering new sites, chasing fish, watching the activities of everything around us. In the Caribbean we had no troubles with quarantine because there were always islands where he was allowed ashore. Only Trinidad was a problem. We are now in the South Pacific and he has passed quarantine in French Polynesia

Opinions on cruising with pets are divided, but most of those who have pets believe they make life afloat more enjoyable.

and can go anywhere with us. The only regret is not being able to take him with us to visit the USA or Europe without being re-quarantined. We will avoid going to countries where restrictions are too difficult. The advantages of having our dog are worth all the disadvantages. I think having a dog also enhances our personal relationship by adding another being to love and care for together, without the complications of adding another human ego.'

Jackie's partner Luc Callebaut fully agrees: 'Cruising with a pet on board is so nice that we plan to get a second one so we can even breed schipperke dogs! Obviously it is better to have a small pet on a big boat than a large pet on a small boat.'

Luc also pointed out that a dog is an additional safety factor as it will keep intruders away. This is also the comment made by singlehander Michelle LaMontagne, who found that her barking dog kept uninvited guests away in remote anchorages. But as Zoltan Gyurko, also a singlehander, pointed out, 'a fake recording of a barking dog would do the same trick without messing up the decks'.

Conclusions

Cruising has become considerably more expensive than two or three decades ago, and in most places visiting sailors are expected to pay their way. Indeed, visiting yachts now make a substantial contribution to the local economy in many places and their role is increasingly recognized, and their presence encouraged, by local businesses and authorities. The only costs that do not appear to have risen in real terms are living expenses, and the good news is that you can eat well and cruise in some comfort for comparatively less than you needed a decade ago. With the exception of a few countries, the rise in the cost of food has not kept pace with inflation; international flights are also relatively cheaper – as are other expenses, such as postage, car rental, and even fuel in some countries. Where costs seem to have risen is in countries closely linked to the USA, such as Puerto Rico, Turks and Caicos, the Virgin Islands and Bahamas, where the US dollar is in circulation but prices are often higher than in the USA.

Those who have to cruise on a limited budget will find that their financial constraints may limit some of their choices, but there are still plenty of places in the world where you can cruise happily without a fat wallet. What *is* a mistake is to leave home with the idea that cruising around the world is free. Unfortunately there are some costs that cannot be avoided, such as the fee imposed on cruising boats in Greece, clearance fees in the Bahamas and most Caribbean islands, quarantine fees in Australia, or the cost of a cruising permit in Indonesia, to name just a few. Similarly, it is difficult to avoid paying the transit fees for the Suez Canal or Panama Canal, unless one is prepared to make a long detour. This is easier in the case of the Corinth Canal, which can be bypassed by a detour of some 200 miles, but one wonders if the detour is worth the money saved.

The need for the boat and crew to be well prepared was stressed again and again by those surveyed, and this included financial arrangements. Terence Brownrigg has this advice for anyone planning to follow in his wake: 'This sort of trip has to be regarded as a once in a lifetime experience, and one has to be prepared to spend whatever is necessary to enjoy to the full some of these places where one is unlikely to come again. However, if you have to go on a tight budget, think again; but if you do decide to go, then be prepared not to count every penny.'

As lifestyles and individual requirements vary so widely, it is impossible to make an accurate assessment of cruising costs generally. However, based on the figures provided by a large number of cruising sailors as well as participants in various rallies, which have been mentioned in detail in the previous pages, for comfortable cruising I would suggest an annual allowance of approximately $15,000 (£10,000) per person. This sum includes all normal living costs, those associated with routine boat repair and maintenance, as well as going out and travel expenses. Many sailors cruise successfully on considerably less, and just as many manage to spend a lot more. Like the trade winds, which rarely blow at the *average* force 4, financial averages usually mean different things to different people.

11

The Human Factor
PSYCHOLOGICAL ASPECTS
OF LIFE AFLOAT

"Nothing can spoil the pleasure of a voyage more than problems with your crew."
FABIO COLAPINTO

"A boat is not the place to fix anything wrong with a relationship, whether it is with a partner, a child or a friend. If someone irritates you ashore, they will irritate you more on a boat. Some people are not emotionally geared for life aboard. They are not wrong, or misfits, they are just not boat people."
SAUNDRA GRAY

The above statements are unfortunately true, and in my own experience the most common reason for an unsuccessful voyage is rarely the boat, the breakages suffered, or some other emergency, but the atmosphere on board. Having often been forced to step in to solve a crisis and attempt to restore peace, I have learned much about this problem from my dealings with skippers and crew in the various rallies. Furthermore, in some of the surveys I examined the effect of living in a confined space during an ocean passage. The frankness with which my questions were answered both by the skippers and their crew gave me an insight into the psychological side of life aboard, an aspect rarely considered when the beauty of cruising is discussed. Although various problems were reported, in most cases they were described as not serious, but merely the normal tensions to be expected when people are forced to spend a long time together in a small space. Looking at those boats and their crews more closely, it was interesting to note that in almost all cases where clashes of personality were reported, very few were among members of the same family, but overwhelmingly among crew unrelated to each other. Almost without exception, on boats where previously unknown people were taken on as crew, the atmosphere on board was tense, both skipper and crew seeing only the other person's faults and never their own. In contrast to this, the atmosphere was visibly more harmonious on boats crewed by people who had been sailing together for a long time, whether they were related or not. A similar congenial atmosphere was also found on boats with large crews, who had a strong motivation to sail together, and one of the happiest ships that I ever came across was crewed by a group of young Norwegian teachers who had pooled their savings for a voyage around the world.

ON PASSAGE

A long ocean passage has different effects on people, with some of those interviewed describing such voyages as boring, while others complained of what can best be described as 'cabin fever' after about ten days at sea. The situation can be exacerbated by rough weather, which forces the crew to spend longer periods inside the boat. Under such conditions, the availability of a separate cabin can make a great difference, as the lack of privacy was the main cause of irritation on the boats where tempers flared. The lack of a personal cabin was deplored even on boats crewed by the same family, and one teenage girl complained bitterly about having to share a cabin with her younger brother. The lack of space was usually worse at sea than in port, because many people slept longer than normal while on passage. The most usual ways of trying to overcome the monotony of the voyage were by playing games, listening to music, watching videos, reading or fishing.

The atmosphere was noticeably lacking in friction on boats where the crew took an active interest in sailing the boat as efficiently as possible, changing sails often, or steering by hand. Not surprisingly, these were also the yachts that made faster crossings. Several skippers of such boats remarked that this pleasant atmosphere often deteriorated in port, when there was less to do, with the crew squabbling over the dinghy or other minor things, and the lack of space being evidently more irritating than when the crew were on watch at sea and rarely meeting each other.

Some of these aspects were re-examined during one of the ARC surveys, particularly the boredom factor, which can create problems during an ocean passage. Undoubtedly the fact that the ARC is treated as a race by some skippers takes care of the boredom factor by keeping the crew on their toes to put in a good performance. Even among skippers who were not driven by the competitive spirit, the ARC added a new dimension to the Atlantic crossing and there were far less complaints about boredom than one might have expected. The weather always plays an important part on a long ocean passage and many crews were frustrated by the slow progress when the trade winds failed to blow as expected. One of the larger yachts was so effortless to sail that boredom was kept at bay by watching videos. According to the owner, the only problem encountered was the daily debate among the crew as to which film to watch!

THE ARC SKIPPER

One important rule in the early days of the ARC was for the owner to be on board for the Atlantic crossing but, as many boats are owned by companies, the ruling was waived so frequently that eventually it was dropped. While owner-skippers continue to make up the majority, there are several other categories of skippers who sail in the ARC. Owner-skippers usually sail with a crew comprising family members or friends. These make up the majority of ARC participants and continue to ensure the unique nature of the ARC. There are also a number of owners who take on paying guests, which is now a permanent feature not just of the ARC but of all offshore rallies. While taking on paying guests in this fashion may not be described as a charter, the rallies also attract professionally operated charter yachts, properly set up for this kind of business. Occasionally there is a bareboat charter, when a group of friends charter a boat to sail across the Atlantic.

Age is no barrier in sailing, and many people only start full-time cruising when in their sixties.

The owner ruling was brought in initially to avoid having delivery skippers in the ARC, and this rule was justified, as right from the beginning there were problems with these kind of participants and, in fact, one of the only two boats to be lost in the ARC was wrecked ashore on the windward side of Barbados by an inexperienced delivery skipper and his equally inexperienced crew. The worst combination is a delivery skipper, who, either from his own initiative or with the permission of the owner, takes on paying guests for the Atlantic crossing. Often such boats are ill prepared, and a few have been turned down by the organizers as they did not meet the minimum safety requirements of the ARC. In one such instance the boat was being delivered to the Caribbean by a professional skipper with the help of a crew made up of paying guests. Each of the latter owned their own yachts back home and appeared to be qualified sailors. Learning of the disqualification for safety reasons, they pleaded to be allowed to sail in the ARC and committed themselves to bring the boat up to the required standard in the few days left before the start. So determined were they to fulfil their dream of sailing across the Atlantic that they bought all the necessary safety equipment out of their own funds, and also made all the modifications required by the organizers. The boat passed the safety check the day before the start and made it safely to St Lucia, where the crew were awarded a special prize for their determination.

The ARC has been accused of attracting inexperienced sailors who otherwise would not attempt crossing the Atlantic. A survey conducted by *Yachting World* magazine among the participants in ARC 2000 proved that this view was completely wrong as the majority were in fact experienced sailors. The majority (62 per cent) had been sailing for over 20 years, and relatively novice sailors only made up 10 per cent of the total. Almost half the skippers were retired or had sold their businesses to go cruising, while the rest had either taken a year off work or managed to keep their businesses running while they were away. About half of those surveyed planned to be away from home between six months and one year, one-quarter for less than six months, and the rest for two years or more. Only one-tenth intended to carry on around the world, with the majority planning to spend their time in the Caribbean, and sail back to Europe after one or two years, or possibly spend one season cruising the US east coast.

So what are the basic requirements of a skipper planning to do the ARC or, for that matter, any ocean voyage? Determination is certainly an essential ingredient. Some skills in navigation are just as important, although in these days of GPS navigation, offshore sailing is infinitely simpler than in the past. A well-built, properly equipped and thoroughly prepared boat is undoubtedly an essential requirement. Good preparation is the main element in enjoying an offshore passage to the full. The survey mentioned above showed that most skippers had made thorough preparations for the voyage. On half the boats, the preparations had taken between six months and one year, 12 per cent had needed between one and two years, 15 per cent over two years, and 26 per cent less than six months. Most boats were therefore well prepared and, as a result, their crews managed to deal effectively with any breakages and emergencies that occurred during the Atlantic crossing.

Taking on crew

The comment quoted at the beginning of this chapter by an experienced sailor on completion of his second circumnavigation echoes the countless complaints I have heard over the years from disgruntled skippers. While I admit that many skippers did indeed have problems with their crew, some of them quite serious, there were probably just as many problems that crews had with their skippers. It is indeed a problem that cuts both ways and I have come across many examples that show that, like everything else in life, there are two sides to every story. Although I may tend to look at this subject from the point of view of the owner-skipper, I have deliberately made the effort to assess the situation objectively and also look at the problem from the crew's point of view.

Most cases where serious problems were reported involved boats where crew were taken on at the last moment before a passage. This often happened in the ARC, as finding crew for the Atlantic crossing does not appear to be a problem; on the contrary, it is a voyage that attracts many enthusiasts. Most of the crewing arrangements are made well ahead of time, and in most cases crew join the boats by flying out to the Canaries. All charter boats being delivered to the Caribbean are usually crewed by unpaid hands, with the exception of the skippers, some of whom had been doing this shuttle service for years. There are also a number of boats on which the crew pay for the passage, this often being part of a navigation or sail training scheme run by yacht clubs or sailing schools.

By and large, the days when crew were welcome aboard without any financial contribution are gone and, as shown by the findings of the surveys mentioned in the previous chapter, most owners expect the crew to at least cover the cost of his or her food. In fact, some people cruising on a tight budget try to supplement their funds by taking on additional crew, who are expected to make a reasonable contribution both towards their own upkeep and that of the ship. Although it cannot be described as chartering, the difference is not that great, and unless the conditions are spelt out clearly at the beginning and both parties know exactly what to expect, either the crew or the owner may end up disappointed. One other area in which it may be possible to find a temporary crewing position is on board charter boats being delivered to another base at the end of the sailing season. Finally, some of the large yachts employ permanent crew, but this is a paid job and the crew are expected to work hard for their money.

Skippers should be aware of the problems they can encounter by taking on crew without careful consideration. Half an hour's conversation on the dock before leaving on a voyage of several weeks is not enough to make an assessment of suitability. This also applies in reverse, as many crew only discover in the middle of the ocean why a particular skipper had problems finding crew. The main points to be considered by the skipper are the obligations assumed by the owner of a vessel towards a crew member, such as liability in case of injury, death or other unforeseen occurrences. The skipper is also legally responsible to repatriate the crew should this become necessary, and to the crew's country of residence – not the port where he or she was taken on. This is the reason why some skippers insist that their crew are in possession of a valid return ticket to their countries of origin from the intended port of destination. If a ticket is not available, some skippers play it safe by holding the equivalent sum of money in bond until the crew leaves the yacht. Some skippers go even further by drawing up a formal contract which spells out both their obligations and those of the crew, and which both sign in front of an independent witness. I came across this practice early on in my cruising days when I met an Australian skipper who changed his crew frequently, but made sure that every time a new crew joined his boat, a pro-forma contract listing both his obligations and those of the crew was signed by both parties. In my own case, I was quite surprised when a close friend, who had agreed to sail my boat to South America while I was busy with the Millennium Odyssey, handed me a formal letter spelling out everything that had been agreed between us verbally. At the time I found this quite strange, but later on, when a disagreement arose over a certain matter, it was good to be able to refer to the letter and remind ourselves of what had been agreed. The matter was resolved instantly and that letter probably saved our friendship.

Countless stories have come to my knowledge over the years, and two examples that occurred during the Millennium Odyssey when the fleet reached Tahiti should serve as a lesson to anyone. One skipper had taken on a young crew in Ecuador to help on the long passage to the Marquesas. On arrival in Papeete, the crew went straight to the immigration office and informed the authorities that he wanted to leave the boat and demanded the owner to pay his passage home. Although the officials sympathized with the owner and saw that it was a clear case of blackmail, they had no choice but to enforce the rules. Pretending to be reasonable, the crew then suggested that the owner only paid for a cheaper flight to Australia, as he preferred to go there rather than the UK. However, the owner refused to play the game and made sure the reluctant crew was packed off on a flight to London. When a similar situation arose a few days later, and another skipper had to pay for his crew to fly home, some of the other skippers with non-family crew took my advice and asked their crew to deposit with them the equivalent of their fare home.

In spite of many similar stories that buzz around the cruising grapevine, I never fail to be amazed at the number of people who are still willing to take on crew on the spur of the moment only hours before an ocean passage. It happens every year in the ARC, and I can usually guess the outcome from the speed with which the owner and crew part company minutes after the boat arrives in St Lucia. One such skipper suggested to others who may be faced with the same situation to think very carefully before taking on somebody they do not know for a long passage. Having two young children on board, he and his wife decided to take on another couple so as to have some extra help during the Atlantic crossing. The problem was not that the new crew did not get on with the owners of the yacht, but that the couple themselves did not get on with each other and fought and quarrelled all the time. The situation got so bad that the skipper decided to put into the Cape Verde Islands to rid himself of his crew, but strong headwinds made this impossible so they had to carry on all the way across the Atlantic. He warned others to be very careful about taking on crew for a passage during which it would be impossible to stop en route to change crew. The advice is equally valid for crew as there are probably just as many cases of crew that have been taken on by a difficult skipper, and wanting to get off at the earliest opportunity. This question of a clash of personalities on board a cruising boat must be considered very seriously as it can lead to grave consequences, even murder in a few documented cases.

As a general rule, from the cases I have encountered during the years, skippers appear to be most content with crews who have had some sailing experience, preferably including a longer passage. Ultimately the atmosphere on board is set by the personality of the skipper and, in contrast to the problems mentioned, I have also seen many boats where people have come and gone, yet were always welded into a happy crew by the talent and character of the skipper.

Crew size

The size of the crew may well play a part in both the boredom and the tension factor on a long voyage. According to the statistics of yachts clearing into the Bay of Islands area of New Zealand, the majority of boats (41 per cent) were crewed by just two people, 20 per cent had three, and 13 per cent had a crew of four. The average number of crew per boat worked out at 2.9. This is quite close to the results obtained from the boats that visited the island of St Helena. This small island in the South Atlantic is one of those places that are rarely visited by anything apart from cruising yachts and one or two ships. A total of 184 yachts called there in 2000, among them 152 cruising boats, of which 40 were cruised by couples, and 15 were singlehanders. The remaining 32 boats were South African racing yachts from Cape Town. The average crew on the 137 cruising boats, not including the singlehanders, was 3.34 per boat.

By comparison, in an earlier ARC survey, the average crew size worked out at nearly four per boat. In fact, the number of permanent crew on many boats was two, but more than half the boats had doubled their crew just for the transatlantic crossing. On the majority of boats (60 per cent), the permanent crew was made up of members of the same family, in most cases by couples. The situation was quite different in ARC 2001 in which family crews were no longer in the majority.

The ideal crew size was examined in the Global Cruising Survey in which opinions were sharply divided between those who are used to sailing as a couple, and may occasionally take on additional crew for an offshore passage, and those who prefer to sail the boat fast and efficiently with a crew of adequate size. Zoltan Gyurko, who often sails on his own, describes his ideal crew as 'the smallest crew possible is best, as arguments and hard feelings grow exponentially with more people'. Three-quarters of the skippers surveyed indicated that their ideal crew on their ideal boats would be two. 'Sweet, knowledgeable darling of a partner' were the exact words used by John Neal, and most others would agree, as several specified that a couple would undoubtedly make the ideal crew. Don Babson was one of them: 'Two – no more, no less. She tells me what to do, I do it, and there is no one else aboard to argue the issue.' Arthur Beiser agrees, and explains why: 'I would not like to own a boat that Germaine and I could not manage by ourselves; most of the time we cruise by ourselves very happily. Nevertheless, we often take one or two others on long passages. I think an ideal boat should not need more than two to run her, but should be able to accommodate two to four others.' David Beauchamp also prefers to sail whenever possible as a couple: 'Glynn and I seem to be able to handle any situation that has come our way so far. We have handled some real nasties and have come through unscathed – mainly, I hope, due to good preparation. When there are two of you and you get on so well, who needs more?' Luc Callebaut also prefers a couple, but is more specific about his requirements: 'A well-balanced couple where both are qualified to handle all aspects of cruising.' Antti Louhija agrees, but highlights the drawbacks of a small crew: 'Two is ideal, but makes for too little sleep and sometimes difficulties when manoeuvring in harbours.' Several skippers who prefer to cruise as a couple mentioned the need for additional help, especially on long passages, mainly to ease the burden of night watches. This point was stressed by John Wicks, who had just completed a voyage from Europe to Australia with only his wife, Alison, as crew. On the longest leg of the Millennium Odyssey, from Galapagos to the Marquesas, their autopilot broke down and the two of them found hand-steering very tiring. The Italian yacht *Jancris* arranged a rendezvous in mid-ocean, transferred two sailors to help out and, it was rumoured, also a massive supply of pasta!

For Skip Novak, 'the ideal crew is a couple, possibly with another couple coming and going from time to time. If you are making exploratory cruises, it is good to have four on board, as two people can guard the boat while the other two go off to hike or tour. For me, the rule of thumb is the less people the better to cut down on aggravation in trying to satisfy everyone's ambitions at one time or another. A cruising boat of a reasonable size should be able to be sailed efficiently and safely by two people for long periods, otherwise the design and concept must be in question.'

Carlton DeHart prefers to sail as a family: 'We have always sailed with just our family. We did our circumnavigation with my wife and our two daughters. It would be nice to have a few strong lads on board during a reefing session, but the added aggravation of having them on board while in port has prevented us from taking crew. We had two autopilots that we claimed equalled four crew members that didn't eat, didn't have an opinion, and didn't need airplane tickets. I suppose that as I get older, I might reconsider that opinion. As for now, I would rather do all the work and enjoy the intimacy.'

Carlton DeHart prefers a family crew, and sailed around the world with wife Jody and daughters Amy and Caroline.

Among the more sporty, and not surprisingly also younger skippers, opinions differed. As a professional skipper, Steve Spink knows exactly what his ideal crew would be: 'Ideally four people, on a single watch system. The ideal crew would be a fairly laid-back character and someone who can keep it together under pressure. Plus, it is essential to have someone who can fix most things on a yacht. And, of course, a good cook.' Quite a tall order, I must say, unless all those sterling qualities do not have to be necessarily vested in the same person!

Michelle LaMontagne, who normally sails on her own, also prefers the crew to be skilful at most things: 'Mechanical and electrical skills are a definite bonus. I can teach a willing person almost everything, and anything they do is something I don't have to do myself, but teaching a beginner can be a pain.'

One-quarter of those surveyed mentioned a crew of four as ideal for longer passages. John Ellis is one of them: 'The ideal number is four including skipper, preferably mixed sexes. This is more than enough to cover watches and, if someone falls sick or is injured, you still have enough people. Also, four is an easy number to cook for. One can still have privacy with this number, but there are also enough people for company. For me, crew selection and compatibility is probably *the* most important factor for successful and happy cruising.'

Cruising couples

As shown by the statistics obtained from various cruising destinations, as many as 50 per cent of boats are crewed by couples on their own. The percentage is even higher in certain places, such as the Bahamas, where many couples from the USA and Canada spend long periods of time on their boats – a much more enjoyable retirement than living in a condominium in Florida. The number of couples sailing on their own in the ARC has diminished over the years, and in ARC 2001, of the 219 boats only 14 were sailed by a couple on their own, with an additional four boats being crewed by a couple with children.

The attractions of sailing as a couple were highlighted by many of the skippers interviewed in the Global Cruising Survey. It was highly revealing that so many of them described their ideal crew to be a couple. As this is such an important part of cruising, and because the success of a voyage, and of life afloat generally, is so dependent on it, the 20 women interviewed in the Sailing Women Survey were asked to comment on this subject. Their views are quite significant as 15 of them stated that they usually sail as a couple. Among the others, three women are sailing on boats with larger crews that are involved in expeditions or charter work, although occasionally they sail the boats just with their partner. Without exception, every one stressed that sailing as a couple was a most enjoyable and rewarding experience.

Lois Babson commented: 'We sail as a couple and are happy with our closeness while cruising.' Saundra Gray was among those who pointed out that there were occasions when being just the two of them was not perfect: 'We enjoy being alone on the boat, but on long passages, especially during rough weather, it is nice to have extra experienced hands.' However, Saundra also described some of the problems one may have with additional crew: 'The relationship between people changes as others are introduced into the equation. Often we have guests aboard. Our guests are usually people who want to be helpful, but often do not know much about sailing or boats. So we try to have guests when we hope to be in an area that will be pleasant and benign, but there have been times when weather or other matters have complicated the situation. Otherwise we prefer to be just the two of us.' Glynn Beauchamp agrees: 'We sail alone, as a couple. This is our choice. Passage making can be, and is, exhausting and even boring at times.'

Jody DeHart knows the drawbacks of sailing shorthanded, but 'the pecking order is already established, our privacy is intact, we have no other opinions to deal with, nor drunk crew stumbling on board in the wee hours. Sometimes it gets tough while sailing, but the rewards while in port are worth the effort.'

Ann Harsh agrees wholeheartedly: 'We have done both and prefer sailing alone. Our first thought was that for long passages, having an extra crew was a desirable safety factor in case of bad weather, illness, etc. Having made many long passages, we find that is not really necessary. The key is to share the watch schedule equally and to have a boat that can be handled readily by one person, so the other can sleep, and, of course, sailing in appropriate weather conditions. Combining these factors, we find sailing as a couple preferable. We found that because we are a couple, even though the crew is included in conversations, meals, etc, he or she is still lonely and feels to be the "third person out". We also know our boat, how we like to sail, and what we expect. This is often difficult to instil in another person. Finally, when we decided to go cruising, we were concerned about spending unending hours together, in a relatively confined space, as previously we had both worked, had separate social lives, and frankly had not spent that sort of time together. We now find that we enjoy all of our time together and the intensity has not been a problem.'

Michael Frankel, who sailed as crew on *Hornblower* for the duration of the Millennium Odyssey, made this very point when he said: 'More than a year of living with others as a sailing partner is too long and strains a friendship.'

As I was putting the finishing touches to this book I met Arthur and Germaine Beiser as they were preparing *Ardent Spirit* for their usual summer cruise in the Mediterranean. In a few days' time they were planning to set off from France for Croatia, and I asked Arthur if he didn't find handling the 58-foot yacht on their own a bit too much. He looked almost offended when he replied, 'This boat has been set up to be easily handled by just the two of us. Recently I even had a remote control installed to activate the electrically operated jib furling gear, so handling the boat is really no problem at all, and it is nice to have a large comfortable yacht with enough space to accommodate all our grandchildren.' His comment filled me with admiration and later I remarked to Gwenda: 'I cannot think of a better example than this couple in their seventies to serve as an inspiration to anyone being concerned that age might interfere with their cruising plans . . . myself included!'

The age factor

The make-up of the crews in the various surveys remains very much the same mixture of young and old, male and female. In the ARC, three-quarters of the boats have at least one woman on board, and several boats have children on board. The ages of the ARC 2001 participants spanned the entire spectrum from 20 children to half-a-dozen participants over 70 years old. In fact, several of the younger crews in the ARC were astonished to be outperformed by people more than twice their age, whom one of them had dismissed as 'old codgers'. On the sea, experience and endurance sometimes matter more than physical strength.

The people I meet cruising, whether in one of the rallies or cruising on their own, are of all ages – although the majority tend to be over 50. For an assessment of average crew ages I referred to Michael Frankel's survey conducted in Tahiti, where he pointed out that 'from dockside conversations I estimated that the average age among all participants in the Millennium Odyssey was about 47. The average age of owner-captains was around 59. The tendency toward older owners and crews may be due to modern technology that requires much less muscle power to operate larger boats. About a third of the boats were crewed solely by a couple. Apparently, well-designed 50 footers with plenty of power-assisted gadgets present no special handling problems for their 50- and 60-something owners and mates.'

The youngest crew in the Millennium Odyssey was six-year-old Ginevra Abbandonati on the Italian catamaran *Cush*, while the oldest skipper was 71-year-old Duke Marx of *Distant Drum*. He was accompanied by his wife Betty and they celebrated their fiftieth wedding anniversary when the rally reached Tahiti. This was quite significant as this was also the place where they had spent their silver wedding 25 years previously. As Michael Frankel commented: 'their enthusiasm for the adventure and tireless boat handling and maintenance were an inspiration to all those who wonder what they will do when they get older'.

A question I am frequently asked is what is the best age to go cruising. My usual answer is 'there is no ideal age, but I know that, if at all possible, the best time is now, as tomorrow may be too late'. The following examples will bear this statement out fully. Indeed, age is certainly not an impediment to long distance voyages, and in all round the world rallies there were several captains and crew over 60, and even over 70. In the ARC there are several prizes awarded to the older participants, and in the latest ARC nearly half the skippers were over 60, and the oldest was 72. Other special prizes for determination were awarded over the years to some outstanding ARC participants, such as to the Swiss owner of *Three Generations*, a 70-foot Jongert. As he was in his late seventies and also had a serious heart condition, he was advised by his doctor not to even think of setting off on an Atlantic crossing. Undeterred by this, he continued with his preparations, but then had a skiing accident, so his doctor now insisted that he call off his voyage. 'If you are all so concerned with the state of my health,' he apparently told his doctor, 'then you, the cardiologist and the orthopaedic surgeon must come along, because I am definitely going!' And he did – as well as the three doctors!

Just as remarkable was the story of an Austrian crew whose skipper had a heart attack two days before the start of the ARC. Naturally we expected, and demanded on medical advice, that they withdraw from the ARC. The crew, however, came to see us and insisted that they knew what they were doing and were determined to accept any risks involved. The skipper himself was a doctor, and he also begged us to allow him to sail in the ARC. Faced with such determination, we relented. It was only on their safe arrival in St Lucia that the crew told me that their skipper was terminally ill with cancer, and the attack he had suffered in Las Palmas had been caused by his rapidly deteriorating health. His lifelong dream had been to cross the Atlantic on his yacht and, with only a very short time left to live, this was his last chance. There were tears in the eyes of those of us who knew the background to this story when that special award for determination was presented to him at the prize-giving ceremony in St Lucia.

That someone should not postpone their dream indefinitely was shown beyond any doubt by three incidents that occurred in the Millennium Odyssey. Within only a few months of each other, the owners of three different yachts were

John and Alison Wicks sailed in the ARC before embarking on a round the world voyage.

diagnosed with various types of cancer and had to abandon the rally. All had to return home for urgent treatment, but fortunately their own crew, or sailors borrowed from other boats, took over the yachts and continued with the rally. Two of the owners were eventually fit enough to rejoin their yachts, while the third only did so as the fleet arrived in Rome. He later told me: 'Although I didn't sail all the way around the world, I am still happy that I managed to do part of it. It is so easy to leave things until it is too late!'

These observations reminded me of a comment made by Carlton DeHart who had sailed with his family in the second round the world rally. At a briefing in Fort Lauderdale for potential participants in a new round the world rally, Carlton remarked: 'Whatever you do and whenever you decide to go – don't leave it too late.'

Carlton obviously meant what he said all those years back, as by an incredible coincidence just as I was finishing writing this chapter I received an e-mail from him saying: 'I am longing to get back on the water – the real world – and leave the madness behind. As I must take into consideration my own declining years, I am determined to do it in the next two years. If I am ever going to do it, as I am approaching 60, it must be sooner rather than later.'

Cruising with children

The number of boats cruising with children appears to have gone down in recent years, but if the ARC is an indication of current trends, we may be witnessing a change in this respect. After a drop in the number of ARC boats with children on board in the mid-1990s, their number is growing again. In ARC 2000 there were 16 boats with children on board, whereas in ARC 2001 there were 20 children, with their ages spread evenly between one and fourteen years.

The subject of cruising with children was examined in the Sailing Women Survey, and the women taking part were asked to comment on the pros and cons of bringing up children on a boat. Among the 20 women, 9 had sailed with children and some are now occasionally sailing with their grandchildren. Several had cruised extensively as a family, including two circumnavigations, while Amanda Swan Neal grew up on a boat: 'I grew up cruising and loved it. I think the pros far outweigh the cons. I really enjoyed the early responsibility, independence and freedom I was offered, and many of these attributes I still draw on daily. My six years of correspondence schooling and self-sufficient living has made me very resourceful. I take a great interest in the children I meet cruising. They appear to develop their own personalities very early on, and I think that as a parent you need to be a strong leader and best friend to your children. I would certainly encourage parents not to consider cruising with only one child, as I was glad I had a younger brother. It's an experience that has kept us close as a family.'

Lois Babson has cruised 'with our eight-year-old grandson and it was wonderful. We allowed him to have watch responsibilities and other boat duties. He was always on deck to help anchor or to handle lines when docking. He was taught how to operate the dinghy, and was able to run it by himself. He learned several card games, and beat his grandfather easily.'

Letting children take responsibility and have precise duties was stressed by several women as very important, Jackie Lee among them: 'The kids raised by dedicated parents are usually more mature, practical, used to working, and have better reading and language skills than land kids. I've also seen uneducated, wild creatures. Generally all goes well until the teenage years, when it seems that either the family has to implant itself in one place for the rest of the school years, or the child rebels because he/she wants to stay with friends or wants to be the opposite to what the parents are.'

Jody DeHart, who sailed with her daughter around the world between the ages of seven and nine, feels that 'the pros outweigh the cons by such a large measure that the cons don't really count. Children on a boat learn how to entertain themselves with reading, crafts and schoolwork in a way that kids in schools with a TV could never equal. They learn how to learn from books, which benefits them for the rest of their lives, how to make friends quickly, and how to interact with adults when other children are not around. They get to see their parents making life and death decisions that directly affect them. The cons? Maybe they don't learn to socialize with large groups of children as they would in a big school, but that's the only one that I can think of.'

Ann Harsh agrees: 'The biggest advantage is the broadening of their horizons. The big disadvantage is the lack of social interaction available to them with peers, as there are not very many children actually cruising long-term.'

Saundra Gray, who has cruised with her own children, has seen 'some very successful parenting aboard boats, and some that didn't seem to be working out so well, not far different than land-based parents. A cruising family is like a pioneer or explorer family; they must be self-sufficient, independent and creative. Much maturity on the part of both partners must be exercised to make a cruising lifestyle workable with children.'

Dorothy Walker regrets not having cruised with her children when they were younger: 'Anyone cruising with children is incredibly brave! I wish that we had started when the kids were younger, but when we coastal cruised with them in New Zealand they became bored easily. Having something like a sailing dinghy,

For cruising parents, the most important and difficult task is not to neglect the children's education.

windsurfing board, etc is a great help when they are older. Our daughter seemed to miss the telephone, but our son was happier as he could fish and was also diving at 12, so that helped.'

Germaine Beiser, who had cruised extensively with her three daughters, gave this advice: 'When they are young it is relatively easy, possibly more so if they are girls. They can read, they can play with dolls, they may play strange games. Arthur overheard them one day: "What shall we do now? Let's pretend we're sisters" "Yes! And let's pretend that we are on a boat". So they did. Surreal! You try to keep them from actually killing each other when they fight; easier done if they are girls. With tact and luck you might interest them in the running of the ship and the planning of the voyage. It's quite likely that they will want to learn the language of the country you are travelling through, so they can talk to the kids. But all this changes when they become teenagers. Valium and alcohol for the parents, a big deep-freeze for the young are the solutions. What we did was to encourage each daughter to take along a friend. This makes for a *lot* of teenagers on board, but a much happier atmosphere. They will complain often about the terrible life they are being forced to endure, but ten years on they'll all speak about the wonderful experiences you shared. Your young adults will tell you that they had a much richer childhood than did their friends.'

I asked my daughter Doina to comment on this subject, and she pointed out that reintegration can be the most difficult problem faced by a child who has been away from shore life for a long time. She was nearly 8 years old when we left on our voyage and 14 when we returned and, as she pointed out, 'The problem wasn't so much me having difficulties in adapting to life ashore, but other children not being able to accept me as I was so very different. It was just as hard for Ivan. Children can be very cruel.'

Paulette Vannier, who spent six years sailing around the world with three children, agrees that reintegration can be very difficult: 'The youngest was 4 when we left and the oldest 16 when we returned. It was good having them with us, and to share a lot of things with them, which one cannot do when they are at school and we are at work. The main problem for them is that they don't meet people of their age. We didn't feel the problem on the boat, but realized it back in France. They were really afraid to meet people they felt were different from them. The younger they were when they left home, the longer the adaptation took on their return. For everyone in the family, the voyage remains something like Paradise Lost!'

Expectations

Cruising is, for most people, a long-nurtured dream come true, and I am pleased to report that in my experience the number of happy and contented people far outnumbers those who regret their decision to go cruising. The joy of cruising can sometimes be marred by subjective factors, and it is often lack of experience that leads people into such situations. As Fabio Colapinto commented, problems with crew can easily spoil things so everything should be done to avoid this, and the examples mentioned in this chapter, whether involving a cruise of short duration or a circumnavigation, show how easily things can go wrong – but also how it is possible to ensure a happy atmosphere on board. A survey conducted in the Atlantic provided the opportunity to probe deeper into this subject, and the conclusions I was able to draw were later supplemented with observations made during the ARC and round the world rallies.

Crossing the Atlantic is for most sailors a unique experience, and the profound sense of achievement felt by those who have successfully completed such a voyage is entirely justified. For many of those interviewed, this had been their first major offshore passage, so I rounded off each interview by asking the crew, not just the skipper, if the transatlantic passage had lived up to their expectations. Those who expressed disappointment were a small minority, but looking more closely at the various reasons for dissatisfaction, the most often-mentioned cause was that the crossing had been more uncomfortable than expected. A few people also complained about the boredom of being cooped up in a small space for three weeks or more, and this was particularly noticeable on boats that had experienced friction among the crew, usually those who had taken on additional crew for the passage. However, complaints were also made by shorthanded crews who found watch-keeping and interrupted nights very tiring. On the other hand, on yachts with larger crews who were actively sailing their boats, people seemed to get more satisfaction out of the Atlantic crossing.

In a few instances the disappointment expressed by the crew or skippers was clearly due to high expectations of a perfect Atlantic crossing with blue skies, steady 15-knot trade winds, and flying fish waiting on deck for breakfast. In some cases the frustration felt by some skippers may have been caused by lack of experience, which had led them to either choose an unsuitable boat or prepare and provision inadequately, with several crews complaining about the poor diet – and one actually running out of food a few days before landfall.

Lack of sailing experience and its effect on the crew was particularly noticeable in the case of two fathers, who admitted being extremely worried about their responsibilities towards their families. One of them arrived in the Caribbean mentally and physically exhausted, having stayed awake for the last few nights due to his apprehension of the impending landfall. Under these conditions it was not surprising that his greatest satisfaction was not the crossing itself, but his safe landfall. Equally frank about his disillusionment was another skipper sailing with his family, who admitted that he had been looking for peace at sea, but the only thing he had found was apprehension. He was worried about high following seas, and his obvious inability to cope with an emergency should it arise. He was therefore determined to give up the voyage at the earliest opportunity. This was a painful realization for someone who had dreamt for 30 years about such a voyage, but had never considered the practicalities of this dream. It was ironic that his wife, who admitted having been reluctantly dragged along on the voyage because of *his* dream, had come to love the cruising life and was very reluctant to give it up. Nowhere was this problem of one of the partners willing to carry on, while the other pulled in the opposite direction, more poignant than in the case of a couple sailing in the Millennium Odyssey. It became clear quite early in the voyage that the wife was simply not interested in sailing, and by the time they reached Tahiti the crisis could no longer be avoided. They asked me to come and talk about their problem and the woman kept repeating how homesick she was, and that she would have returned home from any kind of voyage. It was painfully obvious that she was not prepared to continue, and I advised the husband to throw in the towel, which reluctantly, but wisely, he agreed to do. The findings of the Sailing Women Survey, which will be discussed in detail in the next chapter, confirm this view as among the 20 women surveyed, 9 pointed out that what they missed most while cruising was their family.

Generally, the surveys showed that those who approach life at sea with a positive attitude were usually the most satisfied, as were those willing to learn from their own mistakes and not surrender at the first difficulty. The same conclusion was drawn when talking to sailors on completion of a voyage, whether transatlantic or around the world. In most instances the main reason for the enjoyment being tempered by a certain disappointment was the lack of preparation, both mental and practical.

Looking closely at this, even if the voyage had been planned well ahead, the actual preparations did not seem to have taken all that long, the average length of time being around six months. In some cases the time spent on preparation had been much shorter, and some boats had therefore left home only partially prepared, their owners planning to get things done en route. Several of them discovered that this was not as easy as they had thought, and regretted not having done the necessary jobs when facilities were easily available. It usually resulted not only in a less enjoyable voyage, but also in frustration and higher costs. The boats taking part in the Millennium Odyssey provided an excellent sample in this respect as it included several perfectly prepared boats, some of which were mentioned in the previous pages, whose owners had worked for at least one year, and had spent a lot of money to prepare their boats for the impending circumnavigation. At the other extreme, one of the boats that had been entered by its owners primarily as a commercial proposition, having a number of paying guests on board as well as a professional crew, was poorly prepared and badly equipped. It is a great credit to her skipper and crew, who spent every stopover repairing the yacht or installing new equipment, not only that the boat completed the circumnavigation safely, but that she arrived in her home port in a much better state than she had left two years previously. A good example, but not one to follow.

Conclusions

The psychological side of cruising is an important part of life afloat, and anyone planning to leave on an offshore voyage would be well advised to take notice of the above comments and examples. It is bad enough to fall out with a crew even if he or she is not part of the family, so everything possible should be done to avoid putting close personal relationships at risk. Showing consideration to others is an essential part of one's general attitude, and this is often reflected in the way the boat itself is equipped. In my own case, as I often sail just with Gwenda, the boat has been carefully planned to be sailed easily by either of us. All essential lines come to the cockpit, where a powerful electric winch allows any manoeuvre to be carried out by even the weakest crew member. A good autopilot and self-steering gear contribute to comfortable passage making. In spite of this, Gwenda is increasingly reluctant to join me on long ocean passages and she makes it very clear why: 'I think it is important to know your interests and limitations, which is the reason I didn't want to do the Atlantic crossing because I knew that I wouldn't really enjoy it. Of course, I can do it if necessary because I've done it before, but if you don't enjoy something you are just a dead weight on the others.'

Cruising with children has many rewards, and although it is now many years since we cruised with our young children, I am still convinced that it was the right decision to take them with us. The six years we spent together have been a valuable and treasured experience for all of us, so I consider many of the comments and advice given in these pages to be extremely valuable. Bringing up children afloat is a heavy responsibility for the parents, but the rewards are great. Both Doina and Ivan assure us that they highly enjoyed their years afloat and, because we made great efforts to ensure that their schooling was not neglected, their education has not suffered.

Over the years I have come to certain conclusions concerning crew, some based on personal experience gained on my own boat, some from talking to other sailors. Sailing with friends as crew can be difficult occasionally, especially if they are older and sensitive about being told the 'do's' and 'don'ts'. Some people take anything that smacks of criticism very badly, so you either end up antagonizing your crew by telling them off, or you make an effort to keep quiet and probably explode later over some minor matter. People who have some sailing experience, and therefore have their own ideas, often don't like to be told how to do certain things. Some people cannot accept the fact that another boat may be run differently to their own. Having learnt to be aware of people's sensitivity, I now tell new crew when they arrive on board that even if they have sailed on another boat, most systems on my boat are probably quite different from what they are used to, so I ask them for patience and understanding if I keep telling them what to do. In fact, I now propose an initial 48-hour truce during which time I am allowed to point out anything they may have done wrong, without any offence being meant, or taken. The alternative is to sail either with inexperienced friends who will accept that being told what to do and not to do is part of the onboard routine, or with paid crew, who can be told off and know to shut up if they do something wrong. Some skippers circumvent this problem with a written list of 'do's' and 'don'ts' that is handed to crew on arrival. This removes the personal factor to some degree.

Sailing with women who are the wives or partners of friends is another situation in which occasionally things may not work out, especially if their expectations are wrong. Short passages or coastal cruises may have a better chance of success, but not necessarily a long ocean passage. On two separate occasions, wives of friends came on a cruise with me only because the husband had wanted to do the trip. The women quite clearly were not enjoying themselves, and even minor disagreements ended up being taken too personally. I realized that one could easily end up losing a friend, and the situation was not made any easier by the husband feeling that he should be siding with his wife.

I leave the last word on the subject of crew to Peter Noble, whose book *The Mind of the Sailor* deals with the psychological aspects of sailing in much more detail than I was able to do in this chapter, and should be compulsory reading for anyone going to sea: 'In recent years the importance of the human factor to the success of a sailing crew has been increasingly recognized. Any skipper thinking of taking on crew, and any crew looking for a berth, will profit from reading this chapter. I fully endorse its main findings: small crews, particularly husband and wife teams, get on best. Compatibility is everything; be reluctant to sail with strangers. A small boat at sea, except possibly for the singlehander, is not an emotional "escape". People take their problems with them. The successful and happy sailor was usually successful and happy before putting to sea.'

12

The Female Angle

WOMEN HAVE THEIR SAY IN THE
SAILING WOMEN SURVEY

"Labour division is a matter of 'pink' jobs and 'blue' jobs. If it's dirty, stinky, messy, has to do with fuel, oil, bilges or breakdowns, it's definitely blue. Pink jobs are usually shopping, laundry or cooking."

JODY DEHART

The last quarter of a century has seen an unprecedented increase in female participation in sailing, both in cruising and racing. However, this new state of affairs has not necessarily resulted in a significant change of attitudes. Some men appear reluctant to relinquish their dominant position on the boat, while many women accept without complaint the passive role assigned to them. In order to find out if the situation has changed significantly since the earlier surveys, various aspects of female participation were examined in the latest Sailing Women Survey. The findings were backed up by observations made during various rallies, especially the Millennium Odyssey, which had a large number of women among the participants.

I had first looked at the cruising life from the women's point of view by interviewing 40 'seawives' in 1979. Five years later, in a survey conducted among 50 long distance cruising boats in the South Pacific, I again had a chance to reappraise how much women participated in cruising life, from decision-making to washing dishes. Over two decades later, in the Sailing Women Survey, I was interested to find out if the majority of women were still cast in a passive role as they had been previously. As I have made clear on numerous occasions, this is an attitude that I regard not only as being counterproductive, but potentially dangerous in an emergency when a woman might have to take over the running of the boat.

All the women interviewed in the earlier surveys were undertaking long voyages, many of them having been away from their homes for several years, so I tried to find out how many of them had been interested in sailing before the start of their voyage. Although more than half had been interested in sailing during their previous land-based existence, in many cases the interest had been superficial and only a few stated that the decision to go cruising had been entirely their idea. On almost half the boats, the decision had been taken jointly by the partners on a fifty-fifty basis, while most of the others admitted that it had been the man's idea, although they had made up their own mind to go along. Some women admitted that they had taken a very small part, or no part at all, in the decision-making process. Marianne Twisdale of *Pelagic II* felt very strongly that 'women should never agree to go cruising just to please someone else, but only if they really want to do it'.

The pleasant side of the cruising life was shown by the general level of satisfaction expressed by those interviewed in the earlier surveys. The majority stated that cruising had lived up to their expectations, and some were very positive in stressing that they enjoyed this kind of life far more than they had imagined. Only three women found that cruising had not lived up to their expectations and was in fact worse. Ironically, one of these dissatisfied women had been one of those who had been keener to leave than her husband. In another of these dissatisfied cases, I was struck by the tension between husband and wife and the vehemence with which the wife described her utter dislike of life afloat. One of those who had found cruising to be much better than she had imagined, was distressed to see miserable women on boats and had this advice: 'If the idea of cruising doesn't attract you, don't even contemplate it.'

The decision to go

There is no doubt that whichever way you look at it, the love of adventure, the urge to explore, to pit yourself against the forces of nature, is very much a male feature. I know myself that it was my desire to travel the world in my own boat that made me take my family along. I was very fortunate that Gwenda herself had a spirit of adventure and had always liked travelling, so my task of persuading her to give up everything and set off into the blue was not too difficult. However, this was often not the case with several couples that I have come across over the years. It usually involved women who could not accept the fact that the attraction of a life afloat was extremely important for their partner, and in some cases putting obstacles in his way or refusing to go along may put a marriage at risk. There is no better example than that of one participant in the Millennium Odyssey who, on reading about the round the world rally, told his wife that he would very much like to do it. The wife objected vehemently, but he refused to be swayed: 'I have spent my entire life being a responsible family man, but now the children have grown up, we are well off, and so I feel it is high time that I did something for myself.' To which the wife retorted: 'It's either the boat or me.' 'In that case, I'm sorry, but it's the boat!' he replied and off he went.

In contrast to this is the story of Sinto Bestard, a retired banker from Mallorca, who decided to sail around the world in one of my rallies, undeterred by the fact that he was blind. His wife not only did not object, but actively encouraged him to do it and insisted that he took their son Rafael along, which he did. Sinto fulfilled his dream of a circumnavigation and the atmosphere on board *Snooty Fox* was one of the happiest that I had ever encountered.

Another remarkable example of a supporting wife is that of Brit Torp, whose husband Ernst has suffered from multiple sclerosis for some 20 years. Although confined to a wheelchair, Ernst sailed his 42-foot yacht *Her Ladyship* in both the first and second ARCs. He is still an active sailor and has won several races in the

Saundra and Charlie Gray have developed a strong bond after sailing for many years together.

2 Metre Class, often competing against able-bodied sailors. Ernst is in every respect a remarkable man, and I am convinced that the fact that he manages to keep his disability at bay is due not just to his determination, but also to the whole-hearted support he has enjoyed from his wife.

There were several men in the Millennium Odyssey who were sailing without their wives, who only joined them for short periods in some of the nicer spots. The rally attracted a number of men, mainly successful businessmen, who felt that this was a rare opportunity to fulfil their long-nurtured dream of sailing around the world, and who had either retired early or had made arrangements to be away for two years. With the notable exception of the Australian example given above, not one of the wives stood in the way of their husbands' plans, an attitude that is increasingly evident in the ARC also, where men often cross the Atlantic with friends, with the wife joining the yacht once it has reached the Caribbean. It is a wise attitude from women who obviously do not agree with the saying 'If you can't beat them, join them'.

How much women take part in the decision-making process was examined in the Sailing Women Survey. Among the 20 women, 18 stated that all major decisions were taken jointly and in only two cases was it found that the skipper decided first before consulting his mate. This is a radical change from the earlier surveys when women stated that, in most cases, decision-making was left to the skipper and the partner was only consulted when a decision had virtually been taken. Times are obviously changing!

Glynn Beauchamp described the atmosphere on *Milady Candida*: 'Wonderful discussions can and do arise when choosing a new route or destination. We both put all our cards, ideas and suggestions on the table, then jointly decide the best option for us taking into account provisions, our health, the boat's safety, and most importantly the weather!' In the case of Astrid and Wilhelm Greiff, decisions are also taken jointly but Astrid qualified her response by pointing out that 'as the skipper is the one with more sailing experience, his initial input has more weight'.

Several women stressed that they have their own input. Although Amanda and John Neal take all decisions jointly, Amanda has an obvious advantage: 'I'd been to more places than John when we first met, so I had some idea of the places I wanted to show him.'

Not surprisingly, the two skippers among the 20 women use their prerogative. Ann Harsh said: 'I do all of the reading and formulate a plan. I then review it with Ralph, including my whys and wherefores as well as alternatives. We jointly discuss it and modify it as agreed.' Annelie Rollfing, who describes herself as co-skipper of *Maresa II*, expects her views to be taken fully into account: 'We discuss everything together and I have my own say.'

Anna Huggett points out that 'on *Koncerto* all decisions about new destinations are taken jointly, but if Clyff has strong feelings about these, we follow his instincts because whenever we have ignored them, we have regretted it.'

Division of labour

In contrast to earlier surveys – in which women were cast, and accepted, a secondary and often passive role – the women who contributed to the latest survey stressed that jobs are shared out more with regard to ability than according to the traditional roles that dominate shore life. This was the most remarkable change that has occurred since similar surveys conducted in the 1970s and 1980s, and shows a different approach to the male/female question. Several women pointed out that the jobs are shared according to ability and physical strength. One area where this equality in roles was evident was that of keeping watches as, with only one exception, on all boats watches were shared equally between partners. Generally, however, as Ann Harsh explained, 'Our division of labour is based on who does what best, and we think it works out to be fairly even. Ralph is the mechanic as he has much more skills in those areas. I have studied diesel engines and am a good "gopher", but just do not have the same aptitude. Ralph is also the cook as he was at home, whereas I am the cleaner. I do all navigation and communications work.'

Judy Hall has the same experience: 'Some of our roles are shared and some individual, each of us doing what we like best or do best. In emergencies we both play a role. As the female, I handle provisioning, communications, navigation, stand watches and, during emergencies, handle the boat when male strength is needed on deck.'

Amanda Neal explained that on *Mahina Tiare*: 'John and I try to divide the labour about fifty-fifty. We are both capable of running and maintaining the boat ourselves, though we each take responsibility for different areas. Many of the jobs we do together as it's often quicker.'

Lois Babson commented: 'Our roles are very equal. Although Don does most of the navigation, I can do it also if need be. Don hoists the sails, but I tell him when to reef the main and when to furl in the headsail.' Teamwork was also of essence on *Sea Gem*, as Saundra Gray commented: 'We both work hard. We have a somewhat traditional division of labour as I tend to do most of the more domestic chores, while Charlie does most of the heavy maintenance and engine room work. This division is not set in stone as we share work as required. Many times the engine room chores require two people, and general deck work is shared.'

On *Ardent Spirit* duties are also shared along more traditional lines, as Germaine Beiser explained: 'Arthur takes responsibility for the maintenance of technical systems and navigation. I am in charge of household chores, provisioning and cooking. All other work is shared equally.'

Jackie Lee describes the system on *Sloepmouche*: 'We each have our speciality areas and generally it works out pretty equally. I do bosun work such as splicing lines, checking rigging, etc. He does engine maintenance; I do sanding, sanding, and more sanding, and detail work with epoxy. He does the brute sanding and epoxying; I do patient detail work, he gets on with things that need to be done quickly.'

As Lucy Misayat explained, on *Kaprys* work is shared along traditional lines: 'I do the jobs inside the boat, he does those outside.' Marilyn Morgan explained that on *Sheerwater II*: 'John is responsible for overall planning and upkeep of the boat and I am responsible for reprovisioning, keeping a daily log, and doing e-mails.'

It was interesting to notice that women seemed to know much more about technical matters than in previous surveys. Dorothy Walker commented: 'Although I do no engine or maintenance work, I know how to check the oil and water, how to change fuel tanks, and run the engine, etc.'

Jody DeHart has it all worked out: 'The division of labour comes down to "pink" jobs and "blue" jobs. If it's dirty, stinky, messy, has to do with fuel, oil, bilges or breakdowns, it's definitely blue. Pink jobs are usually shopping, laundry or cooking and cleaning up. All decisions are made equally, but a good whinge can affect the result.'

Onboard chores

The women in the Sailing Women Survey were asked to comment on the various chores and to indicate the percentage of their share. One area where I found women to be almost in full control was the galley. This confirmed earlier findings about the division of labour among cruising partners, as work continues to be shared more along traditional lines when it comes to such household chores as cooking, washing up or laundry. Once again, the latest survey showed that things are indeed changing, as on only one-third of the boats were the women doing all the cooking, whereas in earlier surveys the seawives were usually in charge of the galley, or as Alison Wicks put it succinctly, 'husband: skipper, wife: galley slave'. This was in fact rarely the case, and what was noticeable in the Sailing Women Survey was that although most of the cooking was still done by the women, several men cooked on certain occasions, such as in rough weather, or were in charge of breakfast or the barbecue.

MEALS

Jody DeHart was among those who tried to avoid the galley in bad weather: ' I do all the cooking while in port, where the boat is steady. I also prepare meals at sea except when it's very rough. I have a big problem with seasickness. As some of the cooking had been done beforehand and is kept in the freezer, all I need to do is place the meals on plates, microwave and serve them. This allows me to escape from the galley when it's rough.' This is also what happens on *Que Sera Sera*, as Lois Babson explained: 'I do the cooking unless the weather is bad, and then Don makes peanut-butter sandwiches for both of us. He is the bartender, however, and a darn good one at that.'

Cooking breakfast was a job done by several husbands, such as John Neal on *Mahina Tiare*, as Amanda explained: 'I organize and prepare lunch and dinner with expedition members. Between expeditions, when it's just the two of us, John does all the cooking and washing up.'

Some women actually enjoy cooking, such as Jackie Lee: 'It's because I love cooking almost as much as eating! I like the creativity and learning local dishes. Cooking is recreation for me.' Those who do not wish to cook all the time should learn from Germaine Beiser: 'I used to do most of the cooking. From time to time, Arthur would produce a mean omelette. Now that we have a gas-fired barbecue, life has changed. Arthur barbecues whenever possible, although I prepare the meat or fish and vegetables.'

On *Harmonie*, Ann Harsh never cooks: 'We eat one main meal a day and Ralph is the cook almost all the time. For breakfast and lunch, we generally do our own thing.'

Even if cooking was a shared responsibility on most boats, provisioning continues to be primarily a woman's job, and on only one-third of the surveyed boats was this a shared task. However, several women pointed out that the men did help with carrying the provisions onto the boat. As Lilly Vedana put it, 'Tom is my Sherpa.'

For Saundra Gray, 'Shopping in foreign ports is one of the most interesting parts of cruising. We enjoy shopping together, and most of our provisioning is done together.' Jody DeHart, who does most of the provisioning, feels the same: 'It gives me great pleasure to shop in all the little markets, even if it's impossible to find what you came looking for, as you usually leave with something else you didn't even know you wanted.'

This is something that I always thought only happened when the husbands are sent shopping, and is probably the reason why Gwenda usually accompanies me to the market – just in case!

Some women had it all worked out, such as Lois Babson: 'I do the provisioning, but Don comes along to select the peanut butter and to help lug all of the stuff back to the boat.' Silvana Masotti has an even better system: 'I normally prepare the list and Giuseppe goes to the market.'

Compared to previous surveys when no woman got away without doing some washing up, three of the women in the latest survey never did any at all. On nine boats the washing up was shared, while on eight boats the skipper managed to avoid this chore, as Saundra Gray explained: 'When we sail, just the two of us, I do the galley. If there are others aboard we share chores. Captain Charlie artfully avoids the galley.' For Glynn Beauchamp, 'Washing up is generally my job, although Dave usually dries the dishes for me. It's the best time to have a good chat.'

LAUNDRY

One major change that has occurred in recent years is the presence of washing machines, and occasionally even dryers, on cruising boats. In the latest survey as many as one-third of the boats had a washing machine. On most other boats it was pointed out that whenever possible the laundry was done ashore, either at a marina or handed over to be done by a local person. However, on the majority of boats the laundry continues to be entirely the woman's responsibility, and only two women did no laundry at all. Jackie Lee was one of them: 'I only do a little hand washing. Luc does all the laundry on board as we have both a machine and a spinner. They are well worth it. The spinner alone saves arthritic hands and hours of drying time.'

It was interesting to notice that men were much more prepared to do the laundry if there was a machine available. Having a washing machine on board can be a great help, as Jody DeHart explained: 'I do all the laundry, but because we have a washing machine and a dryer on board that work very well under way, even at a 15 degree heel, it's not a big deal. Carlton makes 400 gallons of water on his watch and I do ten loads of laundry on my watch, using up all the water. We always have clean sheets, towels and clothes. When we arrive in port, all the laundry is done, the boat is washed down, and the tanks are full of fresh water.'

Lois Babson said: 'I only do laundry if I cannot send it out to a local laundry. Sometimes it is expensive, but it frees up my time to do other things.' Fortunately most marinas now have coin-operated machines, and even the smaller places frequented by cruising boats nowadays have a laundromat, so washing large items such as sheets and towels is no longer as difficult as it used to be in the past. Amanda Neal commented: 'Often the nearest laundromat is in town, so we run other errands at the same time. If there is no laundromat we use the bucket, but John has more stamina in wringing it out, while I am more fastidious about how securely the laundry is pegged while it flaps in the rigging.'

Saundra Gray commented: 'I think I could write a book on "laundry experiences in strange and exotic places". We have a washer-dryer aboard, but I do not use it too often unless we have access to water. I have found while cruising that you do not have to use so many clothes, you do not have to change sheets every seven days, and towels can be used much longer.'

On boats with extra crew, they were expected to do their own laundry. Even on some boats crewed by a couple, each did their own laundry – as Marilyn Morgan pointed out: 'In port or marina, I do most of it, but at sea we are each responsible for our own.'

MAINTENANCE AND REPAIR

Whereas laundry work still appears to be the responsibility of the woman, the situation is completely reversed in the case of maintenance and repair jobs, as on three-quarters of the boats this was entirely a man's job and on the remaining boats the women only did some of the easier jobs. Jody DeHart said: 'Repairs and maintenance are definitely blue jobs. I help clean up and supply the cold drinks, while Carl does the actual work.'

As in most cases the boats were sailed by couples, many jobs were done together, as Saundra Gray explained: 'Charlie does most repairs and I help if needed. We work together on the items that need extra hands. He does an excellent job of maintaining the boat and its working elements. We also try to schedule routine maintenance work to be done in suitable ports where there are skilled technicians.'

Paulette Vannier, who admits to having no idea how to repair anything on an engine, tries to be helpful 'by handing over tools or cleaning up afterwards'. Glynn

Beauchamp is also 'always on hand to assist where and when required. I am very good at hauling Dave up the mast using the anchor winch. Upholstery and sewing are more my responsibility. I do a little painting, but for some reason it tends to go on inside out or back to front when I do it!' Perhaps this is the reason why some skippers prefer to do the work themselves, as Lois Babson explains: 'No repairs for me; Don likes to do that stuff . . . and is quite welcome to it.'

Although in many cases the women described their responsibility as being the kind of jobs that they would also do at home, such as sewing or upholstery repairs, there were a few women who went well beyond that. Jackie Lee was one of them: 'I do whatever I can. I repair sails and lines, do epoxy repairs, maintain the stuffing box, run the compressor, do underwater work, and assist in maintenance of the watermaker, wind generator and other things.' Amanda Neal, who is a qualified rigger, also shares equally in running repairs and maintenance: 'John does the engine maintenance and repairs to the teak deck. I do rigging maintenance, including braid splicing and sail repairs.'

Some division of labour is obviously dictated by the difference in physical strength, one of the main reasons why nearly half the women in an earlier survey stated that they never touched the anchor. This has changed drastically in the intervening years as most boats in the latest survey were equipped with an electric windlass.

Steering in and out of port was also shared equally on most boats. Overall, the women spent more time at the helm than dealing with the anchor, which appears to be a reasonable arrangement for a shorthanded crew where one member is physically stronger than the other. This view was best expressed by the late Susan Hiscock, who we had the fortune to meet while *Aventura* and *Wanderer IV* shared an anchorage in Fiji: 'Coming into congested ports, for instance, the wife should be at the helm and the man at the lines and fending off. Yet often the husbands try to make themselves look superior. It is only vanity on their part. They want to be seen to be in control.'

One area in which men continue to be in charge is that of dealing with formalities, and in the latest survey only three women dealt with this task. Anna Huggett of *Koncerto* was one of them: 'As we are equally qualified, I do all formalities. I make sure I put myself down on the forms as the captain, as officials in some countries only deal with the captain.'

On 12 boats the men dealt with formalities all the time, while on the remaining 5 the women did so occasionally. Ann Harsh usually deals with officials herself: 'I have better language skills in general, and also find that having a woman do this is a plus in most countries.' Indeed, in many places, having the woman deal with local officials appeared to be an advantage, while a few couples pointed out that they always go together to clear into a new country as officials tend to be more amenable in the presence of a woman.

COMMUNICATIONS

As mentioned in an earlier chapter, improved communications have made cruising both safer and more enjoyable. It was therefore interesting to find out from those taking part in the Sailing Women Survey if they felt that better communications have greatly improved the quality of their cruising life. The opinions were fairly divided on this issue. Judy Hall was among those who declared without

Women are in charge of communications on many boats.

reservations: 'I love having Inmarsat C, SSB and ham radio, plus VHF radio for communications. Every woman I know enjoys being able to communicate with other boaters as well as keeping in touch with family.' Lois Babson shares those feelings fully: 'Hey, I'm a woman, and you know how women like to talk! E-mail has also been a great way to communicate.' Nina Louhija agrees: 'Absolutely more enjoyable. I think most sailing women must feel the same.'

The women were also asked if they considered communications to be an intrusion. For Germaine Beiser, 'The availability of cellphones has made an immense difference. I certainly don't consider it an intrusion to hear from our family. It's a great comfort to me to know that if anything goes wrong with our children they can let us know, and that if something wonderful happens they can tell us too. Cruising is quite exciting enough as it is without making it more so by lack of communications. The cruising life has turned out to be more fun now that we can ring a friend on another boat, discover that they are nearby, and make a rendezvous with them.'

Glynn Beauchamp shares Germaine's enthusiasm: 'Better communications are wonderful. When on passage it may be a pain in the neck doing those regular radio skeds, but what a comfort and help they are if disaster should strike. A radio is not an absolute necessity but, oh boy, it is so comforting to hear those voices sometimes, especially when everything appears to be against you. Good Old Murphy is alive and kicking on our boat! Most, but not all, other sailing women I know are happy to keep up with communications. I don't consider communications to be an intrusion. There is always the OFF switch, after all!'

Jackie Lee feels that: 'It's given me a lot more security being able to keep in touch with ageing family, and to know that help is available when needed, or that others know where we are. Many other women I know are reassured, and women are the more active of the couple on radio or e-mail. The only drawback is that it is easy to spend more and more time gathering information that is not all that essential, and spending less and less time in touch with the outdoors or meeting other cruisers face to face.'

Ann Harsh feels that better communications 'provide the peace of mind that we and our family both want. We certainly do not consider it an intrusion on our cruising lifestyle.' Saundra Gray does not regard communications as an intrusion either: 'There is plenty of excitement out there, and communication is not that frequent or intrusive.'

Jody DeHart feels, 'Better communications is a two-edged sword. You can keep in touch, but you can't run away. We are always in touch with our ageing parents and children. They worry if we can't relay to them that we've arrived safe and sound.' For Lucy Misayat, 'Communications have not made any difference so far. Some other women say they are happier knowing all is well at home.'

Dorothy Walker is not convinced: 'No, because now that we are more in touch with our business, we worry more than on our first trip when we were out of touch for months and the staff struggled on without us and we felt more relaxed. Now every time we open an e-mail we wonder what has happened. I think better communications have made no difference to how enjoyable my personal cruising is, but certainly they have made the business side much easier.'

Lilly Vedana is also in two minds: 'It all depends. For business it's essential as I have a lot of e-mails to write. But as I am not so family oriented, I could do without them. But I know from a lot of other women how important it is for them.'

Dealing with emergencies

Better communications have certainly made dealing with emergencies much easier. The latest survey showed that women are, on the whole, not only keener on improved communications, but are also in charge of communications on many boats. One area of total male domination in the past used to be that of navigation, but this is also changing as on several boats the women were involved in navigation. Even on boats where women played a secondary role in navigation, most were able to navigate, as emerged from the next section of the interview, which tried to assess the way in which women could cope alone in an emergency situation if the skipper had been incapacitated. On nearly all the boats surveyed, the women were confident that they could navigate to a port should such an action become necessary while they were sailing offshore. This was the most marked difference compared to the findings of the previous surveys, when nearly half the women stated that they would not be able to do any offshore navigation whatsoever. This is entirely due to GPS navigation, and this fact more than any other has given women the necessary confidence to deal with a possible emergency.

No such marked changes from the previous surveys were noted in the other aspects of dealing with an emergency situation when women would have to do everything on their own. The majority said that they would be able to sail their boats singlehanded. Several said that they would have a struggle doing some of the jobs, but were convinced that in an emergency they could summon the strength from somewhere. It would certainly be to every skipper's advantage to make sure that, in an emergency, all essential equipment could be handled by the weakest member of the crew.

A case in point is that of June Macauley of *Acheta*, who had the experience of doing all these things in just such an emergency when she had to sail the boat on her own after her husband Mac was struck down with a severe case of hepatitis. Another woman interviewed in an earlier survey similarly had to cope on her own in an emergency. While on passage from Australia to Indonesia, her husband developed blood poisoning from an infected knee and was completely immobilized in his bunk in a serious condition. With great trepidation she took over the role of captain and navigator, as well as trying to nurse her husband, and after two days, with little sleep, she managed to bring the boat in to anchor in Kupang on the island of Timor. She then found it almost as traumatic to deal with all the paperwork and the officials in a country where women do not do that kind of thing. As these examples show, the possibility of the skipper becoming incapacitated while on passage is real, and one never knows where and when an emergency may strike. It therefore pays all skippers to delegate responsibility to their crews and ensure that they know how to sail and navigate the boat on their own if necessary. These incidents emphasize the wisdom of the advice given to other seawives by Pascale Fecamp of *Kalabush*: 'It is a priority for a woman to be able to sail the boat alone.'

Michelle LaMontagne, who often sails on her own on *Wooden Shoe*, made this very point all too clear when she said: 'I meet many wives or girlfriends on boats who know nothing about boat handling other than staying awake on watch to call their partner for help if anything changes, like the wind direction. I ask them if they could retrieve their partner if he fell overboard or if they could drive the boat like a motorhome to shore if something happened. Many do not. I was sailing with someone in foreign waters who became very ill and subsequently died. I had to learn enough of another language to be able to get medical assistance, then had to become the mechanic and electrician for the boat. While most women will never have to do this, there should certainly be a plan as simple as which radio net to call for help and guidance as it can happen to anyone sailing offshore.'

Just as in the previous surveys, the engine remained a mystery to many women, some admitting that they could not cope with the simplest repair, such as bleeding the air out of the fuel system – which is probably the most obvious reason for diesel engine failure. There were some notable exceptions, such as Ann Harsh and Jackie Lee, both of whom were quite confident in taking on a diesel engine. Overall, the 20 women in the Sailing Women Survey seemed to be generally better prepared and more skilled than those who took part in previous surveys, perhaps because all had done a fair amount of sailing, or maybe because they simply have a different attitude and no longer accept being cast in the role of 'just the wife'. This was the criticism once voiced by my friend Muriel Bouteleux, who vehemently objected to 'forever being treated like a passive appendage'. Things have definitely moved on from my very first survey when one of the skippers replied to one of my questions by describing his wife as 'the most useless item' on board his boat. For the sake of political correctness, I must hastily add that the same macho skipper described the bottle opener as the most useful instrument on board his boat!

Life afloat

It was interesting to compare the findings of earlier surveys with regard to what women thought about the cruising life at the beginning of the twenty-first century, and to hear that few of the women greatly missed the comforts of life ashore, especially those cruising on boats equipped with hot water, showers and other basic comforts. What was noticeable in some cases was that the longer a woman had been cruising, the simpler her lifestyle had become. This was the point made in an earlier survey by Linda Robson: 'One must be prepared to do domestic chores as one would have done them 50 or 100 years ago, such as washing laundry by hand in a bucket. If one is not prepared to give up some shore comforts, it's probably better not to go at all.'

Doing away with some of the machinery of modern living does not necessarily mean that most cruising women lead spartan lives. Many of the yachts surveyed were equipped with freezers, refrigerators and washing machines. Nor does the galley on some yachts differ all that much from a kitchen ashore, being equipped with electric mixers or liquidizers, while even microwave ovens are no longer a rarity on yachts. Bearing in mind that many comforts are often taken for granted, the women interviewed in the latest survey were asked to name the things they missed most, as well as those they missed least while cruising. It soon became apparent that it was not the absence of material comforts, or modern conveniences, that most women missed.

Jody DeHart, an anaesthetist for open heart surgery, missed most 'my work-related joys. I love my job, it's very exciting and I do it very well. On the boat, I'm just Mom and what's for dinner?'

Nina Louhija, a best-selling writer in Finland, also missed her work more than anything else. But not Paulette Vannier, who stressed that it was her work that she missed least. What she really missed was a dishwasher, which was perhaps not surprising for someone cruising with three young children. Paulette also missed having space and time to herself, and also 'peaceful nights, as on a boat you are forever woken up by something like the wind getting stronger'.

Germaine Beiser missed 'walks on paths and streets. It's often not easy to get to a path ashore and summer in the Med is often too hot to make walking enjoyable. I do miss cities and nice shops, but we frequently visit places like Venice and Dubrovnik, so it's not too bad.'

Interestingly enough, several women missed the exercise, such as Amanda Neal: 'At sea I miss a daily aerobic workout routine such as swimming, running or dancing. I certainly try and make up for lost time when I hit shore.' This is what Jackie Lee missed too: 'Fun aerobic and flexibility exercises, such as Jazzexercise and dance.'

Anna Huggett missed most 'certain foods, ice cream and shopping in general'. Lilly Vedana's list was similar: 'Chocolate, strawberries, green asparagus . . . sometimes a horse ride.' Lucy Misayat simply missed her daily English newspaper.

Rather than easily identifiable material goods, what some women – such as Annelie Rollfing or Astrid Greiff – missed was 'culture and entertainment'. However, what others missed more than anything else were family and close friends, with several women mentioning their children – and especially grandchildren.

There were some who did not miss anything, such as Glynn Beauchamp: 'Nothing really, except possibly a pet as we've both always had cats and dogs. This, however, was more than made up by the wildlife all around us.' Silvana Italo missed nothing: 'For me life afloat is just a pleasure.'

The list of things that were missed least by the women was just as revealing. Saundra Gray probably spoke for many when she described what she missed least while cruising: 'The constant bombardment of advertising and news, which is so overwhelming in American life.' Ann Harsh agreed: 'TV, news and the telephone.' Amanda Neal was happy to get away from 'the commercialism of society and the boxes people put you into'. For Jody DeHart it was 'traffic, telephones, and the hustle it takes to keep your head above water. It took me a long time to settle down to island time while cruising, but now that I am on land again I can't wait to get back.' Indeed, the hectic pace of life ashore was mentioned by several women as what they missed least. Alison Wicks said, 'The rat race, running a business and employing staff.' Lois Babson feels the same: 'The everyday hectic work day, and responsibilities of running our own company.'

For Anna Huggett it was 'the frustrations of land life and family dramas'. Whereas for Jackie Lee it was 'traffic, paperwork and administration, family obligations, a regular job, wearing shoes!' Lilly Vedana felt the same: 'City stress, noise, phone, tax and other paperwork, having to be fashionable.' Silvana Masotti was happy to be rid of 'traffic jams, polluted air, noise pollution'.

For Lucy Misayat it was just the telephone, whereas for Astrid Greiff it was simply politics. Marilyn Morgan hated the thought of 'petty politics at work', while Glynn Beauchamp knew what she didn't miss at all: 'Probably neighbours!'

SACRIFICES

Looking at the things that were missed most and comparing them to those that were missed least, the Sailing Women Survey provided a good opportunity to find out from these women if they felt that they had made any major sacrifices to go cruising or to live on a boat. And, if so, were those sacrifices justified? It was a question that the women dealt with in a forthright manner, and although a number of women did admit to having made certain sacrifices, there was only one who considered the price to be too high. Nina Louhija explained: 'The fact that I was not willing to make sacrifices is the main reason why I stopped sailing on long ocean passages.' Anna Huggett also had some reservations: 'The major sacrifice was giving up a reliable income to purchase this boat. Time will tell, but we pray and trust that it all comes out right.'

There were others too who felt that they had made a sacrifice, such as Judy Hall, who is a university professor: 'Twice I have quit successful jobs in my career in order to go sailing. But what I gained from the adventure was well worth it. And I was able to return to my field right where I left off!' Saundra Gray understands Judy's point too well as she sailed with Judy both in America 500 and the Millennium Odyssey: 'Any time you leave for an extended period there are sacrifices. My enjoyment and enrichment from the experiences have far outweighed the inconvenience.'

In contrast to these examples, several women stressed that going cruising had not required any real sacrifices, as Ann Harsh explained: 'I don't feel I have made any major sacrifices to go cruising or to live aboard. I enjoy this lifestyle immensely, but I recognize it is not for everyone.'

Glynn Beauchamp shared those feelings: 'No real major sacrifices were made prior to living aboard. We had both gone through marriage separations – the past was behind us. Life began anew! To live aboard a cruising boat you cannot bemoan what you had before or what you left behind. Put it behind you. Kick it in the butt. Face the new challenges afresh and you'll enjoy life. As Dave, now my husband, says, "We don't have problems, only challenges".'

Paulette Vannier put matters in perspective when she stressed that being a mother can be a burden whether living ashore or afloat: 'The major sacrifice is that, with three children, supervising their lessons, correspondence courses, etc, there was no personal life left. This is very important to realize by anyone planning to do the same. The way to justify it is to realize that when you have three children waiting at home when you get back from work, you don't have much personal life either, even if you don't realize it at the time.'

For Lois Babson, 'our only sacrifice was to leave our grandchildren behind for long periods'. Whereas Lucy Misayat misses 'seeing the garden change during the seasons, but that is not a major sacrifice'. Jackie Lee commented: 'Since 1984 we've lived a nomadic life working on the water. Moving onto a boat was actually settling down for us. I can't imagine any other way of life.'

It was quite remarkable that even when certain sacrifices were necessary, which was often the case, none of the women expressed any regrets. Jody DeHart spoke for all of them when she said: 'I have made a few sacrifices to go cruising, but I feel that they were justified for the memories I've taken away with me. I tell my friends that I never feel so alive as when I'm on a boat sailing along, listening to the water rush past the hull, watching the sealife and riding on my magic carpet.'

RELATIONSHIPS

Such an overwhelmingly positive picture is undoubtedly due to the excellent relationship most of these women had with their partners. The women who took part in the latest survey were not the exception, as the importance of a good relationship was stressed by women in all the surveys. 'One should never start off on such a voyage unless you already get on well with each other ashore' commented one of them, while another woman admitted that cruising had been an eye-opener and she now realized that she had hardly known her husband before. Spending 24 hours in such close proximity obviously has an effect on any relationship, and one woman observed cynically in an earlier survey that 'life afloat is very good at pulling people apart'. Another woman commented that the passive role played by some women in the initial decision to go cruising can lead to problems later on, endangering not just the continuation of the voyage, but the relationship itself.

On the positive side, however, it must be stressed that such examples were very much in the minority, and in the majority of cases the cruising life had brought people closer together. The couples who had been cruising for a long time, or had done a lot of sailing together before the voyage, had a noticeably harmonious relationship. This closeness was also shown by the fact that half the women inter-viewed in an earlier survey felt more dependent on their partner than they did ashore, with only two women saying that they had become more independent than previously. Several women pointed out that life at sea was different, in that both partners are dependent on each other to a much higher degree than when ashore, and have to work as a team: 'As it is us against the elements, we both depend on each other more.'

The findings of the latest survey confirmed and reinforced these points. The 20 women were asked whether their relationship has suffered as a result of spending long periods of time together on the boat. With the exception of one woman, who declined to comment, not a single woman stated that her relationship with her husband or partner had suffered. In fact, one-third of the women simply replied that their relationship had improved. Some of the others qualified their response, such as Ann Harsh: 'I would not say it has improved dramatically, as it was fine before we started, but it has certainly not suffered. We enjoy our time together, but a little separation every now and then is healthy too.'

Amanda Neal might not agree: 'Our relationship started on the boat and only gets better. We find that when we return to shore life our relationship suffers more from lack of communication as we have different interests.'

Jody DeHart has no doubts: 'I would say that our relationship has greatly improved. When we are at home, we hardly ever see each other. We both have successful careers, and could probably do quite well without our partner. But when you are alone on a boat, you really need the other person, get to appreciate the other's help and qualities. Without the other standing a watch, you wouldn't be able to sleep, which doesn't sound important until you've gone without it for 48 hours. We have spent many quality hours in the cockpit just talking. We make plans and discuss the future, which we would never get to do in our other busy life. Generally, our relationship has not changed much, as it was good and still is, but obviously we shared strong moments together and maybe the links are stronger. It is not the case on all boats, and we know couples that have been destroyed by this way of life. The minimum is to be really sure that both husband and wife do enjoy the sea and living on a boat. It sounds silly, but a lot of people leave without this condition being fulfilled.' This is certainly not the case of Judy and Bob Hall: 'We love sailing together and have a wonderful, close, loving relationship.'

Dorothy Walker was among those who had to get used to cruising life before fully enjoying it: 'As we already worked together for years we were used to spending 24 hours together – not that this meant that things on the boat were perfect. Far from it! For the first two years my lack of ability and fear of sailing itself did not help our relationship, but after the second year I feel we came through with a stronger relationship than ever.'

Lois and Don Babson had also worked together before going cruising: 'Our relationship is maybe a little better, but we had worked together in our business every day before sailing, so we pretty much have the same relationship now as we had then.'

Saundra Gray feels that 'our relationship is good because we have worked together to make it so. We find being together on the boat is the best time in our lives. We enjoy doing things together. We both enjoy the water and travel and share the same basic interests. There is a lot of give and take in a relationship and a marriage is a "work in progress".'

The crews of Distant Drum and Hornblower *(right to left): Duke and Betty Marx, Bob and Judy Hall and, in the back, Ray Trotta and Michael Frankel.*

One of the best examples in this respect is that of Germaine and Arthur Beiser: 'I can't remember when, in the last 50 years, we didn't spend long periods of time together on a boat. So I can't say what it did to our relationship.'

One woman who felt that their relationship had improved in some respects and suffered in others was Jackie Lee: 'We've never *not* been together ever since we met. We've always had jobs together and we always work better together. Luc is the brain and I am the faithful companion. We are very comfortable being just us two and the dog. Perhaps the only drawback that living on a boat really emphasizes is our totally opposite way of thinking about what and how things should be done, especially boat projects. Sometimes it makes doing a project agony and impossible for us to work together. The result is usually a good combination of our extremes, but it's not reached by co-operation, rather an exasperated giving in on both parts. But at the end of the day, we both agree that we are lucky to have each other and lucky to live this lifestyle.'

Glynn Beauchamp summed it all up: 'When we first went cruising we were in a relatively new relationship. So many people said this would certainly be a test, and it was. We went through very rough weather with rain constantly, winds from 30 to 70 knots, and seas up to 12 metres. Not pleasant. Neither of us had time to get scared, we were just too busy. However, on several occasions we would look at each other and grin and then one would say "we're doing this for fun, you know". This would invariably make us laugh, lighten the load, and set us back on track. We live together on board 24 hours a day, 7 days a week, and still love it. How many people get a new view to see every time they look out of a window?'

SUGGESTIONS

To round off the interview, I asked each woman if she had any specific advice or suggestions for other women who might contemplate setting off on the high seas. Apart from general advice, many women also gave tips from their own experience on ways of making life aboard more enjoyable. Several women suggested that you should have as many comforts as possible, such as a washing machine. One wife advised others to take along practical books on such subjects as preserving food and cooking with tropical ingredients. Several women stressed the importance of women having their own interests and hobbies, especially those that had a relevance to the sailing life, such as diving, shell collecting, painting, photography or amateur radio. Some women used the opportunity that cruising offered to pursue special interests, such as one woman who studied the history and political life of the countries she visited, while another enjoyed learning languages. Several women played musical instruments, and one had a special interest in astronomy – indeed, her boat was the only one on which star sights were taken regularly as part of the navigation routine.

The women taking part in the latest survey were asked to name the three items that would make their life more comfortable either on the present boat or on their ideal cruising yacht. Perhaps, not surprisingly, virtually all suggestions concerned comforts. It is an unequivocal signal to any man as to what their partners regard as essential, or at least desirable, in cruising life. The most quoted items were a large double cabin with en-suite shower and toilet (electrically operated in the case of Ann Harsh). Next was a washing machine, ideally with a dryer. Also high on the wish list were watermakers, good showers, and a generous supply of hot water. Plenty of electricity was also mentioned, although Anna Huggett stressed that she would prefer this to come from solar panels rather than a noisy generator. The galley came in for much attention, with a large oven and a decent cooker mentioned by several women – as was a microwave oven. One woman wanted to have an ice machine, while another regarded air-conditioning as a desirable feature in hot climates. E-mail as well as internet access were also mentioned, in addition to having one's own laptop computer that need not be shared with the skipper. Audio books were mentioned for night watches, and also, for those watches, a powerful, reliable autopilot. Not all women were concerned with creature comforts only, as one specified electric furling gear on both jib and mainsail as her priority, while another one would prefer all primary winches to be electric. Three women stated that their present boats were very comfortable and didn't really need any major improvements. However, Saundra Gray pointed out, 'our boat is about as comfortable as you can get. I think I would like to de-clutter some of the areas as we tend to save too many items, and that is something that makes keeping the boat neat and clean more difficult.'

Jackie Lee also looked at the practical side when she said, 'Materialistically, we have what we need. What I'd really like is to be finished with sanding projects, to have time for some fun projects, not just boat upkeep, and getting a daily massage for my aching bones.'

For Lilly Vedana, the dream is 'to have enough money, to be able to live without charter guests and, for me personally, to live six months on board and six months back home in New Zealand'. Paulette Vannier would also like to have 'a lot of money to travel everywhere inland, go to restaurants, and fly back to France whenever I want'.

None of the wishes seemed extravagant, perhaps with the exception of Lucy Misayat's wish list. She would like something 'impossible – like never having to be in more than force 6, always finding a peaceful anchorage with no noisy neighbours, jet-skis, or dragging anchors in the middle of the night, and having all the clothes on board never needing to be ironed'.

Advice to women/advice to men

Many women suggested to those who intend to go cruising that they should try to find out all they could beforehand. 'Read lots of cruising books before you leave to get an idea of what to expect,' was Linda Robson's advice, while several women suggested that it was a good idea to sail as crew on another boat to see what sailing offshore was all about. 'Charter for at least two weeks and make an offshore passage of several days' was the advice for both men and women contemplating a lengthy cruise. As one woman, who went cruising without any experience, stressed: 'It is often said that ignorance is bliss, but at sea ignorance causes fear.' So she advised women to learn some navigation skills before going offshore, take an interest in handling the sails, know how to use the engine, and how to dock the boat.

As cruising is so different to life ashore, many women pointed out that you had to approach it with a positive attitude of mind and not leave with too many preconceived ideas. Yet another suggestion was to live on board for a while before going anywhere, as most couples had never lived in such close proximity before. One particularly militant woman, who was strongly in favour of more female participation in sailing matters, stressed that, 'Above all, women must believe in themselves. It is the only way of counteracting male chauvinism at sea.' This view was shared by another woman, who stressed: 'Don't accept a passive role and believe that things are too difficult, but take an active interest in everything. There should be no difference between men and women on board a cruising boat.'

To round off the Sailing Women Survey, the 20 women were asked to give one piece of essential advice to any woman setting off on a long voyage, and similar advice to any man planning to leave on a voyage with his wife or partner. The most comprehensive advice came from Saundra Gray: 'First, know if you really want to go. Doing this for someone else will not work. If you do not want to go, you will end up feeling like a martyr – and martyrs are pretty hard to live with. Second, know enough about the management of the craft to enable you to take over if you have to. There is always the possibility of injury or illness, where you would have to assume responsibility. Finally, relax. Enjoy the gifts of each day and treasure being where you are. The major gift of a long voyage is time. Take time to get to know yourself and your partner better. Take time to read, to write, and to think without distraction. Enjoy the solitude.'

Saundra had obviously put a lot of thought into this subject, as had Jody DeHart: 'The most essential piece of advice I can give to any woman is to become one with the boat and your surroundings as soon as possible. Say a long prayer and throw away any fears. Trust the boat and your partner or don't leave. This is really fun, but you won't realize it if you're carrying all that baggage. Being on a boat is much harder than being on land. Therefore, everything on the boat must be nicer than you have at home. This is the year 2001. The technology is there, take it with you.'

Jackie Lee made the same point: 'Make sure it's something *you* want to do, don't do it just for your partner. If you do, participate and learn as much as you can.' Annelie Rollfing agrees: 'Try to look in your heart, and if you feel bad, cancel!' Lilly Vedana feels the same: 'Check it out first, either you like it or you don't.' Dorothy Walker was more specific: 'Believe you can do it, but be honest and say when you want off.'

Marilyn Morgan advises other women to 'be positive even when things are looking a bit grim'. Germaine Beiser agrees: 'It's important to remember that you and the others can get very tired or stressed on a voyage. Hold off on some of the unpleasant things you feel like saying until later, when everyone is rested.' Glynn Beauchamp stresses how important it is to be 'healthy, fit and maintain a sense of humour, which may not always be easy!'

Astrid Greiff feels that 'roles should be as equal as possible on board. But on board men like to fiddle around all the time so women should have plenty of hobbies and find ways to occupy themselves; try to interact with other women.' For this reason, Lois Babson's advice is 'Be involved with every aspect of the boat and the voyage.' When all is done, Silvana Masotti counsels women to 'Take along some good books and leave behind all worries.'

Judy Hall insists that 'one should only go with someone you would like to share non-stop time with. It will make all the difference in how enjoyable the entire adventure will be.' Nina Louhija gave the same advice to both men and women: 'Don't plan too far ahead, and prepare to change plans, points of view and decisions.'

Amanda Neal advises: 'Keep peace with yourself and be strong. Don't be afraid of change, accept your imperfections and don't dwell on your mistakes, live the moment, and do something silly every day.' Paulette Vannier insists that above all else a woman should 'learn to love the sea'.

The advice given to men was just as clear-cut. Judy Hall urges men to 'make sure you have a strong relationship and can share the highs and lows of this kind of lifestyle. If your partner is reluctant but willing, try to ensure that the first few months are sailed at times of good weather, with a minimum of high-risk experiences, until she is more certain of her own ability as a sailor. Be supportive and acknowledge her strengths and contribution to the trip.'

Astrid Greiff feels that men should bear in mind that 'women tend to "suffer" more on board because of the restricted room and lack of comfort. Try to make your partner's life as pleasant as possible, both in your relationship and in material comforts. Don't take anything for granted.'

Glynn Beauchamp stressed that, 'If your wife or partner is keen – do it. If not – think again. You are your own doctor, nurse, cook, comforter, mechanic, technician, and each other's companion. Before going anywhere, doing anything, talk to people who have done it. Read heaps of books and gather lots of information.'

Annelie Rollfing has some practical advice: 'Try your new life on board by chartering bare boat with your partner. Do it a few times and for at least two weeks each time.' Jody DeHart warns men not to 'treat the voyage like Cowes Week. This is not an endurance test. If you're going to get her to go, make it fun and make it her idea.'

Ernst Torp is given a warm welcome by a local character on making landfall in Barbados.

Anna Huggett urges men to 'make sure she is able to handle the boat in an emergency. If the man gets ill, she needs to be able to cope with him and also get the boat to port safely. We have met boats with women who leave everything except cleaning and cooking to their husbands. This is stupid and dangerous.'

Lois Babson, who mentioned her greatest fear to be the fear of the unknown, gave this advice: 'Try to overcome in your partner the female fear of the unknown. Keep your mate involved in where and when decision-making.'

Ann Harsh simply urges men to be patient with their partners, a theme reiterated by Dorothy Walker: 'Believe she can do it, but be patient and compassionate.' Lucy Misayat went further than that: 'Don't become the boss – remember it's a partnership.'

Jackie Lee gave the same kind of advice: 'Use positive reinforcement to draw on her talents, listen to what she needs, don't keep her stupid by doing everything yourself, or criticizing what she does.'

Marilyn Beauchamp warns 'Don't snap at her!' Germaine Beiser makes the same point: 'Don't scream or shout while making a manoeuvre, no matter how stupidly you think she performed. Talk about it later. There's a reason why the "Don't Shout At Me" T-shirts are so popular.' Lilly Vedana fully agrees: 'Don't be too hard on her – she's not a bloke. You wouldn't be the first one who finished the voyage as a singlehander!'

Paulette Vannier takes a wider view: 'Be sure she loves the sea and not only you.'

Amanda Neal stressed that 'when cruising you will need to be your partner's best friend. Communication is the key; you need to be aware and open to her feelings. I've recently met a couple whose wife would not go cruising until her husband went to counselling and learnt to be a better communicator. All our problems occur when we don't voice our feelings, and they build up quickly if left unattended.'

Saundra Gray reminds men that 'this is not just your trip on which she is going. This is her trip also. She is giving up as much of her life as you are giving of yours. It can be a tremendously enriching experience for a couple if they respect each other and realize that it is a team effort. Patience and respect go a long way to smooth any rough spots for both a woman and a man. Go for the dream, your attitude will go a long way to making it succeed. Remember, though, that "Attitude is the difference between ordeal and adventure".'

Conclusions

Nowadays women are playing a much more active role in sailing, as many cruising boats are crewed by couples, daughters sail with fathers, mothers with sons, as well as with friends and partners. From speaking to many of these women, it is evident that some consider it a priority for certain features to be incorporated in their boats to suit their requirements, whether at the building stage of a new boat, or by modifying the present boat. Gwenda has played an active role in choosing and equipping all our boats, and many of the features of our latest *Aventura* were suggested by her.

The first priority on any boat is the ease of handling, such as installing winches powerful enough for the sails to be handled by female muscle, or to winch the man up the mast if necessary. On *Aventura III*, an electric winch has made all the difference as Gwenda is now able to quickly furl in the jib or staysail on her own. The difference in physical size and strength between male and female cannot be ignored, but women have already proved that they can sail singlehanded around the world or participate in major ocean races, so there is no reason why a family cruising boat should not be able to be handled by a woman. It is also a matter of safety for all the crew. As Marcia Davock pointed out, 'In certain situations, women have a capacity for endurance greater than men.'

A divided sail plan with smaller sails, such as a cutter, might be more suitable for family cruising than expecting a woman to be able to handle the large sails on a tall-masted sloop. Furling gear is essential for ease of handling, as is any other aid that can help the 'weaker sex'. Even if the woman does not normally plan to handle the sails, she may have to do this in an emergency. Therefore an electric anchor winch is another piece of equipment much favoured by women. From the surveys it would appear that on many boats the women spend as much if not more time at the helm than men. For cruising couples, the most sensible procedure when entering or leaving a port is for the woman to be at the helm, freeing the stronger male to jump around throwing lines, fending off, dealing with the anchor, or whatever else needs doing. It not only makes sense, but, as Susan Hiscock pointed out, it is also more efficient. Therefore it is worth paying attention to the steering position and the visibility from it. It is surprising how many boats have been apparently designed with tall men in mind, where it is difficult for a smaller woman to have an unrestricted view over the cabin top towards the bow.

Although women participate more actively in sailing, on most boats the galley remains very much their domain. For this reason the galley should come in for critical attention. It is not necessarily an advantage for it to be too spacious; often, the more compact the better. However, several women emphasized how important it was not to get stuck in the galley, and that much more enjoyment could be got out of the cruising life by taking more interest in sailing the boat and navigation. As one of them advised, 'Don't exchange one kitchen for another, but share in all the boat work. You will get more out of cruising that way.'

Moving up on deck, the various aspects of safety should be considered, especially if planning to sail with children. Points to look for are sufficiently wide sidedecks, an absence of things to trip over, grab rails on the coachroof, sturdy pulpits, and strong lifelines. If the boat has a high freeboard, it might be difficult for a smaller woman to get on and off from a dinghy, and quite dangerous if carrying or helping a small child. A permanently installed ladder on the stern or a stern platform are both features that make boarding safer. A stern platform is also useful for swimming from, and can be a safety factor for anyone falling overboard, making it easier to get back on board.

Having been interested for many years in the level of female participation in sailing, and speaking to so many women involved in cruising, has made me realize just how much they have contributed to many outstanding voyages. However, just as in life ashore, in order for their contribution to be recognized, women have to be more assertive, make their voices heard, and not accept being cast in a secondary role. Admittedly, they have to overcome a certain amount of prejudice in what is still a male-dominated world, both ashore and afloat.

13

What Can Go Wrong?
MEDICAL EMERGENCIES AND
EQUIPMENT FAILURES

"It doesn't matter how stupid you are as long as you're lucky."
ROMANIAN PROVERB

Like most sailors, I am rather superstitious, and so it was quite a surprise to notice that this chapter, which I originally intended to call 'The Bad News', has ended up – by sheer chance – as Chapter 13. It is a number that I do not like at all, and try to avoid whenever possible. Fridays are just as bad, and if anything decides to break on my boat it is almost always on a Friday. However, I usually manage to get out of most sticky situations, thus proving the wisdom of the above saying from my native land, which has guided me all my life.

During a long ocean passage neither repair facilities nor rescue services are near at hand, therefore a crew must be prepared and able to deal with any emergency. This chapter will therefore concentrate not only on equipment failure and breakages, but also on that most important piece of equipment, the human machine. The best words of wisdom on this topic I received from a doctor who sailed in one of my rallies. Dr Steenstra remarked that before going offshore, many skippers endeavour to learn everything they can about the working of the various pieces of equipment on board and how to repair them, but often neglect to find out about their most important piece of machinery, which is their own body. When something goes wrong, often they do not know what to do, basically because they have little idea how the human machine functions.

The situation in reality is not quite that bad, as in an earlier survey of 100 boats, on half the boats at least one person had taken a first aid course. On several boats one member of the crew had the necessary knowledge from their profession in the medical field, whether as doctor, nurse, dentist or pharmacist. As a result, virtually all the medical emergencies that occurred on the high seas were resolved successfully. There is no doubt that life at sea is healthier than sitting behind a desk, prey to all the viruses that waft along the office heating or air-conditioning ducts. While infectious diseases might be rare on sailing boats, and the most common problems are usually of an accidental nature, such as knocks, gashes or broken bones, there are several less obvious health dangers lurking even in beautiful tropical anchorages, waiting to strike the unwary sailor. Information about which precautions, vaccinations and immunizations are required for various parts of the world are listed in the latest edition of my *World Cruising Handbook*.

Especially when sailing to more out-of-the-way places, it is wise to check what immunizations may be required, such as yellow fever for some countries in South America. Failure to have the required certificate can result in having to have the immunization on the spot. Vaccinations should be kept up to date against polio and typhoid fever when travelling outside of Europe, North America, Australia or New Zealand. Scrupulous care should also be taken over food, drink and hygiene outside of these areas to avoid not only the risk of polio or typhoid, but also hepatitis. In any part of the world, tetanus is a risk from a wound or open injury and a booster vaccination should be had every five years to protect against this. Not only to avoid tetanus, but as a general precaution against infection, especially in tropical areas, all scratches and cuts, however small, should be washed and disinfected thoroughly, for they can become infected at lightning speed in warm moist conditions. Many of those sailing for longer periods in tropical waters have had problems with infected cuts and sores, leading sometimes to tropical ulcers. The infection is usually due to the staphylococcus bacteria, which is very difficult to eradicate once it is in the bloodstream, necessitating internal antibiotic treatment.

Seasickness

Seasickness can be an ongoing problem that affects both the physical and mental state, and a surprisingly high number of voyagers suffer from it to a lesser or greater extent, the proportion of women being higher apparently than men. Over one-third of the boats in an earlier survey had at least one person suffering from seasickness among the crew. In the majority of cases, the worst bouts of seasickness occurred during the first days at sea after a long spell in port. Several children also complained of it, although as they did not have to play a part in the sailing of the boat, they usually just lay down until they felt better. Most of those suffering only occasionally from seasickness took no drugs and had obviously learnt to live with this disability.

The matter was looked at again during one of the ARC surveys, although the ocean conditions prevailing during the time when the crews were interviewed made their transatlantic crossing rather different from most years, in that many people reported an uncomfortable cross swell. In spite of this, it was again noticeable that most people took a very relaxed attitude to the problem of seasickness, not being too bothered if they were actually sick. As the passage started after everyone had done some sailing, most people who suffered from seasickness had come to terms with their condition. The most common problem was a queasiness at the beginning of the passage until people found their sea legs. Most of those who were prone to seasickness prepared for this by taking some medication before leaving port.

Scopolamine patches and Stugeron were the two most popular medications used, although several people complained that Stugeron made them drowsy. A severe bout of seasickness struck one strapping young man taking part in the ARC. He was so sick that he was on the verge of going into a coma, and his concerned skipper, worried that the young man's life might be at risk if he continued the voyage, made a detour to the Cape Verde Islands from where the sick crew returned home by air. In a similar situation, a crew of *Heaven Can Wait* had to be evacuated in ARC 2001 when prolonged seasickness resulted in colic and kidney stone problems due to severe dehydration.

Various remedies were tried out, and one person who suffered from very severe seasickness took tranquillizers as well as other medication in order to go to sleep. Several people, although admitting that they got queasy from time to time, stated that this did not interfere with their sailing. One diabetic sailor pointed out that diabetics have to be particularly careful not to vomit, as this can upset the balance of insulin in the body, but as far as she was concerned this condition was no reason to prevent her from sailing. Useful advice came from a woman who had become pregnant after unknowingly disgorging her daily contraceptive pills in bouts of seasickness.

Medical emergencies

The list of medical emergencies that have been recounted to me during the various surveys is so long and varied that it could fill a whole book. Fortunately, most of them were not serious and were dealt with quickly and efficiently with the means available on board. In this chapter I have included only examples of some relevance to others. Medical emergencies were often dealt with very skilfully in some of the round the world rallies. In the Expo'98 rally, a Finnish cameraman severed his thumb while freeing a spinnaker sheet during the Atlantic crossing. The skipper obtained professional advice by satellite phone as to what to do and, although not having any medical knowledge, proceeded to stitch back the loose thumb. A rendezvous was then arranged with a nearby tanker, which took the injured crew towards Antigua from where a helicopter lifted him from the tanker and transferred him to a hospital in Puerto Rico. The initial intervention on board had been so skilful that the surgeon managed to save the thumb.

A much more serious emergency occurred in the Millennium Odyssey. While scuba diving off the Sudanese coast in the Red Sea, Javier Visiers, the skipper of *Antaviana*, had to surface too quickly and had no time to decompress properly. Affected by a severe case of decompression sickness, he was close to losing his life unless he could be promptly evacuated to a shore facility with a decompression chamber. Victor Knutzen, a medical doctor and the owner of *Pilar G*, the largest yacht in the fleet, gave Javier emergency treatment, took him on board, and proceeded at full speed towards Jeddah in Saudi Arabia. There, Javier was treated at the local hospital, which was equipped for diving accidents, and was saved.

Two other serious injuries sustained by participants in the Millennium Odyssey involved outboard engines, and both could have had fatal consequences. While swimming close to his *Taratoo* in the anchorage off Mustique, in the Eastern Caribbean, Fabio Colapinto was run down by a local fishing boat. Fabio was badly cut by the propeller and was rushed to the hospital in Martinique for treatment. He fully recovered. While in the Maldives, a young crew who sailed on *Stampede* fell overboard from the dinghy and sustained severe cuts from the propeller. He had to be hospitalized for a while and rejoined the yacht in the Red Sea.

The constant rolling, and the occasionally rough sailing conditions, during the Atlantic crossing caused several injuries, especially among sailors not used to a long ocean passage, although the number of serious emergencies was relatively small. Even so, some of the injuries could well have been avoided with a little more care. Ake Sundström of *Kalea II* was extremely fortunate in that his accident happened on arrival in Barbados. Trying to free a jammed hatch with a knife, the blade broke off and punctured his eye. He was rushed to the local hospital with a collapsed eyeball. Luckily there happened to be a visiting eye surgeon present, who operated immediately and saved his eye. I was extremely pleased to meet Ake in Bermuda a few years later and to see that his eye had completely healed. His accident reminded me of a similar eye injury sustained by a sailor on a boat moored near ours in Whangarei. He was taken to the casualty department of the local hospital where the doctor took him by surprise when he exclaimed, 'You must be off one of the yachts in the harbour.' 'Yes,' replied our neighbour, 'but how did you know?' 'Because only yachties come to us with stupid accidents like this,' said the surgeon and proceeded to patch him up.

There is undoubtedly a lesson to be learnt from the remark made by this Kiwi doctor, and looking at the various injuries that have occurred among rally participants, there is no doubt that many were caused by carelessness. At the top of the list are injuries caused by booms, usually knocks to the head. It has been calculated that a yacht rolls about 100,000 times during the average Atlantic crossing, so it may not be so surprising that having missed it on 99,999 occasions, one of the crew will eventually rear his head at the wrong moment and put it on a collision course with the swinging boom. More culpable was the oversight of one skipper who managed to avoid this menace throughout the crossing, but knocked himself out cold when he stood up to his full height in the cockpit shortly after arriving in port, having forgotten that the boom was now resting low over the cockpit.

Undoubtedly the simplest way to avoid the menace of a swinging boom is to use a preventer, and from the number of incidents reported it is amazing how many people don't actually use one. A quick way of setting a preventer is to tie a line to the outer end of the boom, take the line all the way forward, through a block and back to the cockpit, from where it can be easily handled during a controlled gybe. A good idea is to have a preventer, preferably made of wire, permanently attached to the outer end of the boom, its forward end being made fast to the underside of the boom near the gooseneck fitting when not in use. This means that even when running with the mainsheet fully paid out, the preventer can be handled in safety, as a line can be attached to its free end without having to lean overboard. The line is then taken forward, where it can be cleated, or led back to the cockpit through a block. Before a gybe, the line is disengaged from the preventer and another one is set up on the other side. On *Aventura III* a proper boom break controls the movement of the boom in a gybe and, as a precaution, is always set up – not just when running, but even when reaching.

The seriousness of a mid-ocean emergency that could not be dealt with by the crew alone was highlighted by the skipper of an ARC boat who suffered from Crohn's disease. This condition affects the intestines, and although the man had been suffering from it for several years, he decided to risk an Atlantic crossing as his condition had been stable for a long time. Halfway across the Atlantic, the skipper was laid low with an acute crisis with regard to his health. As the boat did not have any long range communication system and only a VHF radio, other ARC boats were asked to close with the distressed vessel and relay advice obtained by radio from a specialist in England. Another yacht in the ARC, the 51-foot *Annie B*, with two surgeons on board, also made haste to assist the stricken skipper, although it was becoming increasingly clear that unless the man could be evacuated ashore he might lose his life. A rendezvous was therefore arranged with a passing ship and the crew made all preparations to transfer the sick man. Sea conditions were very rough, making such a transfer very risky, so the skipper insisted he remain with his yacht. His condition was carefully monitored for the remainder of the crossing and he arrived safely in St Lucia.

That year saw several medical emergencies during the ARC, and the two surgeons on *Annie B*, Barry Esrig and Harold Sherman, had to give so much advice to other participants over the radio that on arrival in St Lucia their yacht sported a huge banner with the letters MASH on its side: Mid-Atlantic Sailors Hospital. It is always good if one can also see the funny side of things.

Burns are another common accident, and the most serious occurred in the Millennium Odyssey on *Que Sera Sera* when a friend who had joined the boat as crew poured boiling hot coffee over herself. She sustained second degree burns to her neck and shoulder and, after excellent emergency treatment in northern Spain, had to return to the USA. In one of the early ARCs one crew also scalded himself with boiling water, which caused severe second degree burns to his chest. Fortunately, he had special burn ointment available, but even so the wound took a very long time to heal and the skin had not fully regenerated one year later.

First aid

The fact that virtually all the emergencies described above were treated on board shows the importance of carrying a well-stocked medicine chest and also of having at least some basic knowledge of first aid. In one of the earlier surveys it was found that on all boats there was a handbook giving instructions on the treatment of injuries and other kinds of medical emergencies. On 40 per cent of the boats the medicine chest was described as comprehensive, on 54 per cent as adequate, and only six skippers admitted that they only had the minimum. Obviously for ocean voyaging the medicine chest should contain a wider variety of medicines than for coastal cruising. People with ongoing medical conditions must make sure that they carry enough supplies of their regular treatment or other drugs that they might require. Complete first aid boxes can be bought from pharmacies, but it is easy to make up your own. A basic first aid kit should include the following:

- Cotton wool and sterile gauze.
- Waterproof adhesive dressings in various sizes.
- Butterfly sutures, Steristrips or plasters that pull the edges of a cut together.

- Sticking plaster, bandages and crepe bandages for sprains.
- Special, non-stick sterile dressings for burns.
- Small scissors, tweezers, safety pins.
- Clinical thermometer.
- Disposable needles and syringes (5 ml is the most useful size).
- Sterile needles with sutures for stitching.
- Skin disinfectant, eg cetrimide, chlorhexidine or iodine tincture.

It is advisable to carry disposable syringes and needles in case you need to have an injection in countries that do not use disposables, as the risk of a serious infection, hepatitis or AIDS from improperly sterilized or shared needles and syringes is considerable.

Medicine chest

Besides a first aid kit, any boat leaving on a long voyage to areas where medical supplies are not available should carry a well-stocked medicine chest. Dr Peter Noble, who advised me on the composition of the medicine chest on *Aventura III*, has compiled a recommended list of essential medicines (Appendix 3).

Regulations regarding drugs vary enormously from country to country and some customs officials confiscate certain drugs, such as strong painkillers like morphine. In several countries, however, the laws are more relaxed, and many drugs that normally are only available on prescription, such as antibiotics, can be bought over the counter. Many skippers use this opportunity to stock up their medicine chest or replace drugs that have passed their expiry date. Some doctors among the skippers interviewed stressed the importance of renewing medicines regularly, especially antibiotics, as their effectiveness decreases with age and storage in tropical conditions. Nevertheless, most antibiotics can still be used after the expiry date, although the dosage might have to be increased. The danger of using antibiotics without proper advice was highlighted by the case of a skipper who was taken severely ill while the boat was anchored near a remote island off the coast of Mexico. His symptoms were described over the amateur radio, and he was advised to take the antibiotic tetracycline. In spite of this, he got steadily worse and finally his wife decided to sail the boat to the mainland on her own, where a doctor diagnosed hepatitis and prescribed the proper treatment. It turned out they had been given the wrong advice, as the strong antibiotic tetracycline should not be used where liver or kidney ailments are suspected.

Medicine may be life saving in an emergency, but may also do harm if used inappropriately, as the above example shows. All medicines should be fully labelled and kept in their original containers. Each preparation has two names: a trade name and a generic name. For instance, Stugeron is the trade name of cinnarizine, which is its generic name. It is essential that the medicine is labelled with both names, as well as the dose. Trade names differ from country to country, and a foreign doctor may not be able to advise on the use of your own medicines if the generic name is not known. Medicines usually carry an expiry date, and it is recommended that you buy medicines with as long an expiry date as possible. Manufacturers usually provide an explanatory leaflet for each product, which explains the indications for use and lists adverse effects. Sometimes there is a leaflet for patients and a more technical leaflet for professionals, so if possible you should try to obtain both. Except in an emergency, prescription medicine should only be used on medical advice, which may be obtained over the radio, satellite telephone or Inmarsat C. Excellent information is available on the internet too. It is also useful to carry a pharmacopoeia for reference.

Families sailing with children should take specific children's remedies. In an emergency, it may be possible to use adult medication for children if the tablets or capsule are divided carefully with a sharp knife so that the reduced children's dose, as listed in the pharmacopoeia, can be administered. It is often possible to improvise. Cotton and linen clothing and sheets can be cut up to make bandages and be sterilized by boiling for five minutes. Sail battens make good splints.

When setting up the medicine chest for a longer cruise, it is advisable to consult your own doctor, who is the best person to give advice on what to take. Most doctors will also prescribe certain drugs, which are on the restricted list, once the reason has been explained. Glynn Beauchamp advised anyone setting off on a cruise to 'talk to your own doctor, nurse and pharmacist, and ask them to advise you on how to prepare for the voyage and what medicines to have on board. We did and it worked very well. We also did a first aid training course and got advice on how to use scalpels, sutures and syringes should the need arise.'

Equipment breakages

The various surveys have brought to light a wide variety of equipment failure. In the majority of cases, the consequences were not serious and the crew managed to effect temporary repairs at sea. Fortunately, only a small number of boats suffered the loss of their mast, which is one of the most traumatic experiences for any sailor. In all of these cases, the mast was lost because of rigging failure. It is comforting to know that the number of offshore cruising boats that lose their masts is extremely small and I suspect proportionately less than it used to be, given the increase in the number of yachts. From the wide range of breakages that have been reported in the surveys, I have selected some of the more significant examples.

CROSSING THE ATLANTIC

Although there are equipment breakages in every ARC, in recent years these have become less frequent, which can only mean that boats are better built, better equipped, but also that their owners are better prepared. Approximately 1,800 boats sailed in the 13 ARCs that I was directly involved with and, on average, breakages were reported on some 10 per cent of them. Basically, the breakages fell into two categories: those that occurred before the ARC and those that happened during the Atlantic crossing. Most of the former were dealt with in Las Palmas, and the excellent repair facilities available there are a major reason why after all these years the ARC continues to start from there. Many of the breakages reported

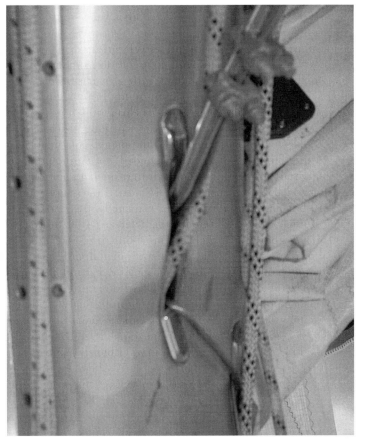

This new boat completed the Atlantic crossing with serious damage to the mast caused by compression.

in Las Palmas were on new boats, some of whose owners had only taken delivery during the preceding months and the trip to the Canaries was their first offshore voyage. Not surprisingly, some faults did show up during those first 1,500 miles. One observation that I made during these years is that major problems were rarely reported on standard production boats coming from a high-output manufacturer, but more likely on boats built by small yards, very often one-offs, which usually cost more than their production counterpart. The standard of after-sales service varies enormously and does not necessarily depend on the price of the yacht or the name and reputation of the builder. Some boatbuilders simply could not care less, even if fundamental things go wrong on a newly delivered boat, and I witnessed many a distressed owner who was incapable of getting any help from a builder or equipment manufacturer for what was very obviously the builder's or manufacturer's fault. In contrast, others will do everything to help, such as sending technicians to Las Palmas to provide after-sales service to their yachts.

The long Atlantic crossing often results in all kinds of breakages and the relatively high rate of gear failure reported in the various ARC surveys, covering a period of only three or four weeks, cannot be described as routine failures. Most of them appear to be caused by tougher than normal sailing conditions, the constant rolling motion in blustery trade winds, showing up weaknesses in equipment that had not been put to such a test before. Also, some breakages were caused by the crews pushing their boats faster due to the competitive element of the rally. The most frequent breakages were those of boom and mast fittings, some of which were not strong enough to stand up to the tough conditions encountered on an ocean crossing. The mainsheet attachment on the boom or the vang attachment broke on several boats and the skippers blamed the weakness of the gear, which in some cases had only been spot-welded onto the boom. Many breakages occurred to spinnaker poles, which were used extensively for poling out genoas, cruising chutes, as well as spinnakers. The constant movement caused end fittings, tracks or mast attachments to break. Again, it was the weakness of the fittings that received the blame, although in some cases the skippers thought the breakage might have been avoided if the pole had been fixed more firmly, with less play at its outer end. Some of the poles themselves were not strong enough, and on two boats telescopic poles collapsed and could not be pulled out again. One of these skippers pointed out that 'maximum force is exerted on a telescopic pole when it is fully extended, yet this is also the state in which the pole is weakest, so it is not surprising that problems occur'.

Spinnaker and whisker poles broke for various reasons, but usually because they were not strong enough for the job they were meant for. Damage to spinnaker poles is usually to the end fittings, due mainly to misuse. In the case of carbon fibre poles, the breakages that occurred were due to side impact, which caused the pole to break clean while its aluminium counterpart might have ended up with a dent or slight bend. Among the dozen or so poles lost during one ARC, at least three were actually dropped overboard. Overall, I got the impression that some of the breakages could have been avoided if the boats had been sailed less hard, and in fact some skippers agreed that they were at least partly to blame for the breakages. The most common breakage in the ARC is that of booms. Although unintentional gybes could be blamed for some of those breakages, many standard booms were obviously not strong enough for the kind of stress they were subjected to during a long ocean passage. The use of preventers would have avoided some of the breakages, and several skippers admitted that most gybes occurred when the boat was steered by the autopilot or windvane.

Long downwind runs also took their toll on halyards and rigging. One halyard broke when the swivel snapped at the masthead while sailing with the cruising chute. On inspection it was discovered that the stainless steel swivel had sheared because of the porosity of the metal. Sub-standard stainless steel fittings could have easily resulted in several boats losing their masts, if it had not been for the crew's vigilance or sheer good luck. In one case the forestay swaged terminal failed at the masthead, the mast being held up only by the jib halyard. As a repair could not be made at sea, a spare halyard was used to replace the forestay. Equally fortunate not to lose the mast was the owner of a boat where one alert crew noticed a wide crack in the connecting piece between the furling gear and the stemhead fitting. An emergency forestay had to be rigged, which necessitated a perilous climb to the top of the swinging mast.

Although the number of masts lost is very small, most of those that occurred were caused by failed terminals. One such failure was blamed on a disintegrating antenna insulator that led to the backstay being lost and, with it, the mast itself. The yacht was being delivered to St Lucia by a very experienced sailor, Alessandro

Mosconi, who had skippered the winning yacht in the first round the world rally. He not only managed to set up a very workable jury rig, but continued to cover in excess of 100 miles per day – and even overtook some boats that were sailing with their masts up!

Several boats completed the Atlantic crossing with damaged masts, and it was almost a miracle that they did not lose their spar altogether. In some instances the fault was caused by compression, and the damage was probably due to poor quality as in all instances the boats were new and the masts were only a few months old.

Steering gear failure is almost as common as rigging failure, also brought on by long downwind runs in which rudders are working hard all the time. On one boat the steering cables broke twice, while on another the entire steering gear was wrenched off its anchoring points because the builders had not provided an adequate backing plate for the bolts holding down the gear. In all these instances the crew managed to replace the cable with spares carried on board while the boat was steered with an emergency tiller. Possibly just as bad as losing your mast is losing the rudder, and some instances of unexplained rudder losses spring to mind. In one such instance the rudder fell off when the 100 mm rudderstock sheared, possibly as a result of a collision with a submerged object, although the crew had not noticed hitting anything. Over the years, four ARC boats that had lost their rudders managed to make it safely to St Lucia by steering with a jury arrangement.

As a result of the proliferation of furling gear, damage to sails is much less frequent than in the past. Some damage during the Atlantic crossing is caused by chafe, but the more serious damage occurs during tropical squalls. Both are of course avoidable, and impending squalls are quite easy to detect by looking regularly into

An ingenious jury rig, made easier by having two spinnaker poles on board, helped this boat complete its Atlantic crossing.

the direction of the wind for the telltale black line under an approaching cloud, which is visible even on dark nights. Several ARC boats blew out sails or tore them badly, although in most cases the skippers put this down to the age of the sails or to their own negligence in not having paid enough attention to chafe. Very often, older sails parted along the seams when stitches gave way as a result of continuous exposure to ultraviolet light, the sails not being protected by a UV guard. Some skippers suggested that self-adhesive patches are useful not only to repair a torn sail, but also to strengthen older sails or to protect vulnerable areas from chafe.

Chafe and the prolonged use of spinnakers and chutes caused all kinds of failures to halyards, blocks and swivels, and on several occasions the only solution was to send somebody to the top of the mast to make the necessary repair or to replace the broken halyard. From their comments, it was obvious that many skippers had not been prepared for the effect of several weeks of rolling. Their equipment was not prepared for it either, as many mast and pole fittings could not take the strain of the continuous rolling and broke. Chafe, particularly on halyards, was repeatedly described as a main cause for concern. Sometimes sail problems can be compounded, as in ARC 2001 when one boat ripped a spinnaker that fell in the water, the guy and sheet getting wrapped around the propeller. In the dark, the skipper had to be lowered over the side to clear the lines, after which the crew had to get up the mast to retrieve the spinnaker halyard.

Furling gear breakages were rarely reported, but when they were it was usually due to too much strain being put on the gear, often by an electric winch. Broken booms, apart from the eventual cost of the repair or replacement, were not a serious problem and some improvisation saw the boat safely across. Rigging failures were not too common, but when they occur they can have serious consequences. Most failures are at the terminals and were usually caused by the rigger not having made proper allowance for the terminal to have both fore-and-aft, as well as lateral, movement. On several occasions a vigilant crew had detected a broken strand and, by taking adequate measures, had most probably avoided losing the mast.

Although there were a few emergencies that required outside help, most breakages were fixed with the means available, the ARC skippers showing a great knack for improvisation. It is a talent that offshore sailors must possess if they are to survive the challenge of the sea. Several instances gained my admiration for their ingenuity, like that of one skipper who tried to find a way to charge his batteries after the main engine had failed to start. First he took the alternator off the engine and tried to turn it with a hand drill. When this failed, he tried to turn it using the back wheel of a bicycle by pedalling furiously sitting astride the bike. When this also failed, he attached the alternator with a spare fan belt to the flywheel of his outboard engine, which was mounted on a bracket. To cool the outboard engine, the drive unit was immersed in a water container. Meanwhile he had to hold the alternator in a sling made from plastic shopping bags to protect his hands from the heat generated. The exercise was exhausting, but succeeded – and the batteries received enough charge to start the main engine.

In the field of electronics the most common failure was to autopilots, which might cause some inconvenience but was far from being life threatening. Ad hoc repairs are usually impossible, so the remedies are limited: either to carry a spare, take on a larger crew or, probably the best, fit a wind-operated self-steering gear as well. Most autopilot failures were caused by the gears being undersized for the work they were expected to do, the less powerful autopilots being unable to cope with continuous use in strong trade wind conditions.

Both before and during the ARC the most frustrating failures were attributed to generators, which was also the case in the round the world rallies. In many cases the problems were caused by poor installation. Various generator problems were reported in ARC 2001, potentially the most dangerous being the one on the yacht *Fruity Fruits*. One week into the crossing, the seawater inlet pipe split, filling the bilge with water. Fortunately, the boat had a bilge alarm and the crew were alerted. After the broken pipe was repaired, the generator caught fire, but this emergency was also dealt with promptly.

Diesel engines also broke down, and in many cases it was the crew's own fault. Every year boats arrive at the finish line in St Lucia with the engine out of action, usually because of flat batteries, so they have to be towed into the marina. In almost all cases the reason was simple: as there was no separate dedicated engine starting battery (which should be standard), the batteries were completely drained and could not start the engine when needed. This is another argument in favour of having other means of charging the batteries. Occasionally the refusal of the engine to start was caused by dirty fuel, as sediment from the bottom of the tanks was churned up by the constant rolling and clogged up the fuel filter or, worse, blocked the fuel supply line. More serious engine breakages were caused by water finding its way into the engine, usually through the exhaust. A proper installation should have prevented following breaking waves making their way into the engine. Two recent incidents involved brand-new boats. On one the engine wiring harness caught fire, while on the other the starter motor failed just one day into the crossing. In both cases, as the boats had no other means of charging the batteries, they were left without electricity and any means of propulsion.

It must be stressed that the above examples are only given as an example of what can go wrong during an Atlantic crossing, and that over 90 per cent of boats that cross with the ARC do not report serious breakages or emergencies of any kind. As the skipper of *Astridos* wrote on the emergency report that every skipper must hand in on completion of the ARC: 'main halyard snapped; wind self-steering bolts loosened; spinnaker pole badly bent at inward end. All repairs carried out successfully in mid-ocean. Nothing abnormal for a cruising schedule.' A longer list of problems were reported by the skipper of *El Syd* in ARC 2001. On day one their steering broke. On day two the boom broke off at the gooseneck and a jury rig had to be set up for the rest of the crossing. The temporary repair on the steering went again on day three, and several more times afterwards. Then the instruments went down, followed by a broken spinnaker halyard. There were also crew injuries including a cracked rib, a broken toe and a head injury. In spite of all that, the crew arrived in St Lucia in good spirits. Skipper Ian McKinney's laconic comment summed it all up: 'It was tough!' Or, as Mark Twain may have put it, 'the reports concerning my death were slightly exaggerated'.

Most Atlantic crossings are generally lacking in real drama, although – as with everything in life – a dose of good luck also helps, because even if nothing breaks you can still be just as unlucky, as happened to the crew of the Luxembourg yacht *Jason*, who were caught in mid-Atlantic in a large fishing net. It took the crew a considerable time and effort to free themselves and continue their passage to St Lucia. It was ultimately also good luck that saved the crew of the French yacht *Cap d'Ambré*, who were crossing the Atlantic bound for Martinique at the same time as the ARC. Having collided with an unidentified object, the boat was taking on water and slowly sinking. Fortunately, just as the young couple were on the point of taking to the liferaft, *Free Spirit of Herm*, sailing in the ARC, caught up and lifted them off their sinking boat. In spite of having lost their boat, they felt lucky not to have lost their lives as well.

Over the years there have been several man overboard emergencies in the ARC, none with fatal consequences. The most recent occurred in 2000 and did not actually involve an ARC participant, for the Norwegian 33-foot racing yacht *Jaegermeister* had been rejected by the organizers on safety grounds. Undeterred, the crew left at the same time as the ARC. During a manoeuvre, skipper Petter Noreng fell overboard and, as his crew could not locate him, they put out a Mayday on the radio. Several ARC boats responded and spent the next 24 hours searching the ocean. Eventually, just as the operation was going to be called off, the Norwegian couple on *Hildring* spotted the man and saved him. He recounted that several boats had passed within a short distance, but the crew could not see him because of the high swell. What kept him afloat was his lifejacket, which fortunately he was wearing when he fell overboard.

Also saved at the very last moment, just before nightfall, was the owner of a charter boat sailing in the ARC with guests on board, who fell off the stern platform while cleaning an engine filter. The skipper could not turn the boat around because they were sailing with twin jibs at the time, so the poles had to be taken in first. Nor could the engine be started, as it was out of action and was being serviced when the man went overboard. To make matters worse, the steering wheel had been taken off as it was making an irritating clonking noise and the boat was steered by the autopilot. While a crew kept an eye on the man in the water, the others managed to raise the mainsail and install the wheel, although while doing the latter the locating key was lost overboard, so the only way to steer was to keep the wheel pressed hard against the shaft. In spite of all this, the boat eventually turned around, tacked upwind to the man, and fished him out of the ocean.

ROUND THE WORLD RALLIES

Approximately 200 boats took part in the five round the world rallies that I organized between 1991 and 2000 and, looking at the emergencies that occurred in those rallies, what becomes immediately obvious is just how safe sailing around the world has become. One single boat was lost during those rallies, two boats were dismasted, and the single most serious incident was the loss of one life in the Europa 92 round the world rally. While sailing from Galapagos to Marquesas at night and under spinnaker, the Finnish yacht *Cacadu* was caught by a squall. During an uncontrolled gybe, 26-year-old Panu Harjula was knocked overboard by the boom. Eleven other yachts sailing in the rally turned around and joined the search, but the missing man was never found.

The only boat lost, also in that first round the world rally, was the Hungarian *Jolly Joker*. One dark night, as the fleet was sailing through the Torres Straits, the boat strayed off course and the crew were unable to avoid hitting a reef. The situation was undoubtedly exacerbated by the fact that the skipper was not on board for this leg and the crew were probably not experienced enough to navigate through such a difficult area.

No other lives or boats were lost in any of the subsequent rallies, although there were a few close calls – such as the grounding of the Austrian *Amadé* on a reef in Tonga. Fortunately, the well-built aluminium yacht survived the ordeal and sustained only superficial damage to its hull and rudder, and was able to continue its voyage after emergency repairs in Fiji. During the Millennium Odyssey, *Taratoo* grounded on a coral head in Fiji, but the aluminium-hulled yacht only sustained damage to the hydraulic ram and rudder, which were repaired in Australia. Another grounding without serious consequences was of the Canadian *W.E. Penny* in the Amazon estuary during the Expo'98 rally. There were three incidents during the Millennium Odyssey involving yachts that had sailed the southern route to the Antarctic Peninsula. *Risque* suffered damage to its rudder, and *Futuro* to its keel, when they ran aground in uncharted waters, but potentially the most grave incident involved *Vegewind*, which was caught by a change of wind on a lee shore. Had it not been for the superhuman efforts of the crew, the yacht could have been lost as it was being pushed by the ice onto a rocky shore.

Collisions with whales were also reported, such as the ones involving *Allegra B* and *Risque*. The Australian *Foxy Lady*, also sailing in the Millennium Odyssey, collided with a large whale off Dominica. The fibreglass rudder was totally destroyed and had to be rebuilt in St Lucia. A collision with an unidentified object, possibly a large whale, was reported by *Company* while crossing the South Indian Ocean. There were also a number of collisions with other yachts, the most serious occurring in Darwin where the 130-foot *Act IV* demolished a home-built steel yacht. Apparently the large yacht, which had just left a boatyard where it had had some work done, was unable to stop in time to avoid hitting the smaller boat. Apparently the propeller on *Act IV* had been fitted the wrong way around, although this was never proven.

The 36 boats taking part in the first round the world rally suffered a variety of equipment failures, but almost without exception all were dealt with efficiently and thus any serious consequences were avoided. Rigging failure was potentially the most serious, and it was almost a miracle that no masts were lost. While sailing up the Red Sea, *Elan Adventurer* could have lost its mast when the forestay masthead fitting broke. 'Thank God, the mast was held up by the two spinnaker halyards which are always clipped on the pulpit, or we would have lost the mast,' commented a very relieved skipper Julian Wilson. On the same leg, the crew of *Gulkarna II* discovered that both cap shrouds and one lower stay had started parting at the swage fitting. 'The problem was probably caused by the fact that the turnbuckles had not been fitted with toggles. This made the rigging very rigid with no allowance for fore-and-aft movement,' explained skipper Peter Bunting. The builder Hallberg Rassy promptly sent replacement rigging to Port Sudan and, when the boat arrived in Malta, Hallberg Rassy decided to play it safe and arranged for *Gulkarna*'s entire rigging to be replaced.

The boats taking part in the latest round the world rally didn't fare much better, and equipment breakages that occurred during the two-year circumnavigation with the Millennium Odyssey are listed in Appendix 4. Margaret Reichenbach and

Aventura's mast steps helped promptly retrieve a broken spreader, seen here held up by a flag halyard, on the way to the Falklands.

Matt Rollberg, who prepared their *Santana* thoroughly for their circumnavigation and wrote extensively about their experiences, give the following advice to anyone planning to set off on a long voyage: 'First, be aware that some gear simply does not hold up to the rigorous demands of ocean cruising. Second, some manufacturers may not understand installation necessities and ocean passage conditions on a sailboat. Third, it makes sense to buy from manufacturers that offer – and deliver – global service. Fourth, gear will only last so long. You should plan to replace worn-out gear, just like tyres on your car.'

Finally, two potentially serious incidents that had occurred in one of the round the world rallies should also be mentioned: the arrest of *Jakes Fantasia* in Eritrean waters during that country's conflict with Ethiopia, during the first round the world rally, and the attempted attack by Somali pirates on the yacht *Nori* during the Millennium Odyssey, thwarted by the presence of other boats in the convoy. All in all, not a bad record for a period spanning ten years, and involving some 200 boats and 1,000 sailors.

DAMAGE CONTROL

Among the preparations that some skippers had made for damage control was the provision of a set of wooden plugs of various diameters to be used if one of the through hull fittings failed. In case the hull was holed, some boats carried plywood and other materials for emergency repairs as well as underwater epoxy. On one boat a 6-foot octagonal piece of Dacron with grommets was kept in readiness to be fitted over a damaged hull. Alternatively, one could use a sail to cover the hole from the outside, while cushions could be used on the inside. One skipper suggested using an inflated dinghy seat to plug a hole from the inside.

Large-capacity pumps to use in such emergencies were highly recommended. On the yacht *Brydie*, a powerful 2-inch diameter pump was permanently mounted on the main engine for just such an eventuality, whereas Arthur Beiser preferred an independent petrol (gas) driven high-capacity pump.

Lessons to others

To round off the Global Cruising Survey the skippers were asked to describe the most significant incident in their sailing lives, which, in their opinion, could serve as a lesson to anyone intending to follow in their wake. I had expected Bill Butler to mention the way he decided to run his *Siboney* onto a sandy beach during a typhoon in the Philippines, and thus managed to save his boat – only to lose her a few years later when she was sunk by pilot whales 1,000 miles west of Galapagos. Nor did he dwell on the loss of *New Chance* off Newfoundland, which was due to the negligence or inexperience of his crew. It is perhaps understandable why he preferred to describe instead his 'two primordial rules for cruising safety, both learned the hard way: trust no crew member, no matter how fabulous his sailing career and credentials, until he is fully proven aboard, and you know that he does not sleep on watch, keeps a sharp lookout for all hazards, and is dependable under all circumstances. Besides that, stay glued to weather forecasts. Develop contacts with shore stations that can provide long-term forecasts.'

Mirek Misayat recalls that 'all the significant incidents in my 50 years of sailing were associated with unnerving situations. In 1951 while making a passage with four other inexperienced crew from Boulogne to Newhaven in a 26-foot charter boat, we were caught by gale-force winds off Beachy Head. The engine broke down, the sails were torn, and we were drifting towards the rocks of Beachy Head. Just as we were about to be smashed to pieces, the tide turned and the boat drifted into Newhaven harbour. The moral: listen to weather forecasts, as that gale had been predicted but I had neglected to listen to the radio.'

Antti Louhija: 'There are hundreds of incidents with great importance and mostly positive, but as a lesson to would-be cruising sailors, my shipwreck in the Red Sea in April 2001 is probably the most significant. During the darkness of a moonless night we hit a coral reef 40 miles offshore. We had been heading for a GPS-waypoint and the course had been laid so as to bypass the small islet and reef of Barra Musa Kebir by 2 miles. We struck the reef where it should not have been, and the boat eventually became a total loss. Luckily nobody on board was hurt. GPS is a wonderful tool, but do not trust the charts.'

For Arthur Beiser, the most significant single incident in his long and eventful sailing life was 'the loss of my Nicholson 70 ketch *Isle* in mid-Atlantic in November 1987. We had bought the ten-year-old yacht a few months before and taken her to what everybody said was the best yard in the Newport area for a thorough overhaul and installation of new equipment. The joiner work and painting were indeed excellent, but the yard's engineering work turned out to be terrible, and as a result, the boat sank. Many elements of bad workmanship contributed to this event: batteries not properly secured, non-watertight wiring connections in the bilge, rubbish not cleared from the bilges, hoses whose clamps were not sufficiently tightened, and on and on. The boat was big, and too much was going on for me to be able to check everything, and I was concentrating on the rig, sails, winches, and other deck gear. So I hired a Lloyd's surveyor to keep an eye on the work. Result: catastrophe. Reason: general incompetence and lack of meticulous attention. Lesson: I will never again have a boat so large and complicated that I cannot with my own eyes and hands check everything regularly and be able to fix almost any defect that may arise. Equally significant was the first cruise Germaine and I made when we were 23 and just married, in a 21-foot boat. This was so wonderful an experience that since then we have been unable to imagine life without a boat.'

Tom Williams could have easily shared Arthur's experience of having a boat sink under his feet, when 'we developed a stuffing box leak in mid-ocean and then had the bilge pumps fail. I connected the engine seawater intake to the bilge, pumped out the water, made the necessary repair . . . and we came through.'

David Beauchamp describes a situation where he nearly lost his boat: 'We had several days of mainly gale force winds pushing us along using only the staysail. The preventer I had rigged for the boom, being unused, was neglected. During the night the seas we were shipping released one end of the line from its cleat and washed it overboard. Finally, we made landfall just after daylight and, as we turned to go through a narrow passage in the reef, there was just enough of the line trailing in the water to wrap around the prop. The engine stopped dead. We did get away with it, but only narrowly. The moral here is: do not neglect to check every line and halyard that could possibly foul the prop. No matter what other danger or difficulty may distract you, try to take the few moments to work out where the dangers could lie and check them out – before they happen. I do now!'

This is also the advice given by Bob Hall: 'Never assume that nothing can happen even when you are near shore in protected waters. We always have someone on watch 24 hours a day. We have had to make rapid course changes when we have overtaken or been overtaken by a boat with no one on watch. A potential collision was avoided only because we were watchful.'

Peter Förthmann knows too well the risks involved as he was nearly run over by a ship in the English Channel when he fell asleep on his watch. Zoltan Gyurko describes a similar situation: 'I crashed on a reef once while being asleep. For hours I thought the boat was lost in the surf. But I kept trying to save the boat by doing all sorts of weird tricks, and miraculously I eventually got it off. It was on a remote island in Vanuatu where I never saw anyone. Amazingly, there was very little damage to the boat. I think that most boats are stronger than most people think – and so is the human heart. Never give up hope, even in terrible situations.'

Charles Gray is in complete agreement: 'We arrived at dusk in the Escape River in the Northern Territory of Australia, planning to anchor overnight and co-ordinate our arrival into nearby Albany Pass with its 10-knot tidal current the next day. We were tired, and the 110-lb Bruce stuck hard in the bottom mud. At 4 am we were thrown out of bed as a 25-knot wind blew us abruptly up on the shore. *Sea Gem* was lying almost on her side. The tide was going out. I had to walk out two anchors at low tide in crocodile-infested waters at night, in order to kedge off

with the tide. Since we had her built in 1986, we had never before had to kedge off. That night we were tired and lazy and depended on our always faithful Bruce. The lesson? Always put out two anchors in a tidal river.'

Luc Callebaut describes a similar experience but with worst consequences: 'We lost our previous boat when her mooring broke loose during tropical storm Felix in Saba, and she grounded on the shore reef instead of drifting out at sea. We weren't on board. The mooring was supposed to be hurricane proof, and we had checked the line the week before. No matter how well you prepare yourself for unpleasant surprises, skill and experience are not enough, you will also need some luck to avoid disasters.'

Skip Novak recalls the situation 'when we lost the rudder on *Pelagic* 700 miles west of the Magellan Straits coming from New Zealand. We had to rig a spinnaker pole sweep out of raw materials on board. It took us 12 hours to rig it in a dying gale, but once rigged we were able to continue into the Straits and dock without assistance in Punta Arenas. This was incredibly satisfying. The lesson: know your boat and your abilities. Think of the worst-case scenario and how to cope with that in the worst-place situation. For world cruising, self-reliance is the key and part of the pleasure. There are too many rescues being called out unnecessarily.'

Barry Esrig fully agrees: 'The most significant incidents in my sailing life revolve around distress calls. The mobilization of the sailing community, the Coast Guard and the commercial vessels is quite impressive and reassuring. When you

The Hungarian Jolly Joker was lost in the Torres Straits during the first round the world rally.

are on your own, you always have someone at the other end of the SSB or VHF ready to aid you if you are in trouble, and mobilize whatever is necessary to help. What we need to avoid are those incidents that get us in trouble but are preventable and avoidable. Do your best not to put yourself in harm's way.'

Chris Harding's advice concerns the preparation of a boat for a long voyage: 'Having set out on *Futuro* knowing that the boat was not really prepared for a circumnavigation, I have learned the hard way how much work is involved in trying to put right a boat while on the move, and how much this costs in comparison to having the work done by professionals before leaving. While it is possible to get many technical and structural problems solved in some of the strangest places in the world, the quality of the work and the materials used are rarely up to standard and very often cause more damage and work than the original problem. This can have a major effect on the seaworthiness of a vessel. I have seen first-hand how a badly prepared boat was turned into a floating hulk with almost no means of propulsion in a few short hours of a moderate storm. None of the damage by itself was catastrophic, but the combination of the damages taken together was enough to completely disable the vessel and present a serious risk to those on board.'

Terence Brownrigg shares that view: 'Fortunately I have not lost a yacht, though I have been dismasted three times. I therefore think that eternal vigilance is essential. If one always goes down the "what if the worst" scenario, you probably wouldn't put to sea at all. There is no substitute for experience – even being dismasted!'

David Hersey would probably agree: 'A thousand miles from Cocos Keeling en route to Mauritius at seven in the morning while sailing at 8 knots in over 2,000 metres of water, we hit something that stopped the boat dead in her tracks for a few seconds and left a series of parallel gouges like big teeth marks in the leading edge of the keel. As it happened, we didn't take on any water and so continued happily on our way. But maybe it could have been a different story had the giant squid or submerged container, or whatever it really was, hit us in a slightly different way. These are things you have no control over, and it is very easy to become complacent when you are used to day after day of beautiful idyllic sailing. You have to always be ready for the big surprise around the next sunrise.'

Clyff Huggett is in complete agreement: 'one Sunday, Anna and I went fishing just a three-hour sail from Gulf Harbour, in New Zealand. Just as we had finished fishing, I was taken very ill and totally incapacitated. Anna had to find her way back to Gulf Harbour and dock the boat on her own. The lesson is simple: both husband and wife must be able to handle the boat under sail or power on their own, and be able to transpose a reading from a GPS to a chart, and set a course for the nearest port should one of the couple become incapacitated. We also have a policy of clipping on in the cockpit at night. This saves the embarrassment of being a crew member short in the morning.'

John Ellis knows the feeling after 'the loss of a crew member overboard in the first round the world rally. On another occasion, I was involved in trying to rescue two guys from another yacht in the Solent who had been washed overboard. We were not successful. So my advice is: at night and in rough weather, always clip on.'

Javier Visiers agrees that personal accidents can be even more dangerous than equipment failures: 'My diving accident in the Red Sea has taught me that one should be well prepared in every respect if one wishes to go scuba diving. Otherwise it is better not to do it at all.'

Eduardo Gallardo confirms the wisdom of the Romanian proverb quoted at the beginning of this chapter: 'My first transatlantic crossing and real blue water passage was from Las Palmas to Antigua in 1978 on a 32-foot boat, with nothing but a VHF radio, a compass and a sextant, and absolutely none of today's amenities. Although I knew how to use the sextant, I had no practical experience. I crossed in 21 days and arrived at my destination without any major problem or inconvenience. The moral of the story is that all the preparation in the world cannot replace dumb luck.'

Much valuable advice was given concerning decision-making. Carlton DeHart pointed out that 'the most significant thing I did was to make up my mind to do it, cut all ties, get on the boat, and *leave*. Too many people plan all their life to sail away and never go for whatever reason. As I have told many people, three-quarters of our trip around the world was over the day we left town and sailed away. Neither the boat nor the amount of gear you have really matters, just get out there and do it. Leaving is the most difficult thing we ever did.'

John Morgan is in complete agreement: 'I find the two most anxious moments were connected with indecision about whether to go on or turn back. This is a personal problem. We all have a weakness somewhere, and it's how you deal with it that counts. In each case, I continued – and felt better once the decision had been made. Courage is when you have a choice, brave is when you don't. I am fortunate in that my partner complements my character.'

Klaus Girzig fully agrees: 'The most important and difficult action is putting your dream into practice. The highlights arrive by themselves.' For Don Babson, 'the most significant decision for us was to join a rally. Had we not joined America 500, there would have been no crossing for us in 1992. Without that experience, and without the Millennium Odyssey, there would have been no round the world voyage for us either. Without those rallies, the friendships among the whole fleet, which will last for many years, would have never developed. The shared accomplishments will live in each of us for ever.'

Michael Frankel, who sailed in the same rally, would like others to know that 'cruising around the world is not as difficult as it first sounds. More people should just do it, spend less time worrying about it, and start actually planning their adventure.'

Richard Walker tried to put the whole matter in perspective: 'The most significant thing is to forget storms, boardings by pirates, anchor dragging or hitting reefs. The most significant act was the day we non-sailors bought our boat and set off.'

For John Neal, the most significant moment of his sailing life was 'arriving in the Marquesas at 22 and experiencing the epiphany of discovering that paradise existed'.

14

Where on Earth Are They Sailing?
WORLDWIDE YACHT MOVEMENT AND STATISTICS

"Most yacht owners nowadays prefer to keep their boats in marinas that are easily reached by air, or in areas with good cruising opportunities and benign weather, and not waste time on long offshore voyages. In other words, the more nautical tourism there is, the fewer true navigators there are."
JUAN FRANCISCO MARTIN

In this age of space technology, mass tourism and fast communications, the sea remains a great challenge, and there is little to equal the satisfaction felt by every sailor on the successful completion of an ocean passage. This challenge, coupled with the temptation of exotic destinations beckoning from beyond the horizon, acts as a magnet to which many are irresistibly drawn. Thousands of sailors do indeed set off each year in search of adventure. Some outstanding voyages have been accomplished in recent years, and cruising yachts have reached the most remote corners of the world, from the frozen icescapes of Antarctica to the steaming upper reaches of the Amazon. Such remarkable voyages completed in small boats have spurred other sailors to follow their example.

Although the number of people undertaking offshore voyages has steadily increased, this increase is smaller than anticipated. As a result of the development of navigational equipment and the general improvement in yacht design and construction, the number of sailing boats with the potential to undertake offshore voyages has increased dramatically in recent years, even if relatively few of these actually leave on cruises of long duration. In parallel with the increase in the global yacht population, or as a result of it, there has also been an expansion in yachting facilities; the improvement of port facilities for yachts and the building of marinas in attractive locations have encouraged many sailors to cruise abroad. Another relatively recent development is the large number of yachts that are based permanently abroad, especially in the Mediterranean, Eastern Caribbean and Bahamas. This applies particularly to owners from countries where, due to the climate, the sailing season is short; or those lacking a coastline, such as Switzerland and Austria. The reduction in air fares and the availability of berthing facilities in marinas developed in pleasant cruising areas have encouraged many owners to base their boats away from home. Often these owners move their base from season to season to provide a greater variety to their cruising. This applies particularly to the Mediterranean where the choice of good wintering facilities is very large.

Yet in spite of the increase in the number of cruising boats that undertake offshore passages, the traditional ocean routes show little variation and the number of yachts that stray away from them is still relatively small. Most sailors seem happy to stick to the well-tried routes, which have their origin in climatic and oceanic conditions. Like migrating birds, cruising yachts follow certain patterns and a useful factor that must be borne in mind when examining their movement is the seasonal character of most trans-ocean passages. Thus, the number of yachts undertaking winter passages in high latitudes is so small as to be almost negligible. Similarly, summer passages in tropical areas are considerably less frequent, mainly due to the danger of tropical storms, the hurricane season coinciding in most parts of the world with the summer months. These factors narrow down the existing cruising routes to well-defined 'lanes' in all oceans. Sailing yachts are much more susceptible than large commercial vessels to prevailing wind and sea conditions, which determine the routes they are likely to sail. For this reason these main cruising routes are unlikely to change greatly in future years.

On a passage from the Cote d'Azur to the Canaries on *Aventura III* in the summer of 2001 we stopped for one night at the island of Formentera in the Balearics. The well-protected anchorage was thick with boats: all kinds of cruising boats flying the flags of various European countries, some very large sailing yachts, a lot of small powerboats and several luxurious power cruisers, some of them so large that they looked like scaled-down versions of the *QE2*. I climbed to the top of the mast to take a photo and estimated that we were amidst some 200 boats. A quarter of a century had gone by since our last cruise in the Balearics when Formentera was nothing more than a small fishing village surrounded by sandy beaches. After two seasons in the Mediterranean, Gwenda and I had decided to return to the Pacific, so we felt that crowded Formentera only confirmed the wisdom of this decision. Three days later we were in Gibraltar where, to my great surprise, the immigration officer who cleared us in remarked that over the years the number of cruising yachts passing through Gibraltar had in fact gone down, albeit by only a few per cent. As Gibraltar is such an important gateway on the world sailing circuit, this could mean that our Mediterranean experience was not so significant in a global context. The only way to find out the real situation was to get hold of some concrete figures, rather than share the widely held belief among cruising sailors that the oceans are becoming increasingly overcrowded.

The first time I conducted a survey of the global movement and distribution of cruising boats was in 1987, when the ARC transatlantic rally was barely one year old and all the cruiser rallies cloned from the ARC were still a thing of the future. As a follow-up to that first survey, a similar one was conducted seven years later in 1994. It was again after a gap of seven years that I carried out a third survey during the latter part of 2001, when I contacted a number of key locations around the world in order to obtain the number of cruising boats that had passed through in 2000 and to compare these statistics with the results of my previous surveys. Whenever possible I also tried to get hold of other interesting details, such as the

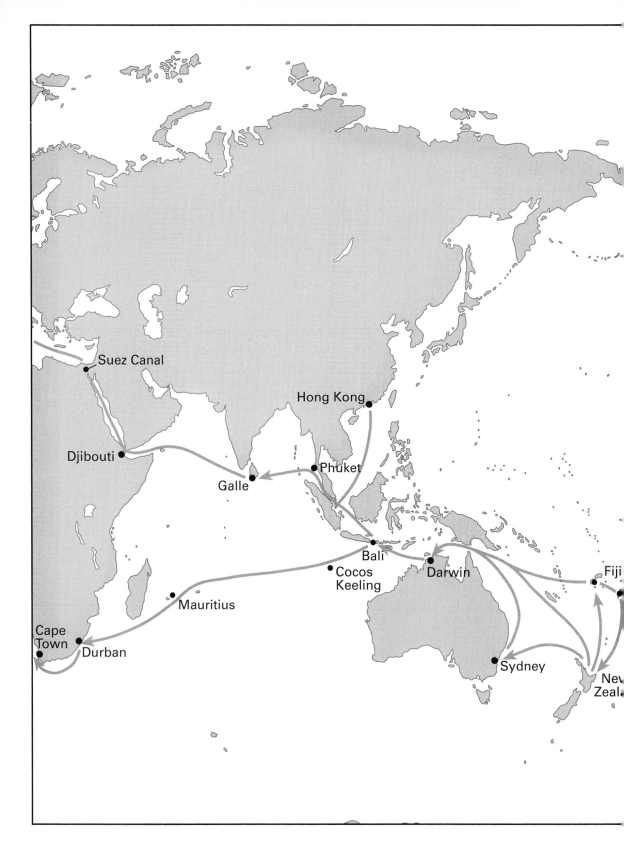

Map 1: Principal passage routes

nationality of the boats, when and where they had come from, and where they were bound for. A global picture started to emerge that often yielded surprising results. As in my previous surveys, wherever possible I tried to obtain concrete figures from official sources, such as port authorities, customs or immigration offices. In most instances, the response was prompt and positive. Occasionally I had to resort to my personal contacts at yacht clubs or marinas to fill in the gaps. Although statistics rarely make exciting reading, this chapter attempts to show where cruising boats go and when they go, and perhaps – just as important, for those who are looking for solitude – what are the places to avoid and at what times.

In an earlier survey on seamanship I drew the conclusion that one of the most important attributes of good seamanship is a strong dose of commonsense. This is what most cruising people are guided by, so when one discovers that less than a dozen cruising boats cross the Atlantic from east to west on the northern routes in any one year, while 1,000 take the more southerly route, it must mean that the vast majority know something that everyone else should know too. By saying this, I do not intend to discourage anyone from attempting less-frequented routes; on the contrary, after reading these statistics some people might be tempted to choose one of the less-frequented routes or ports of call.

Both when collecting this data and in my previous surveys I have been interested primarily in the long distance cruising boats, meaning those that have been away from the home base for at least six months and are undertaking a long ocean voyage. In order to understand the present yachting scene better, and particularly to gain an overview of the most popular cruising destinations, the movement of yachts has been examined in a number of key locations along the principal world cruising circuit, which is depicted in Map 1. Any ocean voyaging yacht must pass through some of these ports during a longer cruise and, in order to present a clearer picture, the results have been processed on a regional basis.

North Atlantic

The northern half of what was known in Columbus's time as the Ocean Sea is where most exploration started, and its two shores still have the largest concentration of sailing vessels in the world. Although the northern routes were plied by Viking ships long before Columbus, most modern sailors prefer warmer weather, and for that reason the tropical and subtropical routes continue to be the most popular.

NORTHERN ROUTES

The transatlantic routes of high latitudes are used only in the summer months by a handful of cruising boats sailing from Northern Europe to North America or vice versa, their number being augmented by yachts taking part in various transatlantic races. Because of the prevailing westerly winds, a crossing of the North Atlantic from west to east in mid-latitudes can be made either non-stop or via Bermuda and/or the Azores. Those leaving from southern ports on the Atlantic seaboard of the United States usually call at Bermuda. Virtually all the yachts heading for the Mediterranean choose to sail there by way of the Azores (Tables 4 and 5).

Arrivals from:	
Eastern Caribbean	531
Bermuda	250
USA	77
Canada	6
South America	17
South Africa	2
West Africa	8
Ascension/St Helena	10
Europe	47
Other Azorean islands	196
Total	1,144

Table 4: Yacht arrivals in Horta in 2000

	1987	%	2000	%
United Kingdom	168	23	326	28
France	187	26	306	27
USA	100	14	126	11
Germany	54	7	101	9

Table 5: Main nationalities calling at Horta

Situated in the centre of the North Atlantic, the Azores are a most convenient springboard for a number of routes. The marina at Horta on the island of Faial is a hive of activity between the middle of May and the end of June when hundreds of cruising boats call there on their way from the Caribbean and Bermuda to Northern Europe or the Mediterranean. More than three-quarters of all the boats that stop at Horta in any year call there during the busy months of May and June, when boats return to Europe at the end of the winter season in the Caribbean. Of the 1,144 boats that cleared into Horta in 2000, slightly more than half arrived directly from a Caribbean island. Altogether it is estimated that of the 1,144 yachts, approximately 900 had completed an Atlantic crossing, whether starting from a Caribbean island or the North American mainland. Even if one allows for the fact that the year 2000 saw the return to Europe of a larger than usual number of boats that had sailed to the Caribbean to celebrate the new millennium, the Azores statistics point to a figure of approximately 1,000 transatlantic voyages per year. The figures from Horta show a steady increase in the number of visiting boats, as in 1984 Horta was visited by only 614 boats, a figure that had risen to 729 boats in 1987 and 931 by 1993. Horta is probably the only place in the world where the movement of yachts has been monitored for well over a century, and they have shown a steep increase over the years, from a single visiting yacht in 1896 (Captain Slocum's *Spray*) to over a thousand a century later.

Early summer is the time when most cruising yachts pass through the Azores, and by looking closer at their movement, on a monthly basis, the last port of call as well as the destination after the Azores, some interesting conclusions can be drawn. One significant change in recent years is the larger number of boats arriving in the

For thousands of sailors the town of Horta and its marina are the main gateway to the Azores.

Azores directly from the Caribbean, and not via Bermuda as used to be the accepted route in the past. This trend was started by delivery skippers on charter boats, always in a hurry to reach the Mediterranean at the end of the winter season in the Eastern Caribbean. Bermuda is also bypassed by a number of US boats that sail from more northern ports directly to the Azores in mid-summer. Their example is followed in August by yachts from Canada that have to wait for warmer weather before crossing the waters near Newfoundland where ice lingers on until well into summer. Arrivals in the Azores from the Caribbean peter out after July and none were recorded between September and January. Yachts crossing from Bermuda also avoid the hurricane season, with a total of only eight yachts arriving in the Azores from Bermuda between September and the following March.

The destinations after the Azores are split almost equally between the yachts that are bound for Northern Europe and those heading for ports on the Iberian peninsula or in the Mediterranean. The number of yachts making east to west passages and stopping in the Azores is small, and the few that did so passed through the Azores in summer. There are, in fact, more yachts using the Azores as an intermediate point on the way from the Mediterranean to Northern Europe. The same also happens in the opposite direction, with yachts calling at the Azores when sailing between ports in Northern Europe or Ireland and the Mediterranean.

The majority of boats sailing to Europe from the Caribbean leave at the end of April or beginning of May. Antigua Sailing Week, which attracts racing, cruising and charter boats for a week of racing and festivities, signals the end of the safe season in the Caribbean after which most boats take their leave. Thanks to detailed statistical records, the eastbound movement of boats in the North Atlantic can be gauged quite accurately. According to the Bermuda Radio Control Centre, which monitors the movement of all vessels in Bermudan waters, the year 2000 was a record year with a total of 1,160 yacht arrivals (Table 6). Although this is an increase of almost 12 per cent over the figures recorded in 1987, when 998 boats cleared into Bermuda, it is none the less not as much as would have been expected for such a popular destination. The breakdown by port of origin and destination shows that nearly half the movement was to or from the US mainland. Most US boats starting off from a port north of Cape Hatteras, as well as virtually all Canadian boats, stop in Bermuda on their way to the Bahamas, Eastern Caribbean or Europe. The same is also true for boats sailing in the opposite direction. Bermuda's traditional role as an intermediate stage on voyages from the Caribbean to Europe has seen a reduction in recent years as increasingly more boats sail directly from the Eastern Caribbean to the Azores.

	From	To
USA	667	505
Canada	22	24
Caribbean	403	224
Europe	64	320
Central and South America	4	2
Total	1,160	1,075

Table 6: Yacht movement in Bermuda in 2000

Virtually all the transatlantic departures from Bermuda were made in the first half of the year, and were predominantly by European boats returning from the Caribbean. The second half of the year is dominated by US boats. Most yacht traffic in July is taken up by US boats returning from the Caribbean or those undertaking a short summer cruise to Bermuda. The other busy time is October and November when US boats head for the Caribbean via Bermuda, 95 per cent bound for the Virgin Islands.

Yacht movement in the first half of the year is extremely seasonal, half the number of boats that call at Bermuda in any one year arriving in the island between the middle of May and the middle of June, whether destined for the USA or Europe. The number of boats heading east across the Atlantic after the end of June is very small, mainly because most skippers try to avoid passages during the hurricane season as tropical storms can affect both the route from Bermuda to the Azores, and even the more northerly direct route to Europe, as was the case in the summer of 2001.

Cold water cruising is becoming more popular in the North Atlantic as more yachts sail beyond the Arctic Circle to Greenland and Spitsbergen, the latter being now a favourite destination among high latitude sailors. According to the Governor's office, where accurate records are kept as yachts are only allowed to visit Spitsbergen with prior permission, ten sailing yachts visited Svalbard (to give it its correct Norwegian name) in 2000. Not surprisingly half of those were

Norwegian. However, by 2001 the island was visited by 21 boats, of which only three were Norwegian, five were British, and two each from the USA, Germany, France, Poland, the Netherlands and Sweden, and one from Canada. The upward trend is expected to continue as more sailors become aware of the beauty of this Arctic destination, but probably also because summer weather is becoming more benign as a result of global warming.

SOUTHERN ROUTES

Most cruising sailors do not like cold weather and this is the main reason why the most frequented routes coincide with the warmer parts of the world. The North Atlantic is no exception, and this is why its southern half attracts more cruising boats. The majority of east to west transatlantic routes have their starting point in the Canary Islands, with only a small number of yachts setting off across the Atlantic from Madeira, or directly from continental Europe. Most passages are undertaken between the middle of November and late December, with only a few boats making the crossing later in winter, although the winds are in fact more favourable in late winter and spring. As the sailing seasons in the Caribbean and Europe, particularly the Mediterranean, are so finely matched, both cruising and charter boats plan their transatlantic passage for the interim period. There are other considerations too, such as the wish to spend Christmas in a Caribbean island and the necessity of avoiding passages during the hurricane season. Therefore transatlantic passages are rarely undertaken after June or before November because of the danger of hurricanes in the western part of the ocean.

The main east to west movement in the North Atlantic has changed little since Christopher Columbus pioneered the best route across and, with very few exceptions, all cruising boats bound for the Caribbean stop in the Canaries to prepare for the 2,700-mile passage. Las Palmas de Gran Canaria continues to be the favourite port of call, not just because it is the starting point for the annual ARC rally, but primarily for its excellent provisioning and repair facilities. Surprisingly, in recent years Las Palmas has seen a slight decrease in the number of foreign cruising boats, which in 1987 amounted to 1,038 compared to the 993 yachts that cleared into Las Palmas in 2000. There is a discrepancy between the actual figures and those reported by the port authority as a considerable number of cruising boats pass through Las Palmas without reporting, and thereby miss being included in the official statistics. Officially, Las Palmas was visited in 1986 by 815 cruising boats, 931 in 1994, and 993 in 2000. In practice, these figures should be augmented by at least 10 per cent to reflect the real situation. Among the boats that called at Las Palmas, the port authority estimates that more than 50 per cent crossed to the Caribbean that same year, even if not on the most direct route. If to the Las Palmas figures are added the boats that leave from other marinas, both in Gran Canaria and the other islands, it means that between 900 and 1,000 boats leave the Canaries on a transatlantic voyage every year, thus confirming the Azores statistics quoted earlier for passages in the opposite direction. Also included in these figures are around 40 motor yachts that stop in either Las Palmas or Tenerife each year to fuel up for the Atlantic crossing.

About 90 per cent of the yachts stopping in the Canaries are on their way to a transatlantic destination, the majority to the Caribbean and a few to ports in South America, mainly Brazil. A survey conducted among participants in the ARC showed that the average time spent in the Canaries was only 13 days. Indeed, relatively few boats spend any length of time cruising the seven islands of the archipelago, usually because they arrive too late and are not prepared to waste any time before leaving for the Caribbean. The situation is gradually changing as the Canary Islands government positively encourages cruising, and yachting facilities have improved in all the islands.

The breakdown by flag of the boats calling at Las Palmas reflects the trend observed at Horta (see Table 5), and shows an interesting reversal as British yachts are now the largest national group, whereas in the 1980s it was the French (Table 7).

	1986	%	1993	%	2000	%
United Kingdom	157	19	218	23	235	24
France	318	39	144	15	188	20
Germany	110	13	103	11	148	15
USA	74	9	43	5	67	7

Table 7: Main nationalities calling at Las Palmas

Although most boats leaving the Canaries are bound for islands in the Eastern Caribbean, some sailors prefer to make a detour to West Africa and even Brazil before arriving in the Caribbean. The former is primarily the haunt of French boats, which were the first to sail in large numbers to Senegal and its neighbours, although in recent years their number has decreased dramatically as the area is no longer considered safe for cruising. Most of these boats continue their voyage across the Atlantic later in the season. Brazil is now included by more cruising sailors on their itinerary, most of whom restrict their cruising to the north-eastern part of this vast country, with only very few continuing towards Rio de Janeiro. A compromise solution for those who do not wish to make a detour to the African mainland, but are tempted to break the long passage to the Caribbean, is a stop in the Cape Verde Islands, which are conveniently situated close to the traditional trade wind route. The most popular port of call is Mindelo on São Vicente Island, which received 96 boats in 2000.

There appears to be a pattern in the choice of Caribbean destination, with North European and American yachts making their landfall in English-speaking St Lucia, Barbados or Antigua, while French yachts and some other Europeans prefer the French-speaking islands of Martinique or Guadeloupe. Mainly because of the ARC, St Lucia is now one of the favourite destinations in the Eastern Caribbean. According to the customs office at Rodney Bay Marina, 534 boats had made landfall there on completion of an Atlantic crossing in 2000. The total number of boats that cleared into St Lucia during that year was a staggering 22,340, but some had cleared more than once as they made their way up or down the chain of islands and included charter boats on a regular circuit.

Over half the boats that arrive in the Caribbean plan on spending more than one season there. It is estimated that at the height of the winter sailing season there are about 6,000 cruising boats spread out over the Eastern Caribbean, with probably the same number of charter boats permanently based there. These figures do not include the privately owned cruising boats based permanently in the Caribbean, many of which rarely leave their marinas, particularly in the French

St Lucia's Rodney Bay Marina is now the favourite transatlantic landfall in the Caribbean.

islands where thousands of yachts had been bought and sailed over from Europe as a result of a tax incentive scheme, which has now been discontinued.

Following several disastrous hurricane seasons, most cruising boats that remain in the Caribbean for at least one year try to spend the critical months in either Trinidad or Venezuela, particularly since insurance companies started stipulating that boats spending the hurricane season in the Caribbean will only be insured if they stay south of 12°N. According to the Trinidad Customs Department, a total of 4,553 yachts spent the 2000 hurricane season in Trinidad, which is a huge increase over 1990 when approximately 1,500 boats visited Trinidad. To cope with this large number, Trinidad has built several marinas and the hard standing areas have been greatly expanded. Most of these boats are only 'parked' in Trinidad for the summer months, and very few of their owners remain on board during the hurricane season.

A large concentration of cruising boats is also found in the Bahamas, where customs report that a total of 22,444 pleasure craft cleared during 2000. This includes many boats that moved to and from Florida, often just for a weekend or short cruise. Nevertheless, the increasing popularity of the Bahamas as a year-round cruising destination is reflected in the steady influx of boats, mostly from the USA, which have cleared into the Bahamas in the last 35 years (Table 8).

1966	1977	1988	1993	2000
5,144	11,295	18,063	19,697	22,444

Table 8: Yacht arrivals in the Bahamas

Many US and Canadian boats spend the entire winter season in the Bahamas, rarely moving from one place, so there is a discrepancy between the number of boats that are virtually stationary and those that are actually cruising. Among the latter, I would guess that even at the height of the winter season not more than 1,000 boats are actually cruising, and possibly even less than that. By far the most popular cruising destination, where these large numbers do appear to be credible, is George Town in Great Exuma. The winter boat population has grown there to a weekly average of around 400, with over 500 boats gathered in George Town for the annual cruising rally at the end of the winter season.

Most of the traffic to and from the Bahamas is from the US mainland, primarily Florida, and can hardly be described as offshore sailing. One of the destinations in the Western Caribbean that has shown a considerable reduction in visiting boats is Jamaica, which only sees around two dozen visiting boats in some years, their number being doubled every two years when the Pineapple Cup Race finishes in Montego Bay. On the other hand, Cuba now seems to be the trendiest cruising destination in that part of the world and, in spite of the US embargo and the numerous restrictions applied to visiting boats, every year more boats visit that island. It is estimated that in 2000 approximately 150 foreign cruising boats cleared into Cuba.

Mediterranean Sea

The number of boats cruising in the Mediterranean has shown a remarkable increase in recent years. An estimated 5,000 yachts are now cruising at any one time at the height of the summer season. This figure includes both boats on longer cruises, and North Europeans who have temporarily left their yachts in one of the Mediterranean countries. An even greater number of North European yachts are permanently based in the Mediterranean, but only a small proportion are actually cruised for any length of time, so these have not been included in the above estimate. No other region in the world has witnessed such an explosion in yachting as the Mediterranean, although this expansion is showing signs of slowing down. To cope with the influx of yachts, both visiting and local, marinas have been built in all countries bordering the Mediterranean, particularly in the most popular cruising areas. One of the busiest among these is the south coast of Spain, while the Balearic Islands are another busy yachting area, with Palma de Mallorca at its nerve centre. However, the largest number of yachts, mostly engaged in coastal cruising, is found along the French coast. To cope with the insatiable demand for space, many new marinas have been created to compete with the older fashionable ports of the French Riviera. A favourite offshore destination for French-based yachts is Corsica, as well as neighbouring Sardinia, which has also developed into a thriving yachting centre.

The Mediterranean has been described as the cradle of western civilization, and for anyone even slightly interested in history there is probably no other area in the world to offer such a variety of interesting places to visit. Top of many people's list is the Aegean, where ancient monuments seem to have been built for the benefit of seafarers. Many ancient sites are easily reached from the sea, both in mainland Greece and its many islands, and along the Turkish coast of Asia Minor. Not surprisingly, the Aegean has also seen a vast expansion in yachting in recent years,

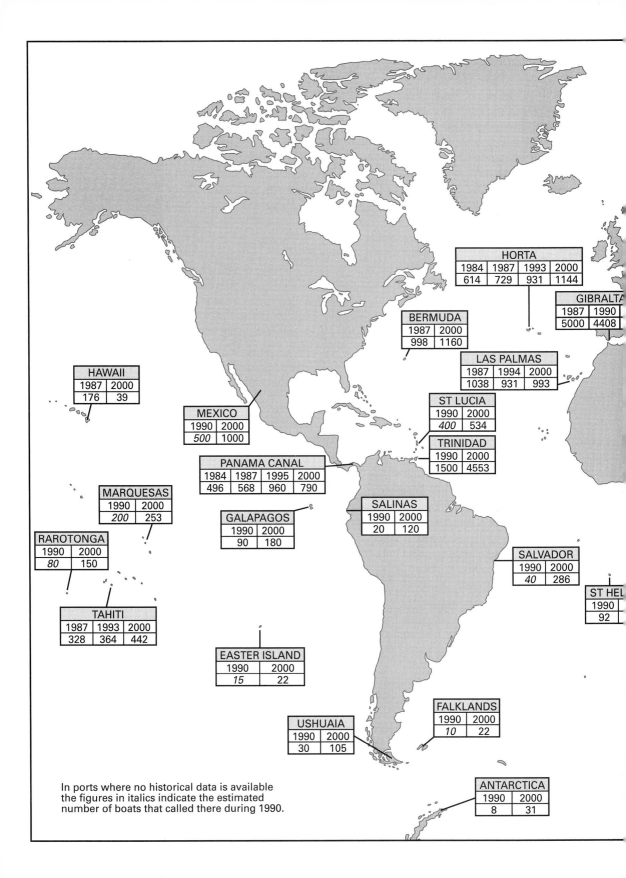

HORTA

1984	1987	1993	2000
614	729	931	1144

GIBRALTA

1987	1990
5000	4408

BERMUDA

1987	2000
998	1160

LAS PALMAS

1987	1994	2000
1038	931	993

ST LUCIA

1990	2000
400	534

TRINIDAD

1990	2000
1500	4553

HAWAII

1987	2000
176	39

MEXICO

1990	2000
500	1000

PANAMA CANAL

1984	1987	1995	2000
496	568	960	790

SALINAS

1990	2000
20	120

MARQUESAS

1990	2000
200	253

GALAPAGOS

1990	2000
90	180

SALVADOR

1990	2000
40	286

RAROTONGA

1990	2000
80	150

ST HEL

1990
92

TAHITI

1987	1993	2000
328	364	442

EASTER ISLAND

1990	2000
15	22

FALKLANDS

1990	2000
10	22

USHUAIA

1990	2000
30	105

In ports where no historical data is available
the figures in italics indicate the estimated
number of boats that called there during 1990.

ANTARCTICA

1990	2000
8	31

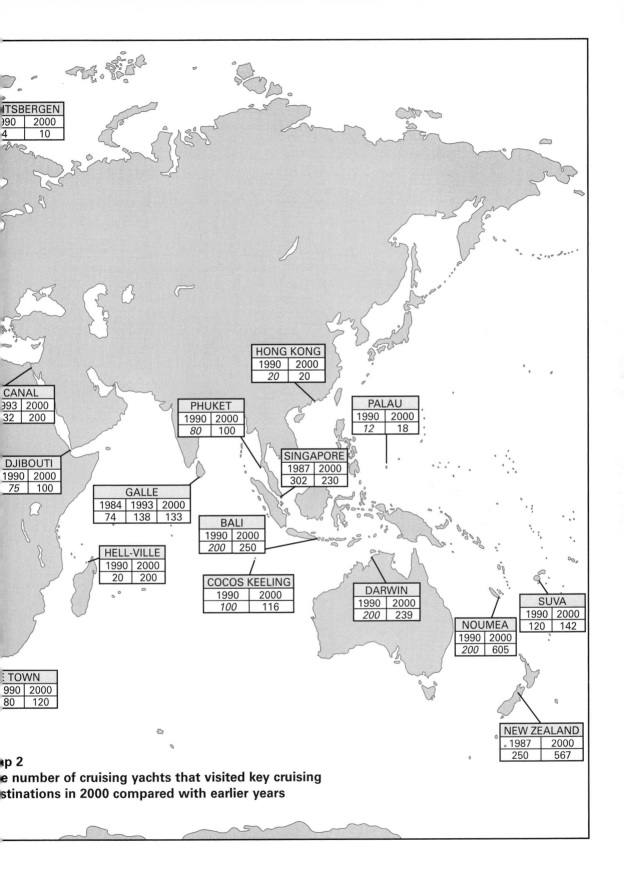

ITSBERGEN

990	2000
4	10

CANAL

993	2000
32	200

DJIBOUTI

1990	2000
75	100

HELL-VILLE

1990	2000
20	200

TOWN

990	2000
80	120

HONG KONG

1990	2000
20	20

PHUKET

1990	2000
80	100

PALAU

1990	2000
12	18

SINGAPORE

1987	2000
302	230

GALLE

1984	1993	2000
74	138	133

BALI

1990	2000
200	250

COCOS KEELING

1990	2000
100	116

DARWIN

1990	2000
200	239

SUVA

1990	2000
120	142

NOUMEA

1990	2000
200	605

NEW ZEALAND

1987	2000
250	567

ap 2
e number of cruising yachts that visited key cruising
stinations in 2000 compared with earlier years

the number of cruising yachts being overshadowed by countless charter boats. Yet another area that is attracting large numbers of cruising yachts is the Adriatic coast of Croatia and its offlying islands.

Although the Mediterranean enjoys good sailing weather from June to November and even in winter it is never too cold, most cruising is restricted to the summer holiday season. For those who do not like crowds, the time to go is spring and autumn, when the weather can be perfect and the ports are not overflowing with visitors. Although most cruising in the Mediterranean is coastal, there are a few well-defined offshore routes, used mainly by boats moving from one cruising area to another. The main point of access into the Mediterranean from the west is Gibraltar, one of the most important transit points for yachts in the world. The busiest time is during the summer months when yachts move in both directions through the strait. Their movement becomes unidirectional at other times, as the spring is the time when yachts call at Gibraltar on their way to the Mediterranean, while the autumn sees a migration in the opposite direction as yachts stop in Gibraltar on their way to the Canaries and the Caribbean.

The fact that the actual movement of boats in the Mediterranean has not increased by the same proportion as the increase in actual numbers is shown by the figures obtained from the Gibraltar Ministry of Tourism. The total number of yachts that passed through Gibraltar in 2000 was 4,643, a modest increase of less than 5 per cent over the figures for 1990 (4,408), but a net drop from the approximately 5,000 yachts quoted to me in 1987. Nevertheless, the trend in Gibraltar is once again upwards, which is not surprising as its facilities are still among the best in the Mediterranean.

South Atlantic

Compared to the busy North Atlantic, the South Atlantic could be described as a tranquil backwater. The main route sailed by cruising boats extends diagonally from Cape Town to St Helena all the way to the Caribbean, and there is little movement outside of this track. Most yachts arrive in the South Atlantic via the Cape of Good Hope as part of a longer voyage, although there has been an increase in the number of cruising boats sailing from the North Atlantic to South America, particularly to Brazil. Most northbound passages round the Cape of Good Hope are made between November and January when sailing conditions are best. There are hardly any yachts sailing the South Atlantic during the southern winter from May to October. Apart from yachts sailing in round the world races, very few cruising yachts sail from Europe or North America to the Cape of Good Hope. The reciprocal route is much more frequented, the northbound route passing close to both St Helena and the Ascension Islands. However, judging from the few boats that called in the Azores during recent years on their way from South Africa to Europe, it would appear that a substantial decline has occurred on that route too. This traditional route, made famous by early circumnavigators, is now almost deserted and it is significant that among all the boats that arrived in Horta in 2000, only 12 had arrived from the South Atlantic: two directly from Cape Town, while the other ten had stopped at St Helena or Ascension.

Another northbound route enters the South Atlantic via Cape Horn from where it heads in a northerly direction before it crosses the equator, but this route is rarely used by cruising boats – it is mostly used by round the world races. However, with an increase in the number of sailors attracted by cruising in Patagonia and even Antarctica, more boats are heading for the South Atlantic every year, some sailing down along the eastern coast of South America, others coming from the South Pacific through the Chilean canals.

According to the Royal Cape Yacht Club, which caters for most cruising boats visiting Cape Town, 89 yachts stopped at that welcoming club in 2000. The total for the area is certainly higher (approximately 120) as there are now several docking facilities in Table Bay. The increase in the number of visiting yachts has been quite remarkable, as only an estimated 30 boats called there in 1974, a figure that rose to 67 in 1984, and to about 80 in 1990. Most yachts that call at Cape Town are on an east to west circumnavigation and are bound for the Caribbean, usually with an intermediate stop in St Helena. That lonely British outpost in the South Atlantic has seen a steady increase in the number of cruising boats in recent years, most of which spend several days there thanks to the greatly improved mooring situation as several mooring buoys have been laid down for the use of visiting yachts. According to the St Helena harbourmaster, a total of 184 cruising boats stopped there in 2000, which corresponds to an increase of over 100 per cent during the last decade (Table 9). This is due to the larger number of boats taking the Cape of Good Hope route, as a result of the uncertainties concerning the North Indian Ocean and Red Sea routes.

	From	To
Cape Town area	155	12
Luderitz and Walvis Bay	22	–
Durban	2	–
Stanley	1	1
Tristan da Cunha	2	–
Luanda	1	–
Brazil	1	71
Ascension	–	30
Caribbean	–	48
Azores	–	11
Cape Verdes	–	6
USA	–	4
Canaries	–	2
Total	**184**	**184**

Table 9: Yacht movement in St Helena in 2000

With one exception, all boats that stopped at St Helena were on a northbound passage, with the bulk bound for the Caribbean, either direct or with at least one intermediate stop in Brazil. Among the latter, the majority were bound for Salvador da Bahia (49), while 14 planned to stop at Fernando de Noronha Island. The figures also include a dozen boats taking part in a round race from Cape Town, as well as a lonely boat on a round trip from the Falklands to St Helena and back.

Flag		%
South Africa	56	30
United Kingdom	45	24
USA	28	15
Germany	9	5
France	8	4

Table 10: Main nationalities calling at St Helena in 2000

The flags of the boats calling at St Helena show that this is an important offshore destination for South African yachts, whereas most other nationalities were undertaking a round the world voyage (Table 10). The island of Fernando de Noronha, where restrictions on cruising boats have been eased, has become a popular port of call now that short stops are allowed without the compulsory Brazilian visa required on the mainland. On the mainland itself, Salvador da Bahia has made great efforts to become the favourite Brazilian landfall by building a marina and improving facilities generally. Several transatlantic and world events now stop there and among the 422 boats reported to have made landfall in 2000, 286 were described as foreign cruising boats, and most of these had timed their arrival to coincide with the world famous Carnival.

Few sailors would consider the windy Falklands as a desirable cruising destination, but in recent years a number of boats that have specialized in high latitude cruising have made Stanley Harbour their winter quarters. Based here between seasons, these boats make regular trips, usually with paying guests, to the Antarctic Peninsula or South Georgia. Slightly more than half the boats that cleared into the Falklands in 2000 were cruising boats exploring the southern part of South America, while a few were merely passing through, such as a Japanese boat that had sailed nonstop from Auckland, New Zealand, and was bound for Bermuda, and a Canadian boat that had sailed from Tasmania en route to Falmouth, in the UK (Table 11).

	From	To
Patagonia	9	4
South Georgia	4	7
Antarctica	2	1
Mainland	5	6
New Zealand	1	–
Tasmania	1	–
Europe	–	2
Caribbean	–	2
Total	**22**	**22**

Table 11: Yacht movement in the Falklands in 2000

An increasingly popular destination in the South Atlantic is Ushuaia. Conveniently located on the shore of the Beagle Channel, only some 60 miles from Cape Horn, in recent years this southernmost town in Argentina has become a busy port for cruise ships and yachts setting off on trips to Antarctica. According

Spectacular anchorage in Antarctica – an increasingly popular cruising destination.

to Daniel Kuntschik, who has been keeping accurate records of all the yachts that have visited Patagonia and Antarctica since 1989, during the austral summer of 1999–2000, Patagonia was visited by the surprisingly high number of 105 foreign yachts, of which 31 sailed on to the Antarctic Peninsula. Among the latter, about half were involved in some kind of commercial activity. Ten years earlier, during the austral summer of 1989–90, the Antarctic Peninsula was visited by only 10 yachts out of the total of 30 that had sailed to Patagonia.

While some of those 105 boats that visited Patagonia in the summer of 2000 had arrived in Ushuaia by way of the Chilean canals, the majority had come from the Atlantic and were planning to reach the Pacific via the Beagle Channel and the Chilean archipelago. Because of the prevailing NW winds that blow in Southern Chile for most of the year, such a strategy does not guarantee the best sailing conditions, even if it provides the chance to enjoy one of the most spectacular and least-frequented cruising areas of the world. The fact that only a handful of boats dare go that far out of their way is borne out by the figures obtained from Chile, where it is estimated that only about 40 foreign yachts cruised north of Patagonia in 2000.

North Pacific

The worldwide movement of cruising yachts is dictated by the trade winds and is therefore predominantly from east to west. Nowhere is this more obvious than in Panama, where the number of Pacific-bound yachts is always larger than that of yachts heading for the Atlantic. The latest figures show that in spite of increased transit costs and various problems encountered by pleasure craft in Panama, the number of sailors who try to avoid the Canal has been insignificant. For anyone trying to reach the South Pacific the only alternative to the Panama Canal is to sail there via Cape Horn. The notable exception are the few boats that are trucked across the continent from the Atlantic to the Pacific coast of the USA or vice versa.

While the situation in the Atlantic Ocean, and especially in the Caribbean and Mediterranean, may confirm the current view that the cruising scene is suffering from overcrowding, the Pacific Ocean continues to be a true sea of tranquillity. The majority of boats on a world voyage arrive in the Pacific by way of the Panama Canal, which in 2000 handled 532 Pacific-bound and 258 Atlantic-bound transits. The total of 790 yacht transits shows a significant drop compared to the 977 yachts that transited in 1999, which is explained by the larger than usual number of yachts that were bound for New Zealand for the America's Cup (Table 12). The predominantly westbound movement becomes even more obvious if one compares the Pacific-bound transits to the Atlantic-bound ones for those two years, as in 1999 there were 261 boats bound for the Atlantic compared to 258 the following year, whereas 716 yachts arrived in the Pacific by way of the Panama Canal in 1999 compared to 532 in 2000. Besides the America's Cup, two other reasons were given for the larger number of 1999 transits: the fact that many sailors had delayed their arrival in the Pacific to avoid the effects of the 1998 El Niño, while others decided to rush through before the transit fees were raised in 2000. Whichever way one looks at it, even the lower figures for 2000 show a considerable increase compared to the 1987 survey when a total of 568 yachts transited the Panama Canal, of which 206 were Atlantic-bound and 362 Pacific-bound. The following figures show the movement in recent years.

	1984	1987	1995	1996	1997	1998	1999	2000
Number of transits	496	568	960	988	1,042	845	977	790

Table 12: Panama Canal yacht transits over the years

Although the above figures show that the number of yacht transits has not increased considerably in recent years, cruising boats waiting to transit the Panama Canal are now experiencing longer delays than in the past. This is due to the Canal operating at its full capacity because of a record number of ship transits. On a few occasions in the past, such as the Millennium Odyssey round the world rally, the Panama Canal Authority agreed to transit cruising boats as one group which filled the locks, and reduced at a stroke the backlog of yachts waiting to transit. However, according to the Panama Canal Authority, the volume of traffic cannot allow valuable locking space to be allocated exclusively to pleasure craft, so there are no plans to modify the current scheduling of pleasure craft transits, which are normally locked with larger vessels and complete the transit in two days. It is also stressed that small vessels take up just as much time and effort to transit as even the largest ships, and the fees paid do not even cover the cost of their transit. As the actual costs of the Canal operations are being re-evaluated, fees for small vessels may be increased.

Sailors on the Pacific coast of the USA are less fortunate in their choice of cruising destinations than their east coast brethren. Although there is a very large number of cruising boats on the USA's western seaboard, particularly in California, most of the sailing is coastal and the only foreign destination within a reasonable distance is Mexico's Baja California. Canadian sailors have been blessed with a much more interesting coastline, but even they have little choice when it comes to offshore cruising. In recent years Mexico's Pacific coast has become a major cruising destination, and many marinas have been built to cope with the ever-increasing demand. It is estimated that well over 1,000 boats, mostly from the USA but also a few from Canada, are to be found cruising in Mexico at any one time. Some of them return home at the end of the winter season, while a large proportion set off from Mexico on an extended voyage, either into the South Pacific or, via the Panama Canal, to the Caribbean and Europe.

The offshore passage that is undertaken by the largest number of yachts in the North Pacific is to and from the Hawaiian Islands. According to the US customs office in Honolulu, approximately 1,000 boats sail from the mainland to Hawaii each year, but as US-flagged boats do not need to complete clearance formalities if they arrive from another US territory, there are no exact records as to their actual number. What is known is that the overwhelming majority return home, most during the same season, while a few spend the winter in Hawaii. Much better documented is the movement of non-US boats, of which a surprisingly low number (22) visited Hawaii in 2000, and only 17 US boats arrived from a foreign destination, while 27 foreign and 20 US boats departed Hawaii for foreign destinations in 2000. This is much less than in 1987, when 72 foreign flagged vessels and 104 US vessels had cleared into Hawaii from foreign ports. The reasons for this steep decline are difficult to gauge, but in the case of US boats it is probably explained by the fact that in the past many US boats limited their cruising to the Pacific Ocean and sailed to and from the South Pacific via Hawaii, whereas now many sail directly from the mainland to the Marquesas, avoiding the detour to Hawaii, and continue westward around the world, eventually returning home via the Panama Canal.

The drastic reduction in the number of foreign yachts visiting Hawaii is more difficult to understand, but it may be just a matter of fashion as, for instance, there are also fewer boats, US or foreign, sailing via Hawaii to Alaska. Also, there are fewer cruising boats generally visiting the western part of the Pacific Ocean, such as Micronesia and Japan. Palau, for instance, received 18 cruising boats in 2000, compared to 22 in the previous year. Such a low turnout may have been the reason why the authorities in Palau decided to ease their formerly stringent restrictions on cruising permits. Other North Pacific destinations, such as the Philippines and Hong Kong, also reflect this trend. The total number of cruising boats that cleared into Hong Kong in 2000 was 80 but, of these, 60 were based in Hong Kong, which was visited by only 20 foreign flagged boats. Even less visited is Japan, which rarely sees more than half a dozen foreign yachts in a year – and often even less. The frustration of being so far off the beaten track was keenly shown by the manager of the Tannowa Yacht Harbour near Osaka, who was elated to welcome three visiting yachts in 2001 after not seeing a single foreign flag during the previous year.

South Pacific

For countless sailors, the South Pacific remains the ultimate destination of which dreams are made, and in the last quarter of a century I have spent long periods cruising among those islands. The main sailing route links the Panama Canal in the east with the Torres Straits in the west and most boats undertaking a world voyage rarely stray more than a few hundred miles from this track. There are many variations to this trunk route, with secondary routes branching off and rejoining it along its entire length. Approximately 200 boats take the route from the Panama Canal to French Polynesia every year, and the westward flow is augmented by an influx of US and Canadian boats, most arriving directly in the Marquesas from the Pacific coast of the USA or Canada. Having passed through the Cooks, Tonga or Samoan Islands, the main route reaches Fiji, which lies at the centre of a number of routes. At the western end the route is joined by boats coming from New Zealand or Australia. As the central part of the route from Tahiti to Vanuatu is liable to tropical storms between November and April, there is very little yacht movement between island groups during that period. The few boats that choose to remain in this area during the tropical summer invariably stay close to a protected port or hurricane hole.

Puerto Lucia Yacht Club in Salinas is now the most popular marina among cruising sailors on the west coast of South America.

Of the 532 boats that arrived in the Pacific by way of the Panama Canal in 2000, about half turned north towards Mexico and California. The rest joined the traditional trade wind route to the South Seas, a long haul of nearly 4,000 miles to the Marquesas. Because of the stringent restrictions applied to cruising boats in the

Galapagos Islands have been eased, most boats take advantage of this relaxation to stop briefly in those islands. As the entire archipelago is a nature reserve, cruising boats are only allowed to make a short stop at one of four designated ports. Those who wish to see more of the islands must either join one of the local excursion boats, or apply for a cruising permit, which is now easier to obtain, although the cost is quite exorbitant.

Increasingly, boats bound for the South Pacific from Panama make a detour to mainland Ecuador. The most popular destination is the new marina at Puerto Lucia in Salinas. Over 70 yachts stopped there in 2000 and the total of cruising boats that passed through Salinas during that year is estimated at 120. Salinas is indeed a convenient and safe stop as well as a good base from which to visit the interior of Ecuador and neighbouring countries.

According to the port captain's office in Puerto Ayora, which is the hub of all maritime traffic in the Galapagos Islands, in 2000 the port was visited by 152 yachts (Table 13). This is an all-time high and the upward trend is expected to continue. Very few of the boats that visit the archipelago miss Puerto Ayora, so the total number for the entire archipelago is estimated to be about 180 yachts. Among the boats that stopped at Puerto Ayora, half came to the Galapagos directly from Panama, while one-third had made a detour to visit mainland Ecuador first. The destinations after Galapagos are more straightforward: the majority of boats were bound for the Marquesas, while the few that were bound for Chile sailed there via Easter Island. A larger than usual number sailed directly from Galapagos to Hawaii, but the nine boats that did so included the six participants in the Clipper round the world race. It is interesting to note that as many as seven boats arrived in Galapagos from French Polynesia and were bound for Panama or California – certainly not the easiest of routes.

	From	To
Panama	75	8
Costa Rica	11	4
Mexico	5	2
Ecuador	50	4
French Polynesia	7	121
Chile	3	4
USA	1	–
Hawaii	–	9
Total	152	152

Table 13: Yacht movement in Puerto Ayora in 2000

Among the boats that called at Puerto Ayora, the largest contingent was from the USA (61), followed by the UK (43), France (10) and Germany (7). From Galapagos, the majority of the boats bound for French Polynesia sailed directly to the Marquesas, but a few were not deterred by the detour to Easter Island (Table 14). The island of the mysterious stone statues is indeed a challenging destination, and among the 22 boats that called there in 2000 more than half had reached the Pacific via the Panama Canal.

	From	To
Panama	4	1
Galapagos	6	–
Chile	8	1
Ecuador	2	–
French Polynesia	2	6
Pitcairn	–	14

Table 14: Yacht movement at Easter Island in 2000

Going west from Galapagos, the main gateway into French Polynesia continues to be the port of Atuona, on the island of Hiva Oa in the Marquesas. Among the total of 469 foreign yachts that arrived in 2000 in French Polynesia from overseas, 253 boats made their first landfall in the Marquesas. The majority had come from Panama and Galapagos, while the rest had sailed from either California or Mexico. The Papeete port authority recorded a total of 504 yacht arrivals in Tahiti in 2000, of which 442 were described as foreign yachts. This figure shows a considerable reduction from the previous year when 696 yachts stopped in Tahiti, the larger than usual number including many boats that were bound for New Zealand and the America's Cup. However, as the figures for 1998 showed only 347 arrivals in Tahiti, even if the 1999 bumper year is ignored, it is safe to conclude that the upward trend is set to continue. Earlier figures for Tahiti show 328 arrivals in 1987, 339 in 1991, and 364 in 1993.

From	
Marquesas	253
Tuamotus	34
Gambiers	36
Tahiti	90
Other Society Islands	29
Total	**442**

Table 15: Yacht arrivals in Papeete during 2000

The statistics kept by the port of Papeete are very accurate, as regardless of the initial point of entry into French Polynesia, all boats must complete full entry formalities on arrival in Tahiti (Table 15). Some of those formalities were recently relaxed as sailors from EU countries are no longer required to deposit the compulsory repatriation bond, a ruling that still applies to non-EU sailors. It is rumoured that the one-year limit imposed on cruising boats may also be lifted. This regulation was introduced in order to dissuade boats from spending the cyclone season in French Polynesia, after several cruising boats had been lost or damaged by cyclones that swept over the Society Islands.

Some of the statistics obtained from intermediate ports along the traditional trade wind route in the South Pacific reflect this westward flow. Rarotonga, in the Cook Islands, saw a record number of 150 yachts during 2000, while the small island of Niue welcomed 138 visiting yachts. During the same season, 142 foreign cruising boats were hosted by the Royal Suva Yacht Club in Fiji's capital (Table 16). From there, the majority of those on a circumnavigation were headed west for Vanuatu and Northern Australia, while the remainder were bound for New Caledonia and the east coast of Australia.

	From	To
Tonga	72	1
New Zealand	25	9
New Caledonia	1	20
Tahiti	3	2
Vanuatu	1	12
Samoa	4	–
Wallis	1	–
Australia	–	4
Other Fijian islands	35	94
Total	142	142

Table 16: Yacht movement in Suva in 2000

The movement in Suva is highly seasonal, with almost all arrivals from New Zealand in May and June, and a pronounced westward movement from August onwards. There is hardly any movement during the cyclone season, with only three boats arriving in Suva between the end of October and the end of March.

Cautious sailors attempt to spend the critical season in areas not affected by cyclones, and by far the most popular destination is New Zealand. As many as 567 yachts arrived in New Zealand for the austral summer of 2000–1, and although this figure includes some returning New Zealand boats, it shows just how popular a cruising destination New Zealand has become. This sailing nation's main attractions are not just its benign summer weather, but its excellent repair facilities where the enforced stop can be put to good use by giving the boat a complete overhaul at some of the lowest labour rates in the developed world. New Zealand's popularity as a cruising destination is shown by the number of foreign yachts that cleared into the Bay of Islands area over the years: 86 in 1974, 186 in 1984, 311 in 1993, and an estimated 400 in 2000. The same year, 2000, saw 670 yacht departures from New Zealand, and the higher figure includes the yachts that had come there for the America's Cup.

Destination	
Fiji	66
Australia	52
New Caledonia	47
Tonga	44
Vanuatu	41
Chile	3
Tahiti	3
Cook Islands	3
Niue	3

Gambier Islands	1
Samoa	1
Hawaii	1
Guam	1
Total	**266**

Table 17: Yacht departures from Opua

The list of destinations obtained from the customs office in the Bay of Islands for the boats that cleared out from Opua between 1 July 2000 and 30 June 2001 shows the many options awaiting sailors who had spent the cyclone season in New Zealand. Several routes originate in New Zealand, and most of the yachts that had spent the summer there return to the tropics in April and May at the beginning of the southern winter. The previous year's movement is now reversed, with the majority returning to Tonga and Fiji to resume their voyage, while those who are in a hurry to reach the Indian Ocean head for the Torres Straits, either via New Caledonia, Vanuatu or Australia. The majority of those crossing the Tasman Sea from New Zealand to Australia continue inside the Great Barrier Reef towards the Torres Straits and beyond.

The anchorage off Hangaroa on Easter Island.

Nouméa, the capital city of New Caledonia, has become a major cruising destination in recent years, as shown by an increase of 41 per cent in the number of boats (605) that called there in 2000 compared to the previous year's total of 429 (Table 18).

	1999	2000
USA	101	177
Australia	85	94
New Zealand	58	79
France	45	58
Europe (except France)	101	158
Others	39	39
Total	429	605

Table 18: Yacht arrivals in Nouméa

Sailors who do not have the time to add one year to their voyage by a detour to New Zealand attempt to be past the Torres Straits by September so as to be sure of avoiding the cyclone season in the South Indian Ocean that sets in by mid-November. The Torres Straits are a major gateway for boats heading west, and the number that passed through Australia in 2000 can be assessed from the precise records kept by the Australian Quarantine Service. Altogether, 802 yachts cleared into Australia from an overseas port during 2000, of which 571 were foreign yachts (Table 19).

From	
New Caledonia	335
New Zealand	136
Vanuatu	73
Solomons	4
Fiji	18
Norfolk Island	1
Tonga	1
Philippines	3
Total	571

Table 19: Yacht arrivals in Australia in 2000

Indian Ocean

There are two major routes crossing the Indian Ocean, both originating at the Torres Straits. For those who wish to reach Europe by the shortest route, the logical way leads through the North Indian Ocean and Red Sea. In the case of those who prefer to reach the Atlantic by way of the Cape of Good Hope, the traditional route leads across the South Indian Ocean to South Africa. Safety considerations often influence the choice of route, such as the recent concerns over the situation in the Middle East generally, and in particular the risks associated with passages through the Gulf of Aden.

Very few boats bound for the Indian Ocean sail by Darwin without stopping, and 239 yachts cleared into the capital of Australia's Northern Territory during 2000. Among the yachts that arrived in Darwin, 230 came from the east (Torres Straits) and only 9 from Indonesia. The situation is completely reversed if one looks at the destinations after Darwin, as the majority of the 225 boats that left Darwin in 2000 were bound for Indonesia (Table 20). Among them, 106 were headed directly for Bali, while the rest planned to stop en route, including in East Timor. The former Indonesian territory was out of bounds in the past, but a number of cruising boats are now attracted to newly independent East Timor.

Destination	
Indonesia	162
Cocos Keeling	30
Christmas Island	12
Singapore	10
Mauritius	2
Seychelles	2
Sri Lanka	1
Maldives	1
Australia	5
Total	225

Table 20: Departures from Darwin in 2000

NORTH INDIAN OCEAN

Yacht traffic along the main route crossing the northern half of the Indian Ocean is dictated by the two monsoons. As most cruising boats undertaking a world voyage move in an east to west direction, the majority of boats cross the Indian Ocean during the NE monsoon, which lasts approximately from December to April, with most passages towards the Red Sea being made in January and early February. Eastbound passages across the North Indian Ocean are made during the SW monsoon (May to September), which is the season of extremely high temperatures in the Red Sea and Gulf of Aden and also of very strong winds east of Socotra, where the frequency of gales is one of the highest in the world. It is therefore not surprising that the number of eastbound voyages is very small.

Most yachts arrive in Singapore either from Indonesia, Eastern Malaysia or the Philippines. According to the Maritime and Port Authority of Singapore, a total of 518 yachts cleared into that busy port during 2000. Among that total, 230 were described as cruising yachts, which is a considerable reduction from the 302 boats that passed through Singapore in 1987. According to Y P Loke, Manager of Raffles Marina, the reduction is due to two main factors: concern over the deteriorating situation in Indonesia and the threat of piracy in the Gulf of Aden, both of which have led many boats to take the South African route.

Approximately 120 of the yachts that called at Singapore in 2000 came from Bali. From Singapore, most boats sail north through the Malacca Straits where Port Klang, home of the Royal Selangor Yacht Club, in Western Malaysia is rarely bypassed by cruising boats, of which 103 called there in 2000. According to the yacht club, approximately 90 per cent of these yachts arrived from Singapore and continued their voyage towards Phuket. This large island off Thailand's west coast is now considered Asia's prime cruising destination. Indeed, yachting facilities have greatly improved in recent years, while on the downside, the Thai authorities continue to create difficulties for cruising yachts wishing to spend longer in the area. According to Andy Stephens, Manager of Yacht Haven marina in Phuket, about 300 boats are based in Phuket at any one time. He also estimated that approximately 100 cruising yachts cleared into Phuket in 2000, which was a record year for both cruising boats visiting Phuket and the additional 100 mostly racing yachts that joined the annual King's Cup regatta. Most of the latter came from Hong Kong and Singapore doing the annual racing circuit.

Whether spending one or more seasons in Phuket or Western Malaysia, when the time comes to leave, most boats do so in the early months of the year when the NE monsoon provides the best sailing conditions for a westbound passage. In spite of ongoing hostilities in Sri Lanka, the port of Galle, on the southern tip of the island, continues to be a popular stop and 133 boats called there in 2000. This compares to 74 boats in 1984 and 138 in 1993. According to Santosh Windsor, who runs a yacht agency in Galle, the year 2000 saw fewer boats than in previous years, and this is almost certainly the result of concerns caused by the reported piracy attacks. In the past, the waters around the island of Socotra were always considered a dangerous area, but in recent years the entire Gulf of Aden, between the Horn of Africa and the Yemeni coast, has been designated a high-risk area, with many reported attacks on both commercial shipping and cruising boats. Most yachts undertaking this passage, whether sailing individually or as part of an organized event, do so as part of a convoy of several vessels, which evidently improves their security. Having passed through the critical area most boats head for Djibouti as the once popular port of Aden, and its surrounding waters, are no longer regarded as safe. The former French colony of Djibouti has retained its close links to France, which maintains a large military presence there. The French Navy keeps a close eye on developments in the Gulf of Aden and will react promptly if a pirate attack is reported. According to the Djibouti Yacht Club, around 100 yachts stopped there in 2000 before tackling the 1,200 miles through the Red Sea to the Suez Canal. Virtually all boats, whether north- or southbound, stopped at Massawa where the Eritrean authorities are making a determined effort to welcome cruising yachts now that the situation in their part of the world has returned to normality. The harbour master estimated that in 2000 Massawa was visited by approximately 150 yachts, the majority en route to the Suez Canal.

Just as in Panama, small boats are not viewed very favourably by the Suez Canal Authority, which is also looking into the real cost of the transits and has recently increased fees. According to the Prince of the Red Sea, the main yacht agency in Suez, out of a total of 200 yachts that transited the Suez Canal in both directions in 2000, approximately 160 were northbound. Among these, 37 were taking part in round the world rallies, so the number of actual cruising boats was considerably less than in previous years. Ashraf Soukar, who handles most northbound yacht transits, complained that the drop is entirely due to the fear caused by the pirate attacks in the Gulf of Aden, which is persuading increasing numbers to sail the longer route around the Cape of Good Hope.

SOUTH INDIAN OCEAN

The port of Darwin continues to be the logical jumping-off point for Indonesia, but the ethnic troubles in many parts of the archipelago have resulted in an overall reduction in the number of visiting yachts, and also the cancellation of the highly popular Darwin to Ambon Race, which now ends in Bali. This is indeed the favoured destination in Indonesia and, for most cruising boats, also the only one as Bali continues to be regarded as a safe destination. According to Bali International Marina, approximately 250 boats stopped there in 2000. Among these, about half continued north towards Singapore, while the others sailed west into the South Indian Ocean, where two main route options awaited them. Those with less time on their hands normally sail the southern route via Cocos Keeling and Mauritius, while those who intended to spend longer in that part of the world take the northern route to Christmas Island and the Chagos Archipelago. The uninhabited islands of this archipelago have become a kind of cruising Mecca, with boats flocking there from all corners of the Indian Ocean. It is reported that as many as 200 boats, many of them from South Africa, limit their cruising to the South Indian Ocean, and for most of them Chagos is the turning point. At the height of the winter season there were occasions when as many as 80 to 100 cruising boats were scattered among the atolls, enjoying the beauty and tranquillity of these cruising gems. The area is occasionally patrolled by a posse of British policemen who are in charge of security of the so-called BIOT (British Indian Ocean Territory), which includes the US military base at Diego Garcia, which is out of bounds to yachts. Those lucky sailors should indeed enjoy the islands while the current situation lasts, as the original Ilois inhabitants, who were forcibly removed to Mauritius, have won a long legal battle with the British government and may be allowed to return to their ancestral lands.

A similarly idyllic destination in the South Indian Ocean is the smaller Cocos Keeling archipelago, a favourite port of call on the traditional trade wind route. A total of 116 yachts stopped there in 2000, a number that is backed up by the statistics provided by the port captain of Port Louis, in Mauritius, which saw 209 arrivals in 2000. More than half that traffic could be described as local, as 139 of those boats had sailed over from neighbouring Réunion. Of the 55 boats that had arrived in Mauritius from the east, many continued to South Africa, although some made a detour to Madagascar, which in recent years has become a popular destination and is also visited by many boats sailing north from South Africa. The customs office in Hell-Ville, on the island of Nosy Be, estimates that some 200 boats cleared into Madagascar in 2000, and the year 2001 saw an even greater number. Some of these boats may have cleared in more than once as they cruised to and from neighbouring areas, but even so, the increase is dramatic compared to the estimated 20 boats that called at Hell-Ville in 1990. The above trend is also reflected by the 220 yachts that visited Mayotte in 2000, as this small French territory is another popular destination in that part of the world.

Current trends

This overview of the principal cruising routes of the world and the movement of yachts along them has concentrated on boats that are cruising away from home.

The highest concentration of cruising yachts is found on routes going in a general east to west direction, namely the southern route in the North Atlantic, as well as the main trade wind routes across the South Pacific and Indian Oceans. Seasonal and climatic factors are unlikely to change in future years, although the attitude of sailors to them may. Following several active tropical storm seasons in both the Caribbean and South Pacific, insurance companies now stipulate that boats must spend the critical season in a safe area. This has resulted in a huge increase in the number of boats heading for Trinidad and Venezuela for the summer season, while in the South Pacific most cruising boats head for New Zealand.

Apart from the weather, political factors can also change cruising patterns in certain areas, as countries make yachts more or less welcome, impose cruising restrictions, or even close certain areas to cruising yachts. On the other hand, some areas, which were long closed, have opened up and more may do so in the future. While certain areas might gain or lose popularity with cruising yachts, overall there has been an increase in the total world cruising population, a trend that is likely to continue. The nations with a tradition of yachting, such as the United States, Britain and France, still dominate the world cruising population, with a higher proportion of Australian and New Zealand boats in the Pacific and Asian regions. US-flagged vessels are in the majority in traditional cruising areas for US yachts, such as the Bahamas, Virgins and Mexico. On a global level, which includes the Mediterranean, British cruising boats probably have the edge over any other nation, including France, whose sailors occupied that position until very recently. The comparatively large number of French cruising yachts is due not only to tradition, but also to the convenient location of French overseas departments and territories, such as Guadeloupe and Martinique in the Caribbean, Tahiti and New Caledonia in the Pacific or Réunion in the Indian Ocean, where French citizens can stop and work for a period of time before continuing their voyage. Sailors from Germany and Scandinavia are also seen in larger numbers, and the general rise in the cruising population has been accompanied by a striking change in the national origins as yachts from countries such as Switzerland, Finland, Italy or Spain are seen in greater numbers.

However, even though there has been an increase in the overall number of people cruising, this has been mostly on a regional basis, and the number of boats completing a circumnavigation has not changed significantly during the last decade. In order to assess the number of cruising boats engaged in a circum-navigation in any one year, I examined the data obtained from a number of significant locations such as: Tahiti, Darwin, Bali, Singapore, Cape Town and St Helena, as well as the Panama and Suez Canals, because any boat sailing around the world is bound to pass through some of these key gateways. My estimate is that the total number of cruising boats successfully completing a circumnavigation is between 150 and 200 per year. At the moment, their number is split equally between the two main routes: via the Red Sea, or around the Cape of Good Hope.

While the global movement is relatively easy to determine, making an assessment of the total number of boats actually cruising is bound to be less accurate. Obviously the total should only include boats undertaking a longer offshore voyage, and exclude those that are engaged in coastal cruising in areas of high concentration (Bahamas, Croatia, Aegean Sea, Balearics, etc). With an estimated 1,000 boats cruising the

Pacific Ocean, and a similar number spread out over the Indian Ocean, the approximately 2,000 yachts actively cruising in the Mediterranean, plus the 6,000 boats that are either crossing the Atlantic or cruising the Caribbean, I believe the total to be between 10,000 and 12,000, with the lower figure probably closer to reality.

Even if one accepts the higher estimate, in most places this is still only about 20 per cent more than the results of my 1987 survey. One person who has observed the movement of yachts for many years is Juan Francisco Martin, commercial director of the Port of Las Palmas and former president of the Canarian Marina Association. His own conclusions confirm the findings of this survey as he believes that 'as charter yachts are now easily available in most parts of the world, people are less tempted to undertake long ocean passages in their own boats. Most yacht owners nowadays prefer to keep their boats in marinas that are easily reached by air, or in areas with good cruising opportunities and benign weather, and not waste time on long offshore voyages. In other words, the more nautical tourism there is, the fewer true navigators there are.'

Looking at the cruising scene on a worldwide basis, the increase in the number of people undertaking offshore voyages has been brought about by three main factors: improved yacht design and construction methods, which have resulted in more comfortable and seaworthy yachts; greatly improved aids to navigation, which have given a greater sense of security to those cruising; and thirdly, the greater prosperity enjoyed by the developed nations, which has changed yachting from a hobby of the rich to a leisure activity accessible to many. More people are financially able to take early retirement, and for many sailors this provides the ideal opportunity to embark on a longer cruise. Those who are tempted to make a longer cruise while still young, but who do not wish to abandon their careers, may prefer the option of a sabbatical leave. With a wide choice of reasonably priced flights to all parts of the world, people with restricted time schedules often plan their cruises in stages, returning when necessary to their business or professional commitments. This trend is becoming widespread among professional people, and several ARC participants are doctors, architects or businessmen who are taking a few months off to undertake a voyage that could not be fitted into a normal annual leave. This kind of attitude is contributing more than anything else to an opening up of the oceans to more cruising boats. However, this does not mean that the oceans are getting as crowded as a motorway on a holiday weekend. Fortunately for those who are prepared to make a detour off the beaten track, there are still plenty of unspoilt places and, as the statistics quoted on the foregoing pages have shown, there are still many places where the number of cruising boats has hardly gone up. It is a phenomenon that few would have predicted 10 or 20 years ago.

The results of this latest survey therefore hardly justify the concerns of those who believe that the world's oceans are getting too overcrowded. Some popular areas are more crowded, especially during the high season, but as the figures show, even popular destinations have not yet reached saturation. It has been said that the definition of a pessimist is a well-informed optimist. I will therefore end this overview with the same words as I used ten years ago – when I expressed the hope that my findings should make both optimists and pessimists happy!

15

Looking into a Crystal Ball
GLOBAL CRUISING SURVEY ON THE FUTURE OF CRUISING

*"The future of cruising? We in the US have the baby boomers now starting
to reach the age to cast-off, so look out, world – here they come!"*
DON BABSON

*"The true delights of sailing and cruising will remain for the few connoisseurs,
of which there are several kinds: racing sailors, true cruising people with a
goal, and the vagabonds of the seas going from nowhere to nowhere."*
ANTTI LOUHIJA

No question caused a more lively debate among the sailors who took part
in the Global Cruising Survey than the one concerning the future of
cruising. Their thoughts and comments make fascinating reading, and in
most cases their answers are quoted in full. Bill Butler, who has the doubtful
distinction of having wrecked two of his boats, one of them twice, sounded quite
upbeat in his statement: 'Cruising sailors will be around for ever, sailing every
imaginable type of craft, slowly increasing in number, with many of the least
seaworthy completing long passages while well-found boats are lost. The mix of
sailors will continue to consist of new and old salts, some better prepared than
others, all bitten by the lure of the sea. It will most probably continue to be the
safest mode of transport.'

Eduardo Gallardo agrees with that view: 'Sailboat cruising, offshore as well as
coastal, will continue to grow as it becomes easier to purchase boats and as more
of the world's economies allow people to retire earlier and in better financial
conditions. Cruising to faraway and exotic places is in the mind of most men. As
it becomes more accessible to more people, sailing will continue to grow.'

This view is shared by Don Babson: 'More people will set off in all kinds of
vessels. We in the US have the baby boomers now starting to reach the age to cast-
off, so look out, world – here they come!'

Michelle LaMontagne takes a less optimistic view: 'My first thought when the
September 11 tragedy occurred was: cut the dock lines. When economic
downturns happen – cut the dock lines! Besides all that, boats are getting more
comfortable, navigation is getting easier, the baby boomers are retiring with more

money and need to de-stress. Of course cruising will continue, although I feel that some people will decide that it isn't what they romanticized.'

Carlton DeHart generally agrees: 'Very little changes with the sea. The old adage, the more things change, the more they stay the same, applies here. Mistakes are quickly turned into lessons on what not to do again. The boats that are built too light or the gear that is not up to the job will soon disappear. My only hope is that with the growing numbers of sailors, there will be an equal growth in consideration to others. In our travels, we have seen all too many sailors who were only looking out for themselves. As to sailing itself, it will only grow in popularity as the media coverage grows and more people are exposed to the reasons we all like sailing. I believe that the boats will become larger as gear develops, new facilities will be built, and since fibreglass boats don't go away, there will be more and more boats. It is my hope that the freedom that sailing represents to me, will never be taken away.'

This opinion is largely shared by David Beauchamp: 'As more boats are being launched and very few seem to be actually scrapped, more and more folk are taking to the sea, yet fewer and fewer of them seem to be instilled with a genuine respect for the sea. It becomes just another medium to be used for leisure – a right, not a privilege. There lies the danger. Bureaucracy will try to make laws forcing people to have the knowledge for making safe voyages. I hope they succeed, but I doubt that they will. In any event, all those lovely, lonely places will eventually become lonely no more. I am glad that by then I shall be cruising no more.'

John Morgan expressed similar concerns: 'I'm glad I'm cruising now because I can see it becoming more and more restrictive and loaded with controls. As an Australian, I can sail without any qualifications or insurance almost wherever I like, subject to the occasional visa. I worry that boats will become larger and more expensive, and cruising will become more elitist.' John Wicks holds the opposite view: 'There should be some sort of licensing for sailors possibly run by organizations like the Royal Yachting Association in the UK. Permits should be introduced in areas of special beauty and significance such as the Galapagos. There should be improved waste disposal on boats and sailors should be prepared to pay for this, as they seem to expect to get everything on the cheap.'

Klaus Bartels's only concern is that 'there is definitely going to be more sailors, and more will be setting off on long voyages'. Michael Frankel, on the other hand, is more concerned about 'boats having too many complex gadgets, especially electronic gadgets, and people become too dependent on them. Boaters ignore the psychological rewards of self-reliance associated with cruising.'

Keeping boats simpler is what Peter Förthmann would like to see: 'Blue water cruising is in, round the world cruising is out. Because of that, I'd like to see more boats of moderate size, but of sturdy construction, ideally in metal, which can be easily handled by small crews. As to equipment, it should follow the KISS* philosophy' (*Keep It Simple Stupid).

Javier Visiers feels that 'the size of yachts has increased tremendously in recent years. Larger cruising boats are being built to sail to faraway places. At the same time, even such large boats can now be easily handled by small crews.' John Neal also feels that 'boats will be gettting bigger, people will be cruising for shorter lengths of time, but will have more expendable income'. Helmut von Strahlen

An ecstatic Ann Harsh receives her trophy from former British Prime Minister Sir Edward Heath for leading the Millennium Odyssey into London.

foresees a future in which 'multihulls will come into their own as ideal cruising boats, with everything onboard being computerized for easy sailing'.

Antti Louhija foresees a very different future: 'As long as the seas are free there will always be cruising. The popularity of cruising will probably not increase much in developed countries, although the popularity of owning a boat seems to increase. Most boats will continue to stay in marinas. Many people dream of cruising, but it takes a special kind to actually do it. More countries are entering the sailing scene, mainly from Eastern Europe. Most ideas in the development of boat design seem to derive from racing, which is not bad as such. We have now better boats than ever, but the safety factor seems to be often ignored. On the other hand, the tendency to ask for every possible living comfort in a cruising boat, meaning comforts belonging to homes on dry land, such as washing machines, dryers, freezers, microwave ovens, television sets, air conditioning, etc, does not bode well for the future of cruising. I am not against comforts, but I am afraid this attracts the wrong sort of people to the seas, people who will eventually be disappointed. The risk is that they will more than ever sail from one marina to the next, making repairs. They forget why they are at sea in the first place, and no longer enjoy the excitement of using natural navigational skills and a simple life while observing a grandiose nature. The true delights of sailing and cruising will remain for the few connoisseurs, of which there are several kinds: racing sailors, true cruising people with a goal, and the vagabonds of the seas going from nowhere to nowhere.'

Skip Novak also believes in a more traditional attitude to sailing: 'My main argument is not to make cruising boats too gadget-oriented – as I see time and time again people sitting in marinas trying to fix this or that, with technicians on board fixing equipment that they really do not need. Why clutter your life when the sailing and getting away is the important thing? The real problem is that this gadget mentality is designer-led, and to keep a new boat simple you have to fight like hell with them, the builders and the gear suppliers, who always insist "you really must have one of these . . ." I think cruising folk need to ask themselves some fundamental questions like, why are they going cruising in the first place and what do they want to achieve – if it is to get away and see a different part of the world, then my advice is to cut out the junk on board. I find it a joy and a pleasure to have less than more. In this way, you will find you will be doing more sailing and less agonizing.'

Luc Callebaut, who is based in French Polynesia where he witnesses a steady stream of cruising boats, agrees with Skip's view: 'Many more people will go cruising in the future. People will tend to be older, as many will wait until retirement to go, also more the intellectual type and therefore less physically inclined, so designers will produce boats needing less physical activity to handle. Electronics will become more and more important, like in automobiles, with less possibility to be fixed on location. Also, cruisers are becoming more like regular tourists: more superficial, less contact with nature, more dependent on shore services and activities, more in a hurry. It's going to become more like "home"! The more people have equipment and computers, the less they will interact with each other and they will have less of that pioneer spirit. We already see a lot more cruisers socializing only with members of their little group and being less and less interested in meeting other cruisers.'

This is a view shared by Clyff Huggett: 'Eighty per cent of the people you meet cruising, you would like to have as long-term friends. Ten per cent know everything about everything and you can't get rid of them fast enough. The remaining 10 per cent are one of the reasons you have to lock up everything. I think there will always be people who do not sit around and dream, but just get up and do it. As long as boats are affordable, people will sail them and go to places they want to see.'

Mirek Misayat, who is based in the Mediterranean, sees things rather differently: 'Cruising as such has become more accessible to a larger number of people, many without adequate experience and training. Anchorages, harbours and marinas are becoming overcrowded at a very rapid rate. Numerous marinas are being built everywhere to cope with the demand. To avoid overcrowding one would have to sail to some remote area, which is hardly a solution for most people.'

Also based full time in the Mediterranean is Giuseppe Italo Masotti: 'Soon there will be a lack of places to visit. Traditional places are already overcrowded, and so people now go to Antarctica, Alaska, Spitsbergen. Also, boats will get bigger because more boat means more comfort and more safety. If you shop around you can get the perfect push button boat. All the gadgets to make life on board easier will be cheaper and cheaper. Are you worried they can break down? Don't. Carry a back-up. You already do it with GPS. Actually, the future is here already.'

Bob Hall does not believe things are as simple as that: 'There is a trade-off between having more amenities aboard and the maintenance required to keep them working. As more people sail as couples, it will be important to have the boat able to be handled easily by two people with limited physical prowess.' Charles Gray, who sails just with his wife Saundra, agrees: 'I think there will be more attention to building safer, faster blue water sailing boats with convenience in mind for sailing couples. The ideal boat will be 44 to 55 feet in length and designed to be sailed by two people. There will be more couples ready to buy that kind of boat and simply sail away. Although some of the world is in turmoil, there are many beautiful areas of the world to enjoy.'

David Hersey believes that the future belongs to larger boats: 'Boats are getting bigger, more comfortable and easier to handle in most conditions. They still take a lot of looking after, although many of the systems on bigger boats are not much more trouble than on smaller ones. More and more people are cruising each year so it remains to be seen how recent political events will impact on the cruising life. After a 40,000-mile circumnavigation, I was really appreciative of just how good things were on our return to Greece.'

Richard Walker takes a more sarcastic view: 'Passages are getting shorter and faster – hence more time at anchor and, God forbid, more time in marinas. So we can expect more fast craft with lots of cockpit glass holders – a landing craft comes to mind, and who will sail it? Just about anyone who can pay the high marina fees and push the "goto" key.'

A true blue sailor like Tom Muller could not agree more: 'There are too many caravans on the water. Boatbuilding standards often suffer because of the cost factor, poor management and negligence. This is quite obvious from the number of poorly built plastic tubs built on both sides of the Atlantic. Compared to the automotive world, boatbuilding is in an extremely bad state these days.'

Wilhelm Greiff does not agree with this pessimistic view: 'Boats are becoming better equipped, faster and more sophisticated. However, people sailing in them should still be able to handle these boats and not forget seamanship and sailors' crafts.'

This is also the advice given by Steve Dashew: 'Neophytes need to spend more time learning the basics of seamanship before setting out. All the modern gear and electronics are not a substitute for practising boat handling!'

Matt Rollberg takes a wider view of cruising: 'It's a good way to live for a period of time, before you are too old and have too many body failures. As boats and systems get more and more complex, it makes it increasingly difficult to maintain them. Also, the trend to bigger boats makes it more difficult for two people to go on their own.'

Marc Labaume has certain concerns: 'Boats are more and more well equipped, even if their design is not always well adapted to blue water cruising. I am thinking especially of mass-produced catamarans that are designed for charter in the Med or the Caribbean, rather than round the world voyages. It seems to me that more people are envisaging offshore cruising now than in previous years. What has changed is that offshore cruising is no longer restricted to some wealthy retired people, or, on the contrary, some broke and young hippies, but that more and more ordinary people can embark on a life of adventure. If you dream it, you can do it!'

Arthur Beiser agrees with Marc: 'Sailing long ago ceased to be an elite recreation, so there is no huge untapped reservoir of potential cruising sailors. Almost every-where the explosion of yachting, much of it in power boats, has created a shortage of permanent marina berths that deters newcomers. On the other hand, there is much more money around and people are retiring at younger ages. And whatever happens to the prices of new boats, fibreglass boats have long lives, and the cost of secondhand boats will surely remain reasonable as time goes on. So, broadly speak-ing, I would not anticipate a major increase or decrease in the cruising population.'

John Ellis with Lois and Don Babson on completion of the Millennium Odyssey.

Chris Harding disagrees and feels that more people will go cruising: 'Cruising is definitely not going out of fashion and I am sure that, thanks to GPS, cruising has been opened up to infinitely more people. The boats are getting lighter and faster and are cruising farther afield than ever before. More and more of what were exotic locations are becoming flooded with boats, and many such places have become charmless, expensive and dirty. To find the "real" places now you have to travel a lot further north or south of the classic cruising routes. I think this will only get worse as there seems to be a lot of money available nowadays for leisure activities, and sailing is extremely popular. The quantity of people I have met in recent years who have sold up and are setting out on their dream voyage has definitely increased. The boats that these people are buying are becoming extremely technical, and many are relying on professional crew to assist with the running of these boats. I can see the future of cruising as increasing both in number of people and size of boats, while places like the Caribbean are becoming very crowded in certain places; also, tighter and tighter regulations are being introduced to try and control the harm to the environment.'

John Ellis has co-ordinated several round the world rallies, and therefore sees the development of offshore cruising from a different angle: 'Since the advent of GPS the number of cruising yachts has increased dramatically, possibly because the introduction of GPS coincided with an unprecedented worldwide economic growth, where people had cash to burn. At the same time, yachts were being built using high-tech materials, sophisticated hydraulics, electrics and electronics. The result: novice wealthy first-time buyers were purchasing large expensive yachts that were largely automated. Certainly the average size of the cruising yacht has increased; and the ARC confirms this. Seventy-foot yachts are being built now that can easily be sailed by two people, and I think this will be the way of the future. The round the world rallies are a good example as over the years the boats got bigger and crews smaller. High-tech materials and systems tested and used on racing yachts will be used increasingly on cruising yachts as owners search for more performance. I feel that many of the basic principles of safety and good seamanship will be missing from future cruising sailors. Already there is a drift away from self-reliance in the case of many skippers, who appeal for outside help for any kind of emergency, however minor. Twenty years ago, the blue water sailor was a rare breed; a husband and wife, often on a 30 footer, or perhaps a family on a shoestring budget taking ten years to sail around the world, perhaps stopping off and working in countries along the way. The average blue water sailor today is a wealthy, often self-made man or woman, but not necessarily with a lot of sailing experience, who wants to take an early retirement or can afford to take two years out from the business. The future blue water sailor will be much the same as his counterpart today, although cruising will become more mainstream. Because of the internet there is a vast amount of cruising information to draw on for independent cruising. Yachts will keep getting bigger and crew sizes will diminish. More creature comforts from home will become standard on yachts as they embrace more of the high-tech features of the racing world.'

I leave the last word to Barry Esrig, who sees the future in a more optimistic light: 'Cruising boats are becoming faster, lighter, more stable, easier to handle. The equipment is better and more sophisticated. It is, however, becoming more expensive. As it becomes easier, more people will be open to sailing. I believe the camaraderie between cruisers will always exist and flourish, sharing experiences and helping each other. Cruisers will always be unique individuals, no matter what is going on elsewhere in the world.'

Appendix 1

1   *The Suva Survey*. A first cruising survey was conducted in Fiji in 1978 and dealt with various aspects of cruising boat design.
2   *The Cruising Survey*. A more extensive survey was conducted the following year in a variety of places in the South Pacific. Its findings presented a comprehensive picture of life afloat.
3   *The Seawives Survey*. Cruising women on a variety of boats sailing in the South Pacific took part in this survey, which examined the role and attitudes of sailing women.
4   *The Circumnavigators Survey*. Twelve crews from a variety of countries who had successfully completed their circumnavigation formed the basis of a comprehensive survey undertaken in 1983.
5   *The Pacific Survey*. The skippers and crew of 50 long distance cruising boats were interviewed in the South Pacific at the end of 1984 on a comprehensive range of subjects, with particular focus on equipment and instrumentation.
6   *The Atlantic Survey*. Cruising boat design, equipment as well as different aspects of life afloat, were covered in a survey conducted in 1985–6 among 100 boats on both sides of the Atlantic.
7   *The Liferaft Survey*. The skippers of 100 boats who had recently crossed the Atlantic were interviewed in the Caribbean on the subject of liferafts and their design. The survey was conducted in association with Avon Inflatables Ltd.
8   *The Ideal Cruising Boat Survey*. Two hundred participants in the first ARC took part in this survey, which attempted to see if there was a consensus on the essential features of the ideal cruising boat.
9   *The Communication Survey*. The present and future of marine communications were examined in this survey conducted among participants in ARC 1986. The survey was commissioned by Inmarsat, the international satellite communications organization.
10 *The Equipment Survey*. The quality and performance of marine equipment and instrumentation were analysed in a comprehensive survey involving almost 200 yachts taking part in ARC 1987.
11 *The Cruising Life Survey*. Participants in the ARC and TRANSARC rallies supplied the data for an assessment of the daily problems of life at sea.
12 *The World Yacht Movement Survey*. A worldwide survey of the distribution and movement of cruising yachts was carried out between 1985 and 1988. Its findings were based on personal research as well as on data provided by

customs, immigration and port authorities in key locations throughout the world. The survey findings were updated in 1994. Data from all previous key locations, as well as from other popular cruising destinations, was collected in 2001 for the current edition of this book.

13 *Round the World Survey*. Equipment breakages and emergencies at sea were investigated among the participants in the Europa 92 round the world rally. A comprehensive survey was carried out during the Fiji stopover, when the fleet had reached its halfway mark. The results were re-evaluated on completion of the rally in Gibraltar.

14 *Cruising Cost Survey*. The cost of cruising was investigated among participants in the Expo'98 and Millennium Odyssey round the world rallies.

15 *Global Cruising Survey*. A wide-ranging survey was conducted in 2001–2 among 40 experienced long distance sailors concerning the essential features of the ideal cruising yacht.

16 *Sailing Women Survey*. Twenty cruising women were interviewed on the role of women in the day-to-day running of a cruising boat.

17 *Millennium Odyssey Equipment Survey*. The performance and failure of equipment was investigated among the yachts sailing in this round the world rally (1998–2000).

18 *ARC Breakages Survey*. The breakages that have occurred during the Atlantic crossing were examined in a number of ARC rallies.

19 *Bahamas Survey*. Material was gathered early in 2002 on the rig of the cruising boats gathered at a popular anchorage in the Bahamas.

20 *Yachting World Atlantic Surveys 2000 and 2001*. The leading British yachting magazine conducted detailed surveys among participants who had sailed in the ARC in 1999 and 2000 to assess the performance of a wide range of equipment during the Atlantic crossing.

21 *SSCA Equipment Survey 2000*. The Seven Seas Cruising Association conducted in 2000 one of its regular equipment surveys among its members, who rated the performance and reliability of all equipment on board their boats.

Appendix 2

TABLE OF SKIPPERS IN THE GLOBAL CRUISING SURVEY, DETAILS OF
THEIR CURRENT YACHTS, AND ESSENTIAL FEATURES OF THEIR IDEAL
YACHTS

Owner	Name of yacht	Design	LOA	Draft	Year	Material	Flag	Essential features on ideal yacht
Don and Lois Babson	*Que Sera Sera*	Hans Christian	43	6'	1988	GRP	USA	Good sails Dependable engine Power davits Watermaker
Klaus Bartels	*Cythera*	Albin Nova	33	5'8"	1985	GRP	Germany	Shower Dinghy davits Outboard motor Bowsprit for asymmetric spinnaker Stern platform Solar panels
David and Glynn Beauchamp	*Milady Candida*	Lothar Kruger	42	6'	1975	Steel	New Zealand	Powerful engine Furling headsails Efficient galley Deckhouse or bimini All essential spares
Arthur and Germaine Beiser	*Ardent Spirit*	Moody	58	8'2"	1987	GRP	USA	Electric windlass Electric jib furling Electric winches Autopilot Refrigeration Watermaker Washing machine High-capacity bilge pump
Terence Brownrigg	*Fiskery*	Warwick	46	6'	1993	GRP	UK	Autopilot Windlass

Owner	Name of yacht	Design	LOA	Draft	Year	Material	Flag	Essential features on ideal yacht
Bill Butler	*Teresa*	Hein Garberg	41	6'4"	1951	Steel	USA	Furling headsail Fridge-freezer Heater/air conditioning Watermaker
Luc Callebaut and Jackie Lee	*Sloepmouche*	Norman Cross trimaran	46	5'	1980	Plywood	Belgium	Strong anchor windlass One electric winch Good propane stove with oven SSB radio Bilge pumps for each compartment
Steve Dashew	*Beowulf*	Dashew Offshore	78	7'9"	1995	Aluminium	USA	Furling headsail Electric windlass Fridge-freezer Watermaker Inverter Power davits
Carlton and Jody DeHart	*Miss Muffet*	Bowman	57	5'10"/11'	1992	GRP	USA	Power windlass Power winches Hundested propeller High modulus sail cloth High modulus running rigging MaxSea weather routing software
Barry Esrig	*Annie B*	Baltic	51	10'	1980	GRP	USA	Watermaker Washer-dryer Convection microwave oven Fridge-freezer Electric winches Breadmaker Icecream machine
								Electric winches Electric windlass In-mast electric furling system Autopilot Bimini Power davits Reverse cycle heater/air conditioner

Owner	Name of yacht	Design	LOA	Draft	Year	Material	Flag	Essential features on ideal yacht
Michael Frankel	*Sabra*	Sunbird	32	4'	1979	GRP	USA	Electric winch Good outboard motor DSC for VHF Radar warning system Walk-in lockers accessible from deck Extra water tanks
Peter Förthmann	*Windpilot*	Hanseat	33	6'4"	1977	GRP	Germany	Windvane Autopilot Furling headsail Radar RIB dinghy Davits
Eduardo Gallardo	*Argo*	Morgan	46	5'3"	1983	GRP	USA	All sails to be handled from cockpit Electric winches Power furling gear Bimini Watermaker Large fridge-freezer
Klaus Girzig	*Alparena II*	Glaser	50	7'6"	1989	Aluminium	Germany	Comfortable sea berths Two shower/toilets Hot water Electric windlass Good tender Powerful outboard
Charles and Saundra Gray	*Sea Gem*	Gulfstar	54	5'2"	1986	GRP	USA	Autopilot Electric winches Power furling Watermaker Inverter Electronic charts AC/DC refrigeration
Wilhelm and Astrid Greiff	*Octopus*	Via 42	42	3'8"	1989	Aluminium	Germany	WhisperGen One electric winch Davits Large bimini Heating Microwave oven

Owner	Name of yacht	Design	LOA	Draft	Year	Material	Flag	Essential features on ideal yacht
Zoltan Gyurko	*The Way*		35	5'		GRP	USA	Night vision binoculars Radar Forward-looking depthsounder Good outboard Good snorkelling equipment SSB radio
Bob and Judy Hall	*Hornblower*	Morgan	46	6'	1988	GRP	USA	Power furling Bowthruster Double headsails Diesel generator Autopilot Easily handled whisker pole
Chris Harding	*Futuro*	Swan	65	9'6"	1982	GRP	Germany	Electric winches Power furling Air conditioning Dinghy garage SSB and weatherfax Bowthruster Electric windlass
Ann Harsh and Ralph Nehrig	*Harmonie*	Amel Super Maramu	53	6'6"	1996	GRP	USA	Electric windlass Electric toilets Power furling
David Hersey	*Company*	Wauquiez	52	7'10"	1993	GRP	UK	Power winches Power furling Reliable autopilot Electric windlass Power davits Workshop Bowthruster Watermaker Radar
Clyff and Anna Huggett	*Koncerto*	Freebird 50 catamaran	50	3'3"	1993	GRP	UK	E-mail Iridium phone Autopilot Radar Workshop Large modern galley

Owner	Name of yacht	Design	LOA	Draft	Year	Material	Flag	Essential features on ideal yacht
Giuseppe Italo and Silvana Masotti	*Freedom*	Grand Soleil	41	6'8"	1982	GRP	Italy	Electric winches Electric furling Bowthruster Generator Watermaker Dishwasher
Marc Labaume and Paulette Vannier	*Istar*	Kennex 380 catamaran	38	3'8"	1989	GRP	France	Good fridge Watermaker Diesel generator Davits Stereo hi-fi system Electric winch
Michelle LaMontagne	*Wooden Shoe*	Hans Christian	43	7'6"	1978	GRP	USA	Good tender Good outboard motor Efficient awning Good tools
Antti and Nina Louhija	*Pegasos*	Finnsailer	34	5'6"	1982	GRP	Finland	Electric windlass Seawater chain and anchor wash Twin furling genoas on separate stays Easy access to every side of engine Efficient electric fridge
Mirek and Lucy Misayat	*Kaprys*	Hallberg Rassy 46	48'6"	6'2"	1997	GRP	UK	Electric winches Electric furling Colour radar Satellite phone Watermaker Washing machine
John and Marilyn Morgan	*Sheerwater II*	Duncanson	29	6'	1976	GRP	Australia	Satellite phone Large double bed Efficient toilet Comfortable settee berths Furling headsail
Tom Muller and Lilly Vedana	*Miz Mae*	Joubert Nivelt	60	5'4" / 10'6"	1983	GRP	Sweden	Powerful autopilot Watermaker Large freezer

Owner	Name of yacht	Design	LOA	Draft	Year	Material	Flag	Essential features on ideal yacht
John and Amanda Neal	*Mahina Tiare*	Hallberg Rassy 46	48'6"	6'2"	1997	GRP	USA	Good inflatable; Outboard motor; Diving compressor; E-mail; Radar
Skip Novak	*Pelagic*	Patrick Banfield	53	3'6" / 9'6"	1987	Steel	BVI	Powerful anchoring system; Dependable headsail furling system; Fridge-freezer; Radar; Watermaker; RIB with 15 hp outboard
Volker Reinke	*Vegewind*		56	7'6"	1997	Steel	Germany	Powerful engine; Pilothouse; Internet access; Coffee grinder amidships for main, reefing lines, back-up for windlass; Double spinnaker pole system; Heating; Odour-free vacuum toilets; High-output bilge pumps; Davits; Efficient galley
Matt Rollberg and Margaret Reichenbach	*Santana*	Beneteau 405	41	6'	1992	GRP	USA	Electric windlass; Air conditioning; Chemically treated, automatic sewage system; Watermaker; Internet access; Bowthruster
Steve Spink	*Company*	Wauquiez	52	7'10"	1993	GRP	UK	Large-capacity watermaker; Washing machine; Electric winches; Bowthruster; Good tender and outboard; Autopilot

Owner	Name of yacht	Design	LOA	Draft	Year	Material	Flag	Essential features on ideal yacht
Javier Visiers	*Antaviana*	Lagoon catamaran	47	3'6"	1997	GRP	Spain	Autopilot Watermaker Fridge-freezer Power winches Satellite phone Hi-fi system
Richard and Dorothy Walker	*Mariposa*	Westsail	53	6'6"	1981	GRP	New Zealand	Large double bed with access from both sides Large tender Failsafe alarm system covering the whole boat Depth alarm
John and Alison Wicks	*Dreamtime*	Westerly	43	6'	1997	GRP	UK	Electric winch Inverter Standby autopilot Fridge-freezer Large comfortable bed Video/TV
John Ellis	No boat at time of survey						New Zealand	Electric winch Breadmaker Efficient awning Waterproof cockpit cushions Seawater anchor wash Icemaker
Helmut van Straelen	No boat at time of survey						Germany	Silent diesel generator Powered davits Stereo hi-fi system Large fridge
Tom Williams	No boat at time of survey						Jamaica	Electric winches Electric windlass Autopilot Watermaker Diesel generator Freezer
Thomas Wilm	No boat at time of survey						South Africa	Amateur radio Weatherfax Watermaker

Appendix 3

RECOMMENDED MEDICINE CHEST
(PETER NOBLE, MA, MD, FRCP)

The list of medication that could be carried is almost endless. The following information is intended only as a guide and lists examples of standard medications and doses for common conditions. In addition, crew members should take adequate personal medical supplies to treat any pre-existing conditions such as diabetes or heart disease. It is difficult to advise on quantity. Medication for minor ailments is likely to be used repetitively, so take enough for several episodes. Any boat embarking on an ocean crossing should take at least two weeks' supply of all major emergency items such as antibiotics. Whenever possible, both English and American generic names are listed, those marked with an asterix being the names commonly used in the USA.

Medicine chest

LOCAL ANAESTHETICS
The injection of a local anaesthetic (lidocaine/Xylocaine 20 ml ampoules) may assist the cleaning and suturing of a wound. The eye requires a specific anaesthetic such as amethocaine eye drops.

EYE INFECTIONS
Chloromycetin ointment or eye drops. Gentamycin* or Tobramycin* (triple dose).

INFECTIONS OF THE EAR CANAL (otitis externa)
Gentamycin drops (may also be used for eye infections).

SKIN CONDITIONS
Eczema and localised allergic rashes: hydrocortisone cream 1%. Bacterial skin infections: neomycin sulphate cream or powder. Fungal infections and athlete's foot: clotrimazole as ointment or dusting powder. Cold sores on the lips: Zovirax cream.

ALLERGIES AND ITCHY REACTIONS TO BITES AND STINGS
Promethazine hydrochloride tablets (Phenergan 25 mgm) or chlorpheniramine (Piriton/Clortrimeton* 4 mgm). Acrivastine (Semprex 8 mgm) is less sedative.

ANTI-SEASICKNESS REMEDIES
There are dozens of remedies and every skipper has views on what does, or does not, work. Cyclizine/Meclizine* 50 mgm and hyosine 300 micrograms are two

standard preparations. Hyosine skin patches (Scopoderm/Transderm scop*) may help those who are too nauseous to swallow and retain tablets.

ANALGESICS (pain relievers)

Aspirin 300 mgm and paracetamol 500 mgm are helpful for pain, fever and inflammation. Aspirin, for those who are not allergic to it, is a most useful drug and may also be used to prevent complications following a stroke or heart attack. Ibuprofen (Motrin) 200-400 mgm is used particularly for joint and muscular pain. Naproxen 250 mgm is an effective analgesic. Tramadol (50 mgm by mouth, but also available as an ampoule for injection) is a strong analgesic.

INFECTIONS

It is recommended to carry two weeks supply of each of the following three powerful antibiotics: Clarithromycin 250 mgm, 2-4 tablets daily. Alternatively a dose of Biaxin XL* 1000 mgm once a day only. Co-amoxyclav 250 mgm, 3-6 tablets daily or Augmentin* Ciprofloxacin (urinary tract infections) 250 mgm, 2-6 tablets daily

VAGINAL CANDIDIASIS (Thrush)

Canesten (Nystatin*) cream or pessaries.

VOMITING AND DIARRHOEA

Most episodes are due to food poisoning and settle within 24 hours without treatment. The anti-seasickness remedies will help nausea and vomiting. Anti-diarrhoea preparations include codeine phosphate 15 mgm, lomotil 2-4 tablets. Vomiting and diarrhoea may produce dehydration, particularly in children, which needs to be corrected by fluids by mouth. Sips of water (with a cup of fruit juice and a pinch of salt added to a pint of water to replace lost minerals) or rice water (water in which rice has been boiled) are helpful.

SEDATION

Valium 5 mgm may be used for anxiety and insomnia. Valium is a muscle relaxant and is particularly helpful in insomnia secondary to muscle and joint pain.

SUNBURN

Take plenty of sunblock and also calamine lotion for sunburn. Antihistamines will help allergic reactions to sunburn.

MALARIA

Fortunately, the mosquitoes that carry malaria do not fly out to sea. If you intend to explore countries where malaria is endemic seek up-to-date advice on the best antimalarial preventative. Mefloquine* (Lariam) 250 mgm is a common anti-malarial preventative. It should be taken one per week as prophylaxis starting one week prior to, and for four weeks after potential exposure.

Quinine sulphate 200 mgm may be used in an emergency to treat a serious malaria attack, but should only be used with other antimalarials. Other recommended treatments: Pyrimethamine* (Sulfadoxine*) or Fansidar*, 2-3 tablets taken only once; Chloroquine sulfate 500 mgm, one tablet followed by another tablet 6 hours later, then one tablet daily for two days.

Appendix 4

Rarely was the saying that all roads lead to Rome more true than in the case of the sailors in the Millennium Odyssey round the world rally, which finished at Easter 2000 with the handover of the Millennium Flame to Pope John Paul II. For Australian Brad Burke, finishing the rally – let alone winning it – was, in his own words, the highlight of his entire life. His *Foxy Lady* was one of six boats that took the symbolic start in Israel in August 1998, after the crews had attended a ceremony at the Church of the Holy Sepulchre in Jerusalem where every skipper had a special Millennium lamp lit.

Most Millennium participants had been attracted to the idea of sailing around the world with more of a purpose than simply completing a circumnavigation. Outstanding among them were Charles and Saundra Gray, who joined the rally at the Fort Lauderdale start in February 1999 on *Sea Gem*. Three other Millennium boats were former America 500 participants: *Que Sera Sera*, *Hornblower II* and *Distant Drum*. Another America 500 veteran, Michael Frankel of *Sabra*, sailed on *Hornblower* as crew. Both *Distant Drum* and *Hornblower* chose the Cape of Good Hope route, while Lois and Don Babcock on *Que Sera Sera* opted for the Red Sea route and Rome finish, and were rewarded not just by witnessing the moving Vatican ceremony, but also by winning the Concordia Cup, awarded to the crew that best reflected the spirit of the event.

Competition was keener among the boats that sailed the cold water route, and the rivalry between the American Swan 57 *Risque* and the Italian Mauric 62 *Taratoo* was intense. *Risque*'s family crew, sailed by Lou and Jackie Morgan, accompanied by two of their children and some friends, led for much of the way. But in the end Fabio Colapinto's obsessive desire to be first won the day. In fact, Fabio Colapinto had sailed in a previous round the world rally in 1994–5, in which he finished second. He vowed to do it again, and win this time, so he completely refurbished *Taratoo* and accomplished the fastest circumnavigation of the rally, for which he was awarded the Sir Edward Heath Trophy at a special ceremony in London.

Seven Millennium boats recrossed the Atlantic from the Caribbean and finished the rally in London. Among those who completed their circumnavigation when they sailed up the River Thames was the American *Harmonie* sailed by Ann Harsh and Ralph Nehrig. As the only female skipper in the Millennium Odyssey, Ann had the satisfaction of having beaten all competition by being declared winner of the group that had started and finished the rally on the Greenwich Meridian.

In order to cover as much of the world as possible, the Millennium Odyssey offered various route options, either via the Panama and Suez Canals, or via Cape Horn and the Cape of Good Hope, with one intrepid group of four yachts actually sailing down to Antarctica, the first ever yacht race to the frozen continent. A total of 40 boats from a dozen countries sailed in the rally. A special edge to the rally was given by the presentation of lamps with the Millennium Flame in all the 40 countries visited. This symbol of peace was handed over sometimes in a secular ceremony, often a religious one. Among the many unforgettable ceremonies, none was more spectacular than the one in Rio de Janeiro. In true Brazilian style, the sailors were collected in a fire engine, and driven under full police escort, an honour normally bestowed only on returning football stars. The Brazilian sculptor Mazeredo had created a stunning 14-foot high statue to hold the Millennium Flame in this vibrant city's cathedral. Just as moving was the ceremony in neighbouring Argentina, where a fleet of vintage cars took the crews of the Millennium yachts to the cathedral in Mar del Plata. The Archbishop accepted the Millennium Flame on behalf of the people of Argentina and used the opportunity to send a message of peace to the people of the Falkland Islands, the Millennium Odyssey being the first sporting event to link the two countries.

No less moving was the arrival of the Millennium yachts in Pitcairn, where the entire island's population of 42 crowded into the small church to greet the visiting

The end of a voyage with a mission: Millennium Odyssey crews in St Peter's Square, Rome.

crews. Tom Christian, a direct descendant of Bounty mutineer Fletcher Christian, accepted the Millennium Flame on behalf of the small community, after which the sailors were treated to some beautiful singing, including two moving goodbye songs that Pitcairners normally sing to departing ships.

The cold and warm water routes converged in Tahiti where the crews of the 40 yachts walked in procession to the cathedral for an ecumenical service. Here they were received in true Polynesian style, garlanded with leis of fresh flowers, while traditional drums and flaming torches accompanied them into the crowded church. A special song had been written for the Millennium Flame, which was sung so beautifully by the choir that there were not many dry eyes in the cathedral that memorable day.

Civitavecchia, the ancient port of Rome, was the perfect setting for the finish of the round the world rally. The Millennium sailors were warmly welcomed in Riva di Traiano marina, named after the Roman Emperor Trajan, who built the original port. On completion of its circumnavigation of the world, the Millennium Flame was handed over to Pope John Paul II at a ceremony in St Peter's Square during the Easter celebrations of 2000.

The Millennium Odyssey was sponsored by the Canary Islands government, who used the round the world rally to promote the attractions of this archipelago.

Report on breakages in the Millennium Odyssey (1998–2000)

Out of the 26 yachts that had actually completed the circumnavigation, only 14 returned completed survey forms.

AUTOPILOTS

* *Allegra B*: Cetrek processor – replaced in Palma de Mallorca; electric motor – replaced in Singapore
* *Pimalo*: Robertson motor broken – replaced in Australia; Autohelm 6000 electronics corroded – unrepairable
* *Dreamtime*: Autohelm pilot broken en route to the Marquesas

DECK FITTINGS

* *Pimalo*: Anchor winch motor – repaired in Australia

DINGHIES

* *Pimalo*: Zodiac glue dissolving – repaired; bottom coming away
* *Futuro*: Inflatable dinghy ripped by leopard seal in Antarctica

ENGINES

* *Pimalo*: Hurth gearbox forward gear – repaired in Crete; Perkins Prima 50: various electrical faults; corroded water pump
* *Aventura III*: Volvo water pump – repaired in Portugal and the Canaries

- *Aventurero III*: Several faults on the main engine
- *Jancris*: Shaft bearing – replaced in Cairns
- *Happy Spirit*: Main engine broken in Brazil (possible water ingression) – repaired in Grenada
- *Hornblower*: Freshwater cooling pump – replaced in Tahiti

FRIDGE/FREEZERS

- *Pimalo*: Fridge short-circuit
- *Aventura III*: Flooded electronics in Le Maire Channel – replaced in Valdivia
- *Taratoo*: Freezer compressor broken – repaired in Darwin, replaced in Cape Town
- *Happy Spirit*: Fridge – repaired in Tahiti
- *Hornblower*: Freezer compressor broken several times due to freon leak

GALLEY

- *Allegra B*: Sealand macerator pump: broken repeatedly

GENERATORS

- *Allegra B*: Onan genset – minor repairs
- *Aventurero III*: Various genset problems
- *Jancris*: Seawater pump on genset – repaired in the Maldives
- *Taratoo*: Seawater pump on genset – replaced in Cairns, repaired again in Mauritius
- *Happy Spirit*: Replaced genset motor in Darwin; new seawater pump in Richards Bay
- *Hornblower*: Kubota fuel pump – replaced in Tahiti
- *Aventura III*: Rutland 913 wind generator ripped off in 50-knot winds in Le Maire Strait

HULL

- *Happy Spirit*: Damaged keel – repaired in Darwin

INSTRUMENTS

- *Allegra B*: Cetrek wind instruments broken
- *Pimalo*: Plastimo compass – replaced in Las Palmas; Brookes&Gatehouse speedometer broken

INVERTERS/CHARGERS

- *Allegra B*: Victron charger replaced
- *Pimalo*: Cristec inverter – replaced in Australia; charger – replaced in Singapore

RADIO

- *Jancris*: Shipmate VHF broken – replaced in Cairns

RIGGING

- *Allegra B*: Broken forestay fitting – repaired in Raiatea; hydraulic backstay – broken/replaced

- *Pimalo*: Lower shroud damaged – repaired in Las Palmas; forestay fitting broken at the head of the mast; furling gear twisted; two lower shrouds damaged; as a result, all rigging was replaced in Tahiti; three lower shrouds – replaced in Singapore
- *Jancris*: Lower shroud and chainplate broken – repaired in Mallorca

RUDDER

- *Taratoo*: Grounded on coral head in Fiji, rudder – repaired in Cairns
- *Happy Spirit*: Rudder flange – machined in Valdivia
- *Risque*: Damaged rudder in Antarctica – repaired in Valdivia

SAILS

- *Que Sera Sera*: Mainsail and staysail clew ripped out in Red Sea
- *Aventura III*: Triradial spinnaker blown out en route to Easter Island – repaired in Tahiti
- *Pimalo*: Two spinnakers blown out
- *Taratoo*: Several sails and spinnakers blown
- *Hornblower*: Drifter disintegrated due to ultraviolet exposure

SPARS

- *Que Sera Sera*: Gooseneck fitting – repaired in Tahiti
- *Aventura III*: Top spreader broken en route to Falklands – repaired in Stanley
- *Aventura III*: Cracked gooseneck fitting – temporarily repaired in Antarctica
- *Taratoo*: Both mainsail and mizzen goosenecks – repaired in Cairns
- *Hornblower*: Whisker pole: several failures

STEERING

- *Aventurero III*: Quadrant broken
- *Hornblower*: Seals on hydraulic ram – replaced twice

WATERMAKERS

- *Hornblower*: PUR multiple failures – replacement shipped from the USA at no cost

WIND SELF-STEERING

- *Pimalo*: Windpilot servo-rudder broken twice – replaced with spares

Appendix 5
DESCRIPTION OF *AVENTURA III*

The previous two *Aventuras* have both circled the globe along the trade wind routes, so when I started planning a new boat and voyage I decided to give the well-trodden tropical routes a temporary miss and do some cold water cruising instead. Having had a foretaste of Antarctic sailing on a charter trip on Skip Novak's *Pelagic* in 1996, I drew up plans for a high latitude voyage that would take my French-built *Aventura III* in one year to the three cold As: Arctic, Antarctic and Alaska. Although the initial plan was to sail *Aventura III* on her maiden voyage all the way from western France to Spitsbergen, a delay in her delivery allowed us to only sail in the summer of 1998 from London to mainland Norway, somewhat short of the Arctic Circle.

On her return to London, *Aventura III* joined the Millennium Odyssey on the first leg to Portugal. The rally followed two routes around the world: a cold water route around Cape Horn and the Cape of Good Hope, and a more benign route via the Panama and Suez Canals. *Aventura III* joined the former and sailed across Drake Passage to Antarctica in February 1999. After three weeks we returned to the South American mainland and, in company with other Millennium Odyssey boats, sailed through the Chilean canals to Valdivia. The voyage continued to Easter Island, Pitcairn and French Polynesia, which was reached in May 1999. In Tahiti, *Aventura III* left the Millennium Odyssey and sailed via several Line Islands to Hawaii and on to Alaska. The rest of the summer was spent in Alaska and British Columbia, and at the end of August, in Vancouver, BC, *Aventura* was loaded on board a special yacht transport vessel and six weeks later was floated off in Toulon, on the French Mediterranean coast.

The following April, in Civitavecchia, *Aventura* rejoined the Millennium Odyssey yachts that had arrived in the Mediterranean by way of the Red Sea. After the final ceremony at the Vatican we sailed to Greece, where the summer was spent cruising the Aegean. The following year *Aventura* briefly returned to the south of France before sailing via Gibraltar to the Canaries. The Atlantic was crossed to St Lucia in December 2001 and was followed by a cruise to the Virgin Islands, Puerto Rico, Turks and Caicos and the Bahamas. The Caribbean Sea was crossed from north to south via Cuba and Jamaica to Panama. Having transited the Panama Canal in March 2002, *Aventura* continued the voyage to Ecuador where she was laid up ashore at Puerto Lucia Yacht Club. Early in 2003 the voyage will continue to Galapagos, Marquesas, Tuamotus and Tahiti. Other South Pacific islands will be visited en route to New Zealand, which should be reached before the end of 2003.

Aventura was built in 1998 by the Alubat yard at Les Sables d'Olonne in the west of France. Alubat is one of the largest producers of aluminium sailing boats in the world. Her hull is number 73 of a production OVNI 43 (OVNI is the French acronym of UFO: *objet volant non-identifié*). The entire OVNI range is designed by Philippe Briand, one of France's foremost naval architects, and runs from 32 to 56 feet LOA. Regardless of length, all boats share a number of basic elements: all are hard-chined, flat-bottomed, and have a centreboard and retractable rudder. This means that with the rudder and centreboard retracted, the boats draw very little, and can dry out on any level ground. The 43-foot *Aventura* draws 3 feet with the board up, and just over 8 feet when the board is down. The centreboard is a flat 1½-inch (40-mm) aluminium plate.

Aventura III was built and equipped with a cold water voyage in mind, so there have been a number of alterations to the standard version. Both deck and hull have been insulated down to the waterline. With hindsight, insulation should have continued right down to the bilges, as in Antarctica, where the water temperature was only one or two degrees above freezing, there was condensation in the lower parts of the boat, and even on one occasion frozen water in the bilges, although the boat was heated and the inside temperature never fell below 6°C. Elsewhere condensation has been minimal, both because of the insulation and also because in the Falklands the insides of all hatches were covered with a thick layer of bubblewrap. This arrangement let through some light, and the bubblewrap created enough of a temperature barrier to stop the worst of the condensation. The boat is heated by a Webasto diesel heater, blowing hot air through ducts leading to four outlets throughout the boat. The first, and hottest, leads to an oilskin-drying locker, which has worked perfectly. Generally, the heater has worked very well and, with a maximum consumption of 2 gallons (8 litres) per 24 hours, it is very economical.

The bare aluminium hull did not need much preparation for occasional encounters with ice. Indeed, several times the boat had to push through large slabs of sea ice at slow speeds, with the only visible damage being an absence of antifouling paint in the bow area. All seacocks have been fitted onto welded pipes to eliminate any protrusions outside the hull that may be broken off by ice.

Aventura's deck layout was carefully thought-out for sailing in extreme conditions. The boat is rigged as a cutter, with both the yankee and staysail having identical furling gears, and the furling lines coming back to an electric winch sited in the cockpit next to the companionway. All lines and halyards are brought back to the cockpit, so that all sails can be handled, and reefed, from the protection of an oversized spray dodger, mounted high enough to allow standing headroom. The entire cockpit can be covered with a bimini.

The electronic equipment includes Brookes&Gatehouse Hydra instrumentation, a Brookes&Gatehouse autopilot, Furuno 1750 radar, and also a weatherfax operated via an ICOM M710 SSB radio. There is a back-up Navico autopilot and a Windpilot Pacific wind-operated self-steering gear. For communications, a Thrane&Thrane Inmarsat C unit was used extensively and provided full coverage in the Antarctic area. An Iridium satellite telephone was acquired in 2001 and is used both for voice communications and e-mail.

One concession to performance was to fit a fully battened mainsail, rather than an in-mast furling mainsail. The latter would have been an easier option, but for a

boat like the OVNI 43, which needs to be driven fast when going to windward, an efficient fully battened mainsail is highly desirable. For light winds, the sail wardrobe includes a 125 per cent genoa, one tri-radial, and two asymmetric spinnakers.

A domestic battery bank with a total capacity of 720 amps is charged by two identical 70-amp alternators mounted on the main engine, a Volvo MD22. One of the alternators is fitted with a smart regulator. Other charging sources are a Rutland 913 wind generator and three solar panels, mounted on deck.

As tenders we use two inflatable Avon dinghies, of 2.40 and 3.10 metres respectively, as well as two Honda outboard engines of 2 and 8 hp.

The distinctive OVNI arch over the stern can be put to many uses, and on *Aventura* it serves as a sturdy platform for the radar, wind generator, as well as GPS, Iridium and Inmarsat C antennae. It also serves as a ready-made davit for the larger tender and outboard. Other useful features are the large stern platform and the open bow well, which gives instant access to the chain or spare anchors. Another highly appreciated feature is the fact that the hull had been left unpainted from water level to the toerail so there are no gleaming topsides to be worried about when tied to rough docks or having unfendered boats come alongside.

In the four years since she was launched in April 1998, *Aventura* has sailed over 35,000 miles. She is a functional, easily handled boat, which has performed very well in the variety of conditions encountered so far.

Aventura III at anchor in the San Blas Islands, Panama, showing her functional stern platform and distinctive arch supporting the radar scanner and wind generator.

Index